THE CATHOLIC UNIVERSITY OF AMERICA
STUDIES IN AMERICAN CHURCH HISTORY

VOL. XVII

THE SECULARIZATION OF THE CALIFORNIA MISSIONS

(1810-1846)

A Dissertation

SUBMITTED TO THE FACULTY OF THE GRADUATE SCHOOL OF ARTS AND SCIENCES
OF THE CATHOLIC UNIVERSITY OF AMERICA IN PARTIAL FULFILLMENT OF THE
REQUIREMENTS FOR THE DEGREE OF DOCTOR OF PHILOSOPHY

by

REV. GERALD J. GEARY, A.M.

Priest of the Archdiocese of San Francisco

THE CATHOLIC UNIVERSITY OF AMERICA
WASHINGTON, D. C.

1934

Library of Congress Cataloging in Publication Data

Geary, Gerald Joseph, 1905-
    The secularization of the California missions
(1810-1846).

    Reprint of the author's thesis, Catholic University
of America, 1934, which was issued as v. 17 of the
Catholic University of America. Studies in American
church history.
    Bibliography: p.
    1. Missions—California. 2. Secularization.
3. Church and state in California. 4. Catholic
Church in California—Missions. 5. California—
History—To 1846. I. Title. II. Series: Catholic
University of America. Studies in American church
history, v. 17.
BV2803.C2G4 1974   266'.2'794   73-3572
ISBN 0-404-57767-9

NIHIL OBSTAT: Peter Guilday, Ph.D., J.U.D., Censor Deputatus.
IMPRIMATUR: †Edward J. Hanna, D.D., Archiepiscopus Sancti Francisci.
May 8, 1934.

Reprinted from the edition of 1934, Washington D.C.
First AMS edition published, 1974
Manufactured in the United States of America

International Standard Book Number
Complete Set: 0-404-57750-4
Volume 17: 0-404-57767-9

AMS PRESS, INC.
New York, N.Y. 10003

TO
MY MOTHER AND FATHER

CONTENTS

FOREWORD

The purpose of this dissertation is to trace the history of the secularization movement which resulted in the destruction of the California Missions. Secularization has always been a perplexing problem of mission history. Its sole result was wanton plundering. Yet certain of the early California chroniclers justified it, and later historians have been prone to regard the evils which it produced as inevitable.

It has been felt that this view has been due to a restricted concept of the problem. The secularization of the California Missions has been too often regarded solely as a local event, the enactment of which filled but a few brief years, from 1830 to 1834, in the longer period of mission history. But today there is a growing tendency to view the whole of California history not as an isolated, self-contained unit but as a related segment of general Hispanic American history. The present study approaches the problem of secularization from this wider viewpoint. Just as the purpose and organization of the mission system were developed during the two centuries and a half which preceded the establishment of the California Missions, so also was secularization and its various implications fully revealed long before it was applied in California. Moreover, when this latter instance actually took place, it was not restricted to a few brief years and to its local setting. A movement to secularize the California Missions manifested itself almost on the first day of their establishment. Though a change of circumstances early forced it into the background, it reappeared in the second decade of the nineteenth century, in Spain, New Spain and, lastly, in California. Thenceforth the impulse for secularization came not from California but from Mexico. There it was but a minor phase of the struggle between conservatives and liberals for political power. Each political change had its corresponding effect on the question of secularization in California, with the result that there gradually emerged two distinct policies concerning it. One sought a gradual modification of the mission system without destroying the good which it had produced; the other aimed at outright secularization regardless of the cost. It was only when the choice was made that the local element entered in and became the determining factor. The evils which then followed were the result of an unhappy set of circumstances rather than of an inevitable decree of fate.

This answer to the problem is not entirely new. Many of its component elements have been already set forth in the numerous works which treat the general history of the Missions. These have been gathered and presented as a unit in the single work dealing specifically with the question of secularization, Miss Kathryn Lee Langston's *The secularization of the California Missions, 1813-1846*, which was presented as a thesis for the degree of Master of Arts at the University of California in 1925. What new elements the writer has ventured to add in the present work, are presented with the hope that they may contribute to a fuller understanding of the Missions, and with the desire that their acceptance should await the judgment of more able students of the question.

The writer wishes to express his gratitude to his Ordinary, Most Rev. Edward J. Hanna, D.D., Archbishop of San Francisco, and to his Coadjutor, Archbishop John J. Mitty, D.D., for the opportunity they gave him to pursue his course of graduate study. He acknowledges gratefully his indebtedness to his major professor, Reverend Dr. Peter Guilday, for his constant guidance and encouragement during the past three years. He also wishes to express his appreciation of the kind attention which Dr. Herbert E. Bolton showed him during the course of a summer session at the University of California; and to acknowledge his obligation to Dr. George Tays, for the great help which he found in his doctoral thesis, *Revolutionary California*. For their willing assistance in the work of translation and proof-reading, the writer is grateful to two of his confreres, Rev. Ernesto Tagle, J.C.L., and Rev. Edwin Kennedy, J.C.B. He also expresses his thanks to his other professors at the Catholic University of America, Doctors Purcell, McGuire, Stock and Auweiler of the History Department, Doctors Smith, Hart and Sheen of the Philosophy Department, and Doctors Deering and Lennox of the English Department.

CHAPTER I

SECULARIZATION OF THE MISSIONS
IN NEW SPAIN

When in 1846 the final blow of an auctioneer's hammer sounded the death-knell of the California Missions, it brought to an end a program of missionary effort that was begun not on the shores of the Pacific in 1769 but on an isle of the Caribbean in 1492. The California Missions were but the last of a great system which traced its origins to the Spanish conquest of America. After great *conquistadores* there had come simple padres to plant the cross in the isles of Española, in the Isthmus of Panama, throughout the whole of the southern continent, and northwards through the Maya country and the Aztec Empire up to what a later race would call the Spanish southwest and the Spanish southeast, Arizona, New Mexico, Texas, and the Floridas. Last of all, they reached Upper California and established there a mission system that was the product of three centuries of development. The methods of peaceful conversion and instruction, the development of agriculture and industry, even the gems of architecture which we of today admire so much in the California Missions, all originated in those earlier establishments. In like manner, it may be said, the forces which caused the decline and death of the Missions began not in California but in New Spain and even in Spain itself. The term, secularization, was in use long before the California Missions were established and in many cases had been applied to earlier missionary establishments with consequences which could have foretold the outcome of its application in California. The story, therefore, of the rise and decline of the California Missions is based on that of the three centuries that preceded it.

I

California can trace its Catholic beginnings to the fact that the first colonizers of the New World were Spaniards and Roman

1

Catholics, "representatives of a powerful nation that was the citadel of a united faith." The French in Canada, the Portuguese in Brazil and the English in Maryland were also Catholics, but none were so profoundly Catholic as was the Spaniard. His was a Catholicism which had been bought with the life-blood of a nation. For nearly eight centuries the Spanish people had fought to preserve its Faith and to win back its land from a Mohammedan invader. When finally on the eve of the discovery of America the last vestige of infidel domination was swept into Africa, there emerged from the conflict a people for whom religion and patriotism were almost the same thing. "The Spaniard emerged profoundly and preëminently Catholic, proud of his Faith, and somewhat fiercely zealous in maintaining and propagating it." [1] But not only was Spain strongly Catholic, its rulers enjoyed unique privileges in relation to church administration. This also was due, perhaps, to the long struggle with the Moors. During the centuries of conflict, necessity had transformed a group of small, independent states into the united kingdom of Spain in which local, feudal powers were displaced by royal agencies.[2] This centralization of the secular government reflected itself in ecclesiastical affairs. Through usurpation, custom, or explicit papal recognition, the rulers of the Iberian Peninsula had obtained for themselves a number of privileges known as the *Patronato Real* which gave them "an enormous power over the Church in their dominions." [3] Thus as late as 1482 Pope Sixtus IV agreed that no candidate should be nominated for any Castilian see who had not been approved by the Spanish sovereigns.[4] Similarly, two years later Innocent VII granted them the patronage of all the churches and convents in Granada and in all the territory that had been or would be conquered from the Moors.[5]

---

[1] Ryan, Edwin, *The Church in the South American republics* (Milwaukee, 1932), 5.

[2] James, H. G., and Martin, P. A., *The republics of Latin America* (New York, 1918), 1–17.

[3] Ryan, "Diocesan organization in the Spanish Colonies," *Catholic Historical Review* (Washington, D. C.), II (1916), 149.

[4] Pastor, Ludwig von, *History of the Popes,* trans. by Fredrick Antrobus (St. Louis, 906), IV, 397.

[5] *Ibid.*, V, 338–339.

When Spain was placed on the threshold of a new world by Columbus' discovery, both of these features of Spanish Catholicism determined her future policy towards it. The struggle that had just ended in Spain was to be carried across the Western Sea where there were not only lands to be conquered and treasures to be gained, but also souls to be saved. The conversion of the Indians was to be one of the chief motives for the Spanish conquest of America.[6] "Wherever floated the banners of Spain, there would be planted the cross of Christ." [7] When arrangements were made for the return of Columbus to the New World, special preparations were made for the establishment of ecclesiastical life there. Missionaries were recruited from the various monasteries and application was made to the Holy See for a vicar-apostolic to guide and direct the work of evangelization. When Columbus embarked on his second voyage, there sailed with him a bishop and a band of priests ready to begin the spiritual conquest of America.[8]

In like manner within the first two decades after the discovery of the New World, the Spanish rulers obtained an extension of the privileges of the *Patronato Real* to their new dominions. In 1493 Alexander VI gave the crown the right of appointing missionaries to the Indies,[9] while a year later he conferred on Ferdinand and Isabella the title of "Catholic" and granted them two-ninths of the tithes throughout the dominions of Castile.[10] In 1501 this latter concession was enlarged so as to embrace the colonies and allow the crown, instead of two-ninths, all the tithes on the condition that the monarchs should endow the churches therein and provide an adequate maintenance for their ministers.[11]

---

[6] Fisher, Lillian E., *Viceregal administration in the Spanish-American colonies* (Berkeley, 1926), 313.

[7] Blackmar, Frank W., *Spanish colonization in the southwest* (Baltimore, 1890), 38.

[8] Walsh, Sister M. Kathleen, "The Origins of Ecclesiastical Jurisdiction in New Spain," *Records of the American Catholic Historical Society of Philadelphia*, XLII (1932), 107.

[9] Pastor, *op. cit.*, VI, 163.

[10] Prescott, William H., *History of the reign of Ferdinand and Isabella the Catholic* (Philadelphia, 1896), II, 26.

[11] Lowery, Woodbury, *Spanish settlements in the United States* (New York, 1911), I, 383.

Finally, in 1508 Pope Julius II by the Bull, "Universalis Ecclesiae Regimini," granted the crown the right to appoint to all benefices without exception.[12]   By these various concessions the Spanish crown was given the broadest of powers over the Church in the New World.   By it bishops, religious superiors, and parish priests were to be appointed, while without its permission no missionary could enter or leave the colonies.   The creation of dioceses, the erection of churches, convents, and schools were all matters that would come under its control.   In time even so small a matter as the transfer or dismissal of a sacristan would become the object of supervision by the crown.[13]

It is true that the concession of such wide privileges would at times lead to an unwarranted assumption of power, interference in ecclesiastical affairs, and the introduction of abuses through unworthy appointments.   Yet if the *Patronato Real* produced some incidental evils, it also produced considerable and substantial benefits.   When the expanse of two continents is considered, it seems that it would have been well-nigh impossible for the Holy See to have undertaken the mission of Christianizing the inhabitants without the aid of the civil government.   "The pope could do nothing by himself in this immense territory; he had not even the means of establishing in it the institutions necessary for the propagation of religion." [14]   The Spanish kings were entrusted with extensive powers, and in the main were faithful to their charge. During the centuries that followed, they devoted the greater portion of the funds derived from ecclesiastical tithes and benefices to the erection of churches and cathedrals, the opening of schools, the establishment of missions, and the maintenance of a numerous clergy.   "Considering the situation in Spain and in Spanish America, one may well doubt whether a church less dependent on

---

[12] Engelhardt, Zephyrin, *The missions and missionaries of California* (San Francisco, 1915), II, 671.

[13] Cf. Moses, Bernard, *South America on the eve of emancipation* (New York, 1908), 125–137; Ryan, *The Church in the South American republics*, 20; Fisher, *op. cit.*, 182–183; Engelhardt, *op. cit.*, II, 670–674; Crivelli, Camillus, "The right of royal patronage," *Catholic Encyclopedia*, X, 260–262.

[14] Moses, *op. cit.*, 119.

the state, left more to her own resources, would have accomplished anything like the noble work that was to be to her credit in the New World." [15] This was to be true particularly of the missions.

II

It was by virtue of the powers contained in the *Patronato Real* that the Spanish crown gradually developed for the Church a definite rôle in the program of new world colonization. In the first days of the conquest the sole purpose of the Church was the conversion of the natives. From the outset a definite policy had been adopted with respect to the native population. As a conquered people they were to contribute to the royal treasury, yet as free vassals their rights were to be guaranteed and protected. Therefore, as early as 1503 an *encomienda* system was introduced into Española for the purpose of attaining these ends. The natives were organized in towns, and each was given a house, farm and cattle for the support of his family. Over these native communities were placed Spanish civilians or soldiers to act as protectors or *encomenderos.*

The encomenderos were obliged to teach, to indoctrinate, and to protect the Indians, to suppress their native customs, and to encourage to a limited degree the intermingling of the two races. The encomenderos were also empowered to exact labor from the Indians, though for pay and as free men, and were to share the profits with the king.[16]

Thus under the *encomienda* system the duty of providing for the instruction and ultimate conversion of the Indians belonged to the *encomendero.* For this purpose he was expected to erect a church in each native community and through priests, introduced and supported by him, to provide for their spiritual instruction and advancement in the ways of Christian civilization. In its first

15 Ryan, *op. cit.,* 8.

16 Hackett, Charles W., *Historical documents relating to New Mexico, Nueva Vizcaya, and approaches thereto, to 1773; collected by Adolph and Fanny Bandelier* (Washington, D. C., 1923–1926), I, 25.

stage missionary endeavor was sponsored and directed by seculars, the ministers of the Church being restricted to their spiritual ministry.[17]

But although in theory the *encomienda* system was intended to combine the ideal with the practical, to protect the rights and save the souls of the Indians and at the same time provide the crown with new revenues, in practice it soon led to many abuses. Exploitation and its attending evils were emphasized at the expense of Christian principles and their mitigating influence. Despite all precautions to safeguard the welfare of the natives, the tendency of the settlers to exploit them to their own advantage to the prejudice of their health and religious instruction, proved too strong to be effectively resisted. Hours of labor in the fields and, still worse, in the remote mines in the interior were lengthened; wages were not regularly paid; and the precepts of kind treatment were neglected. The evils increased after the death of Isabella and unrestricted exploitation of Indian labor made Ferdinand's reign "the worst period in the history of Spanish colonization." The natives of Española were almost exterminated and all missionary projects were brought practically to a standstill.[18]

As a result, the clergy, after a short period of strange inaction,[19] inaugurated a vigorous campaign against the *encomiendas* and their evils. Led by Las Casas they succeeded in having a series of reform measures adopted by the crown and finally by the "New Laws of the Indies" in 1543 in having the *encomienda* system abolished entirely.[20] Although in the face of this official disapproval the system continued to exist for another century, the exposure of its evils "aroused a public opinion which continued to defend the right of the Indian to the position of a vassal of the

---

[17] For the origin and theory of the *encomienda* system cf. Bolton, Herbert E., "The missions in the Spanish-American colonies," *American Historical Review,* XXIII (1917), 42–61; Simpson, Lesley B., *The encomienda in New Spain* (Berkeley, 1929), 26 ss.; Priestley, Herbert I., *The coming of the white man* (New York, 1929), 117–121.

[18] Merriman, Roger B., *The rise of the Spanish empire in the old world and the new* (New York, 1918–1925), II, 233–234; Simpson, *op. cit.,* 34 ss.

[19] Simpson, *op. cit.,* 48.

[20] Priestly, Herbert I., *The Mexican nation, a history* (New York, 1923), 62–64.

crown of Spain, and which ultimately placed him in a class apart, as a ward of the crown with a corps of special officers to take care of him and his rights." [21]

The special corps of agents selected by the crown to take care of the Indian and his rights were the missionaries. The ministers of religion were made independent of the *encomenderos* and were given the office of not only converting the natives but also of protecting them. The basis for this change was laid in 1512 when it was ordered in the Laws of Burgos, the first of the measures enacted against the *encomienda* system, that "the children of thirteen and under of the *caciques* were to be put in charge of the religious and taught religion, reading and writing and at the end of four years returned to their *encomenderos.*" [22] Later measures broadened the powers of the religious until finally they were recognized as the agents commissioned by the crown to protect the Indians.

The significance of this new rôle was revealed particularly after Spanish rule had been extended to the mainland by Cortés' conquest of the Aztecs. While the conqueror introduced the *encomienda* system into New Spain for the purpose of rewarding his followers,[23] the Franciscans and Dominicans, according to the first Bishop of Mexico, Juan de Zumarraga, of their own initiative established numerous centers for the instruction of the natives.[24]

In the building of their convents, they followed a definite plan. The church extended from east to west; on the north, and forming a square with the church was the school with its dormitories and chapel. The large patio between the church and school was used for classes in Christian Doctrine; the adult Indians before going to work, daily received instruction in the patios from the friars. In the patio also, instruction was given to the sons of the *macehuales* or plebeian Indians. The school-building proper was reserved for the sons

---

[21] Cleven, Nels A., *Readings in Hispanic American history* (New York, 1927), 227.
[22] Simpson, *op. cit.*, 51.
[23] *Ibid.*, 85.
[24] *Ibid.*, 100.

of the lords and nobles who lived in dormitories erected near the schools. Some of these dormitories were large enough to accommodate from 800 to 1000 pupils.[25]

While the actual picture of the work accomplished during these early years is somewhat obscured, it seems quite certain that the friars had definitely assumed the office of protecting the sons of the nobles or *caciques,* as they were called in the Laws of Burgos; and probably, when *encomenderos,* who still controlled the lands and labor of the natives, exceeded their powers, the missionaries extended their protection to the other classes of Indians as well. In time, as will be later noted, this interpretation of the office of protector was recognized by the crown.

A half century later the ministers of religion were given a third mission by the Spanish crown. Towards 1550 a great silver lode was discovered in the northern section of New Spain and immediately there began an exodus from the agricultural regions of the Aztecs that surpassed even the gold rush of the later forty-niners. Under the direction of such *adelantados* as Guzmán, Ibarra, and Urdiñola, these new regions were quickly occupied and added to New Spain as the provinces of Neuva Galicia, Neuva Vizcaya and Neuvo León. But while both the mining regions and the older agricultural country were *tierras de paz,* there lay between them a *tierra de guerra,* a barren stretch of several hundred miles controlled by a tribe of hostile nomads called the Chichimecas. Raiding provision trains sent to the mines and often capturing cargos of silver on the way to Mexico City, these hostile Indians prevented the establishment of a safe line of communication between the two important regions. Numerous military expeditions were sent out in an effort to subdue them, but the success of such enterprises was meager.

Warfare against these wild nomads proved quite different from that which the Spaniard had been accustomed to wage

[25] Icazbalceta, Joaquin G., "Education in Mexico during the sixteenth century," trans. by Rev. Walter J. O'Donnell in *Historical Records and Studies* (New York, 1931), XX, 102; cf. Bancroft, Hubert H., *History of Mexico* (San Francisco, 1883–1887), II, 170.

against the more cultured and settled communities of the central plateau. During the conquest by Cortés, the capture of a capital, a treaty with the ruler generally sufficed to control a people. But with the Chichimecas treaties availed little and fighting, instead of a phalanxed attack against a large force of natives, became a devastating guerrilla warfare.[26]

In the face of this failure of arms, the crown now adopted a new policy, that of sending missionaries to pacify the hostile tribes. Accordingly, in 1566 a royal cedula was issued which ordered that instead of soldiers and presidios among the Chichimecas "three or four monasteries of friars should be founded for the purpose of attracting the Indians with gentle methods."[27] The Franciscans undertook the difficult task and, although the blood of martyrs had first to be planted as the seed of Christians, they eventually won the Chichimecas over to the peace of Christ and the more useful ways of civilization. Thenceforth, the missionary was commissioned not only to convert and protect the Indian but also, when the sword failed, to pacify him.

For more than two centuries and a half, down to 1817 when the last California mission under Spanish rule was founded, the members of the various religious orders served as the chief agents of Spanish colonization. During this long period Spain engaged in a vast enterprise of defensive expansion. To protect the rich regions which she already possessed from the attacks of hostile Indians and of more savage buccaneers and to ward off the equally dangerous threats of the French, English and Russians to extend their colonization southward, the crown threw out a far flung line of defensive colonies that eventually stretched across the northern borderlands from the Atlantic to the Pacific. Instead of sending white colonists to occupy these regions, she commissioned missionaries to pacify and civilize the natives. Chief among those who engaged in this work were the Frenciscans and the Jesuits. The former established two great mission chains in the advance northwards, one from Zacatecas along the central plateau through Durango and thence along the Conchos river in Chihuahua into

---

[26] Bancroft, *op. cit.*, III, 13–14.
[27] Hackett, *op. cit.*, I, 155–157.

New Mexico, and the other from Queretaro in an easterly direction through Nuevo León and Coahuila into southern Texas. No less extensive was the work of the Jesuits along the west coast. Starting at San Filipe in 1590, they advanced by decades from tribe to tribe in the series of river valleys that segment the coast line.   In 1604 missions were established among the Suaqui and Tehueco on the Rio Fuerte; ten years later a beginning was made among the Mayos in modern Sonora; in 1636 the Ures were reached in the Sonora River valley; in 1687 Father Kino began the evangelization of Pimeria by establishing Mission Dolores at the headwaters of the Rio de San Miguel; and finally in 1697 the Jesuits crossed the gulf of California to lay the foundations for a chain of missions in the Peninsula which ultimately led to Upper California.[28] "It was a grand movement, executed with infinite pains and patience, achieving vast results; and the laurel wreath of victory for Spanish colonization must ever rest upon the weather-beaten brow of the meek and humble missionary." [29] After being solely the agents of evangelization under the *encomenderos,* the missionaries had become the protectors of the Indians and the commissioned agents of Spanish colonization.   That they were zealous in the fulfillment of this mission is evident from the vast distances they covered; that they were successful is revealed in the methods they followed.

III

To accomplish the conversion and civilization of these numerous peoples, the missionaries developed a well organized mission system.   Its growth took nearly two centuries before it was completed, and was directed by the circumstances of environment rather than by any preconceived plan.   When located among more advanced, agricultural peoples, the organization of the mission was directed chiefly towards doctrinal instruction; when established among the more backward, nomadic tribes, it had to aim

---

[28] Bancroft, Hubert H., *History of California* (San Francisco, 1884–1890), I, 14–33.

[29] Tays, George, *Revolutionary California: the political history of California during the Mexican period* (MS., Library, University of California), 347.

at social as well as religious development; and finally, in one case, the mission system was organized so as to care for religious and social instruction and civil administration as well.

The earliest type of mission was organized chiefly for the purpose of religious instruction, since the first people with whom the missionaries came in contact in New Spain were the Aztecs. Possessed with a civilization that was in many respects little inferior to the European, they were already acquainted with the principles of private property, systematic labor and social organization. As has been already noted, when the missionaries came amongst them their main care was to erect churches and schools in the native communities and concentrate on religious instruction. In like manner, when the advance into the mining regions occurred, the missionaries encountered a peaceful, sedentary people, "practicing agriculture to some extent and living in villages." [30] This was true particularly of the Pueblo Indians whom the Oñate expedition in 1598 found inhabiting New Mexico. Already a sedentary, agricultural people, living in well organized communities, their type of civilization was left unchanged. By 1630 the Franciscans had established 25 missions among them, serving 90 pueblos and claiming 90,000 neophytes, but "there were neither goods of community in the missions nor formal allotment of lands. Each family counted for its own that which its ancestors possessed, occupying and cultivating it according to their necessities or their foresight." [31] Thus far the term, mission, simply meant a church and residence erected in a native village for the purpose of instructing and converting the Indians of the locality.

But this type of mission was rather the exception than the rule. The greater number of Indian tribes met with in the northern advance were of a more primitive class. Nomads and warriors, they wandered from place to place as the chances of the chase or the fortunes of war dictated. Town life and attachment to ancestral lands was scarcely known to them. Missionary work among these presented special problems and developed a new

---

[30] Bancroft, Hubert H., *History of the North Mexican States and Texas* (San Francisco, 1884–1889), I, 106.

[31] Revillagigedo, Juan V., *Carta de 1793*, MS., quoted by Jones, William C., *Report on the subject of land titles in California* (Washington, D. C., 1850), 59.

type of mission. The beginnings of this new type of mission can be traced to the mission at San Filipe which the Jesuits established on the west coast in 1590. There they found a people which while apparently peaceful had made little advance in agricultural or social organization. Accordingly, they were "gathered in little communities, to be baptized and married, to learn the doctrina. The Jesuits taught them to till the soil in a fashion more advanced than that which they had yearned from their forefathers." [32]

> In no mission was a formal distribution of lands made. The governor of these lower missions assigns the portion which each Indian who is the father of a family must cultivate during the year. The Indians are the owners of the harvested crops, of the fruits that are raised and of the products of their small flocks of cattle. [33]

This idea of a mission system based on community life was developed as the Jesuits advanced among the more savage and primitive tribes of Sinaloa and Pimeria, and the Franciscans among the same type of natives in Sierra Gorde and southern Texas. Faced with the necessity of gathering the members of such tribes in one locality to make possible their instruction, they usually persuaded them by gifts and friendly overtures to settle in a site where there was tillable soil, water for irrigation, and building materials. An instance of this was the Jesuit advance along the west coast from river to river. Once gathered in permanent settlements, the Indians, besides being instructed in the fundamentals of the Faith, were taught the rudiments of agriculture, for the missionaries found themselves faced with the necessity not only of saving the souls of the savages but also of providing subsistence for their bodies. Finally, after stability in crop production was attained, there came instruction in building, weaving, and other practical crafts. [34] But what was distinctive of these missions was the fact that the entire organization was based on a com-

---

[32] Bancroft, *op. cit.*, I, 119–120.

[33] Revillagigedo, *op. cit.*, quoted by Cuevas, Mariano, *Historia de la Iglesia en México* (El Paso, Texas, 1928), IV, 308.

[34] Priestley, *The coming of the white man*, 123.

munity of labor and of goods. Early experience seems to have convinced the missionaries that the less civilized the Indian, the less capable was he of grasping the idea of private ownership. Faced with this fact, the religious, themselves trained in community life, solved the problem by introducing a system of community labor and goods under their paternalistic supervision.

> In the upper missions the sowing of the crops was made in common, and the missionaries exercised the office of spiritual and temporal fathers, obliging the Indians to work in the fields, raise their crops and gather them into their barns and store-rooms; they provide them daily and weekly with whatever they need for their sustenance; they supply them with clothes, manage the sale at an opportune time of their fruits and grains, the surplus cattle, and the woolen and cotton clothes made in the workshops established at the missions.[35]

A final development in the mission system occurred when the Jesuits extended their missionary work to the Lower California Peninsula. Since the days of Cortés the Spanish government had made numerous attempts to establish a colony there but without enduring success. Finally in 1686 it invited the Jesuits to undertake the evangelization of the natives. The proposal was enthusiastically received by Fathers Kino and Salvatierra and at their persuasion the new mission field was accepted by the Jesuit superiors. This was done, however, only after an agreement had been reached with the crown that the religious should have complete charge of the financing and civil government of the Peninsula, as well as of its evangelization and pacification. "The entire enterprise was to be under Jesuit control; not only were they to have charge of spiritual interests, but they were also to hire and command soldiers and such other officials or helpers as they might need." [36] Earlier experiences in Sonora, Sinaloa and Pimeria seem to have convinced the Jesuits that the chief obstacles to missionary work were the hesitancy of an embarrassed royal

---

[35] Revillagigedo, *op. cit.*, quoted by Cuevas, *op. cit.*, IV, 308.
[36] Chapman, Charles E., *A history of California: the Spanish period* (New York, 1921), 174.

treasury to finance new missions, the interference of military officials, and the bad influence which the introduction of white settlers often had on the mission neophytes.

As their model they undoubtedly chose the famous reduction system which their Order had developed in Paraguay. There, on a tract of land granted them by the king, they had set up a state over which they exercised complete control in all things, political, military, and financial. Unhampered by government interference, custom, law, and the evil example of white settlers and adventurers, they had succeeded in gathering the Indians into towns or reductions, had converted and civilized them, and trained them for self government and self support. In forty-seven reductions over 300,000 families lived in peace and plenty where formerly savages had engaged in internecine warfare.[37]

In Lower California the same system was followed. At the outset Kino and Salvatierra provided for the independent support of the enterprise by creating through private subscription an endowment known as the Pious Fund.[38] On the Peninsula they followed the usual procedure of establishing missions based on community life with the addition that "the civil system was under the control of the mission authorities. The soldiers were, of course, subject immediately to their own officers, who exercised civil, military and judicial control, but were in turn subject to the direction of the *visitador*. The few settlers in the province came under the same rule and were subject to the Jesuit administration."[39] At times there were quarrels between the missionaries and the soldiers or with the government because of their opposition to the proposed establishment of colonies of white settlers, but in the end this type of mission system revealed itself as the best means for a successful achievement of the various ends of missionary endeavor.

During their seventy years' sojourn in Lower California, the Jesuits. . . . had founded twenty-three—including the chapel of Jesus del Monte—mission establishments, of which four-

---

[37] Blackmar, *Spanish colonization in the southwest,* 116–118.
[38] Cf. Chapman, *op. cit.,* 176–183.
[39] Blackmar, *op. cit.,* 82.

teen had proven successful; they had erected structures of
stone and beautified them; they had formulated a system of
mission life never thereafter surpassed; they had not only instructed the Indians in religious matters, but had taught them
many of the useful arts; they had made a network of open trails,
connecting the missions with each other and with Loreto; they
had taken scientific and geographical notes concerning the
country and prepared ethnological reports on the native races;
they had cultivated and planted the arable lands and inaugurated a system of irrigation. . . . Of their labors in the Peninsula, it has been said with truth that 'remote as was the land
and small the nation, there are few chapters in the history of
the world on which the mind can turn with so sincere an
admiration.' [40]

In a word, in less than a century they succeeded "in an enterprise
which for nearly two centuries had had an almost unbroken record
of failure." [41]

Such then was the manner in which the mission system grew
in the course of more than two centuries. Instituted primarily
for the work of conversion and civilization, the missions were
used by the crown as the means of pacification in the scheme of
defensive colonization. With every step northward new methods
were adopted to meet changing conditions. At first churches and
schools were established among the natives for the purpose of instructing them. Later, when nomadic peoples were encountered,
it was found necessary to gather the natives in settlements around
the churches. Then, with the advance into more primitive regions,
came the necessity of organizing the mission and its neophytes on
a system of community labor and goods. Finally, to avoid the
obstacles which had been revealed in the course of this development, it was deemed advisable to incorporate into the mission
system not only spiritual and temporal authority, but charge over
civil matters as well. This tendency towards centralization and
paternalism has undoubtedly exposed the mission system to criticism. Yet, if these two were aimed at and successfully achieved,

[40] North, Arthur W., *The mother of California* (San Francisco and New
York, 1908), 44–45.
[41] Chapman, *op. cit.*, 172.

it was not because of selfish motives but rather because of expediency. Of all men the missionaries were the most unselfish. They sacrificed everything for their neophytes. As ministers of the Gospel they left homeland and friends to convert them; as their appointed protectors against the encroachments and outrages of soldiers and settlers, they unflinchingly exposed themselves to the enmity and revenge of frustrated ambition and greed; and finally, as the officially constituted agents of Spanish defensive colonization, they produced results, often at the expense of their life blood, which proved to be of incalculable value not only to the Spanish crown but to all future generations in America as well. As one writer has aptly expressed it:

> They rent the veils that enfolded the border beyond; they opened routes for subsequent caravans of trade and industry; through their efforts vast territories were added to the public domain; and they planted nuclei for colonization and fostered their growth by holding in check red and white men alike by their restraining intercourse. More potent than trade or military expeditions, the unselfishness of religion succeeded where the former had failed.[42]

It was this tradition that Serra inherited and brought to Upper California.

IV

But there is a tragic as well as a glorious side to the mission history of New Spain, namely secularization. The term, secularization, originally meant the substitution of secular priests for the religious order priests and the conversion of the mission into a parish. Later it also meant the raising of the Indian community to the status of a self-governing pueblo and, finally, in practice it often resulted in the confiscation of the mission property and lands by white settlers or government officials. Therefore when a mission was secularized it really meant that its status as a mission ceased. It is generally held today that in the legislation governing Spanish colonization there existed from the beginning a

---

[42] Bancroft, Hubert H., *Chronicles of the builders of the commonwealth* (San Francisco, 1891–1892), VII, 468.

law which decreed that after ten years the individual missions
were to be secularized. As one of the first to express this view
has put it:

> The missions were intended from the beginning to be tem-
> porary in their character. It was contemplated that in ten
> years from their first foundation they should cease. It was
> supposed that within that period of time the Indians would
> be sufficiently instructed in Christianity and the arts of civ-
> ilized life, to assume the position and character of *Citizens;*
> that these mission settlements would then become *Pueblos* and
> that the mission churches would become parish churches. The
> monks. . . . were to be succeeded by the secular clergy of the
> national church, the missionary field was to become a *Diocese*
> and the president of the missions to give place to a *Bishop.*[43]

However, this view seems to be contradicted by the fact that
the missions, as has been already noted, were allowed to develop
during the course of more than two centuries into a well ordered
system in which the individual establishments continued to exist
long after the first ten year period. Moreover, this view when
applied to the question of the secularization of the California
Missions seems to justify on the grounds of legality the appalling
evils which it produced. Because of these perplexities the question has been studied anew with the result that the following conclusions have been arrived at: first, that the evidence points solely
to the existence of a law which exempted mission Indians from
tribute or taxes for a period of ten years, that this ten year exemption was extended by commentators to include exemption
from tithes and later from episcopal jurisdiction, but never implied that the missions were to come to an end through secularization after ten years; secondly, that while during the course of
the first two centuries of their history in New Spain many missions were secularized, the impulse came not from a government
law but from private parties, both ecclesiastical and lay; thirdly,
that the first general law ordering the secularization of the missions came only in 1749; fourthly, that on the occasion of the
publication of this law a mistake made by the reigning viceroy

---

[43] Dwinelle, John W., *The colonial history of the city of San Francisco* (San
Francisco, 1863), 20.

of New Spain gave rise to the belief that a ten year secularization law had existed from the beginning; and finally, that when an attempt was made to apply the general law of secularization, the results were so disastrous that its application had to be suspended. Because these conclusions are of importance to the study of the later secularization of the California Missions, they will be treated herein at some length.

The question of tribute or taxation to be levied on the Indians is one which was quite definite in the general laws with which the Spanish crown governed its New World possessions. Since the king of Spain was the conqueror of the New World, its peoples could be obliged in justice to pay tribute as an acknowledgement of his suzerainty and as the means of supporting the ministers and troops necessary for the government and defence of the new realm.[44]   However, on various occasions the crown exempted special classes from this general obligation, such as women, the sick and poor, peoples harrassed by famine, descendants of the royal family of the Incas and all Tlascalans in recognition of the aid which their nation had rendered to Cortés in his conquest of Mexico.[45]   Finally, probably at the request of missionaries laboring in America, a royal cedula was issued on January 30, 1607, and reissued on December 5, 1608, to the viceroy of Peru, in which converts to Christianity were exempted from taxation for the first ten years after their conversion according to the following provision:

> We order that those pagan Indians who of their own free will embrace our Holy Catholic Faith and receive Baptism solely as a result of the preaching of the Holy Gospel, shall not be subject to the *encomienda*, nor pay tribute for ten years, nor be compelled to any service.[46]

According to its commentators this law was not based on the assumption that after ten years the converted Indian would be sufficiently prepared to pay tribute.   As has been already noted, all

---

[44] Solorzano Pereira, Ioannes de, *De Indiarum Jure* (Lyons, 1672), tom. II (*De Indiarum Gubernatione*), lib. I, cap. XVIII, n. 2.

[45] *Ibid.*, tom. II, lib. I, cap. XIX, n. 5 ss.

[46] *Recopilacion de leyes de los reinos de las Indias* (Madrid, 1681), lib. VI, tit. V, ley 3; cf. Engelhardt, *op. cit.*, III, 136.

Indians whether pagan or Christian were obliged to pay tribute to their new sovereign. The law was rather an exemption from this general obligation because it was felt that "in the beginning the converts should be encouraged by mildness lest becoming terrified at harsh measures, they should relapse into their former state." [47] As the same commentator elsewhere remarked, "the Indians would scarcely persevere in their Faith if after having accepted the Christian religion they found themselves oppressed with greater and more irksome burdens and labors than those which they had formerly borne under pagan masters." [48]

At an early date it would seem that this law exempting recent converts from the obligation of paying tribute was interpreted by commentators to include a similar exemption from the obligation of paying tithes. Tithes were to the Church what tribute was to the civil power, an acknowledgment of God's universal suzerainty and a contribution to the support of His Religion.[49] Pagan as well as Christian Indians were bound by this obligation,[50] Charles V having ordered on February 27, 1534, that just as the Indians had supported the worship of idols, so should they contribute to the support of the Church.[51] But if the natives were bound to the obligation of tithes for the same reason that they were obliged to pay tribute, commentators declared those exemptions which had been made in the matter of tribute also applied to tithes. Therefore the ten year exemption for converts was intended to include tithes.

But if the arguments concerning tributes hold for tithes, it seems proper that recently converted Indians should be excused from the payment of tithes since, as we have seen, they are excused for a certain length of time from the payment of tribute. It is true that in many provinces they can no longer be called Neophytes since both they themselves and their parents have been baptized. . . . However, since there are still many who remain to be converted and others who while already

---

[47] Solorzano, *op. cit.*, tom. II, lib. I, cap. XIX, n. 75.
[48] *Ibid.*, tom. I, lib. III, cap. VIII, n. 9.
[49] *Ibid.*, tom. II, lib. I, cap. XXI, n. 4.
[50] *Ibid.*, tom. II, lib. I, cap. XXI, n. 8.
[51] *Ibid.*, tom. II, lib. I, cap. XXI, n. 36.

converted are still weak in the Christian Religion, it is proper that they should be treated with kindness and be freed from the full, strict and rigorous exaction of tithes, as is suggested by that remarkable passage of St. Paul, I Cor., IX, in which, speaking of the obligation that existed to support ministers and preachers of the Holy Gospel, he said, he had not used this power, but had borne all things lest he should give any hindrance to the Gospel of Christ.[52]

This interpretation, advanced by the foremost commentator of Spanish law, was apparently recognized and applied. Recent converts were exempted from tithes for a period of ten years not by virtue of a law but by virtue of the accepted broad interpretation of the law decreeing a similar exemption in the matter of tributes.

But the broadening of the meaning of the law of 1607 did not end with its extension to tithes. It would seem that at a later date, as a result of a controversy between the religious orders and the hierarchy, the law was interpreted to include a ten year period of exemption for missions from episcopal jurisdiction. In New Spain episcopal jurisdiction meant the right which the bishops possessed to pass on the appointment of all priests to *doctrinas,* or parishes and missions, within their diocese. It also included the right of the bishop to visit the *doctrinas,* inspect the records, examine the *doctrinero* or incumbent, correct abuses should any be found to exist, and finally, what is more pertinent to the present question, to receive tithes from the members of the particular *doctrina* for his support,[53] the crown having granted a part of the tithes which it enjoyed under the *Patronato Real* to the bishops for their support.[54]

However, the various religious orders disputed the right of bishops to exercise this jurisdiction in the case of *doctrinas* filled by regulars. When the work of evangelization was begun in New Spain immediately after the conquest by Cortés in 1521, it was at first carried on exclusively by members of the religious orders. Accordingly, a series of privileges were conceded by the Holy

---

[52] *Ibid.,* tom. II, lib. I, cap. XXI. n. 38–40.

[53] Parras, Pedro Joseph, *Gobierno de los Regulares de la América* (Madrid, 1783), II, 295–296.

[54] Solorzano, *op. cit.,* tom. II, lib. III, cap. IV, n. 15 ss.

See which exempted these missionaries from all episcopal jurisdiction and gave them full powers in the exercise of their ministry.[55] However, when with the creation of the diocese of Mexico
City in 1527 the hierarchical life of the Church was begun, the
bishops insisted on their right to exercise jurisdiction in the *doctrinas* of religious as well as those held by their own diocesan or
secular priests. The question was apparently decided when the
Council of Trent in 1563 issued a decree for the universal Church
which declared that "regulars as well as seculars in charge of
doctrinas were immediately subject to the bishop in whose diocese
they were, in the matter of the administration of the sacraments,
jurisdiction, visitation and correction." [56] But the question was
not so easily settled. On March 24, 1567, the former Franciscan,
Pius V, exempted the religious in the Indies from the Tridentine
decree, while his successor, Gregory XIII, took the opposite
stand by revoking all exemptions which had been made from
the law of Trent. This but intensified the controversy. The
bishops insisted on the application of the Tridentine decree while
the religious claimed exemption from it on the ground that
Gregory's revocation of privileges, being general, had not affected
the particular exemption granted by Pius V.[57] Both sides carried
their case to the crown with the result that "numerous royal
cedulas were constantly sent to the various regions of the Indies,
permitting in some the full enjoyment of the privileges granted
by Pius V, and commanding in others the observance of the dispositions of the *Patronato Real* and the Council of Trent." [58]
The question was carried into the next century when it resulted in
the famous controversy of 1647 between Juan de Palafox, the
Bishop of Pueblo, and the Jesuits,[59] and was only settled in the latter
part of the 19th century when an English bishop, confronted with
the opposition of regulars, forced a final decision.[60]

---

[55] For a detailed treatment of these privileges cf. Engelhardt, *op. cit.*, IV,
303–305; Bancroft, *History of Mexico*, II, 160–161.

[56] Parras, *op. cit.*, II, 299–302.

[57] *Ibid.*, II, 305–309.

[58] *Ibid.*, II, 312.

[59] Cf. Cuevas, *op. cit.*, III, 283–312.

[60] Cf. Snead-Cox, John G., *The Life of Cardinal Vaughan* (St. Louis, 1910),
I, 320 ss.

It would seem that it was in the course of this controversy that the tax exemption law of 1607 was interpreted by the partisans of the religious orders to imply exemption from episcopal jurisdiction. A commentator on religious orders in America, referring expressly to the cedula of January 30, 1607, presented this novel interpretation as follows:

> The prelates of all religious orders should know that Reductions, Missions and *Conversiones,* which are all one, are subject *pleno jure* to the Regulars *for ten years,* which period is to be counted from the day on which the establishment of their Pueblo was begun. During these ten years the Kings of Spain have desired to refrain from all interference in them, and have prohibited their Viceroys, Presidents and Governors, Bishops and other Superiors of the Indies from intermeddling in the government of them, ordering them to leave them entirely to the rule of their missionaries. Finally, the King desires that the small tribute which ought to be paid by the Indians as vassals of the King should not be demanded until the mentioned period of time is completed and the pueblos begin to be governed by the laws, for which the missionaries themselves are preparing them.[61]

This new interpretation of the law of 1607 was published in 1783 and therefore was influenced by the developments that had occurred during the century and three quarters that had elapsed since the publication of the original law. The mention of pueblos and pueblo laws reflects the changes that had been introduced during this period, while the asserted exemption from episcopal interference was inspired by the controversy over episcopal jurisdiction. The author had read much into the law of 1607 and it may be doubted whether his interpretation was ever widely accepted.

---

[61] Parras, *op. cit.,* II, 73. This author further states: "In case that in some missions, after the term of ten years, it has not been possible to have all the Indians equally prepared for Baptism, neither the King nor the Supreme Council of the Indies are inexorable but will readily lengthen the time, so that the Indians may continue under the direction of the missionaries alone. In the Province of Paraguay, the governors have an order that the Indians may continue under the sole direction of the missionaries for the first twenty years." *Ibid.,* II, 74–75. However, no reference is made to the source of this information.

But what is of real importance is the fact that not even this broad interpretation of the law of 1607 implied secularization after a period of ten years. Though the regulars and their missions were subject to the jurisdiction of the local bishop, they were not forced by law to surrender their missions to diocesan priests and thereby change the status of the mission and its neophytes. During the first two centuries secularization was governed by custom rather than by law.

Secularization in its strict sense has always been a usual feature in the process of diocesan development. In New Spain, as has been already noted, the clergy was at first composed chiefly of members of the various religious orders. But with the creation of dioceses, the number of secular priests increased. This was true particularly in the more civilized regions around Mexico City, where priests were easily obtained not only from Spain but especially, after the establishment of seminaries, from the native population itself. As the secular clergy therefore increased, the movement began to substitute them for the members of religious orders. There is evidence of this as early as 1554 when it was asserted by the partisans of the secular clergy in Mexico City that "the religious, in harmony with their institutions, ought to withdraw into their convents and leave the parishes which they had erected in the hands of secular priests who were the proper pastors of souls." [62] While this argument was easily refuted by the assertion that the religious life did not necessarily imply the contemplative life, the movement of secularization continued until in the more central dioceses the regulars were for the greater part replaced by diocesan priests.

While the details of this gradual change are obscure, the few instances that are known reveal that the initiative in secularization was taken by the local religious authorities and not by the crown through a general law. Thus in 1640 Juan de Palafox, the Bishop of Puebla, "because of irregularities in appointment and administration, deprived the orders of their missions and established thirty-seven new curacies which had formerly belonged to the Augustinians, Franciscans and Dominicans." [63] In like man-

---

[62] Cuevas, op. cit., II, 153.
[63] Bancroft, History of Mexico, III, 100–101.

ner in 1753 the Jesuit authorities surrendered twenty-two of their establishments to the Bishop of Durango while at the same time the Franciscans gave up a number of their southern missions to the secular clergy in order to use the priests thus formerly employed in opening up new mission fields.[64]   Finally, there is an instance in which the local Spanish element took the initiative in procuring the secularization of a mission.   In 1645 the Spanish community of Parras laid claim to the irrigation water used by the Indians of the local mission with the result that the governor, himself an interested party, deprived the Indians of their water rights.   Thereupon, the natives probably led by their missionaries, appealed their case to the *audiencia* of the province and won a restoration of their usurped rights.   But the Spaniards, not to be defeated, petitioned the viceroy for the secularization of the mission.   As a result secular priests were sent to replace the religious and the water rights were given to the Spaniards.   Within a short time it was found that the mission lands could not be cultivated for lack of water so that as a final outcome the mission fell into decay.[65]

These several instances are illustrative of the general procedure in secularization as it occurred during the first two centuries of mission history in New Spain. While the missions were not forced by law to come to an end after ten years, the normal course of events revealed that they were destined to be but temporary. "The idea of their foundation was that they should serve not as an end but merely as a means. It contemplated their existence only so long as might be necessary to convert, civilize and educate the Indians up to the point of qualification for citizenship." [66] In the beginning the chief emphasis seems to have been placed on the Indians' advance in conversion and civilization with the result that the time element was determined by the standard of native culture which had previously existed as well as by the number of diocesan priests that were available. Thus in central Mexico where the Aztecs and the neighboring peoples were already well advanced in civilization before they came under the influence

---

[64] Bancroft, *History of the North Mexican States and Texas,* I, 587.

[65] *Ibid.,* I, 342; cited by Priestley, *The coming of the white man,* 47–48.

[66] Hittell, Theodore H., *History of California* (San Francisco, 1885), II, 181.

of the missionaries and where at the same time there was a sufficient number of secular priests, the missions as such were brought to an end by secularization within a comparatively short period. In the more remote regions, where the natives were less advanced and the task of the missionary proportionately greater, secularization was generally not attempted till after a longer period of time. The missions continued on the basis of community life sometimes for a century or more. If at times bishops or religious superiors attempted to change the mission status too early, secularization "however successful and profitable when applied to the more civilized pueblos of New Spain, was often attended with failure when applied to the remoter regions." [67] Finally, when secularization was motivated by the greed of white settlers, it resulted almost invariably in the confiscation of the mission goods and lands, a decline in the number of neophytes and the destruction of whatever benefits had been gained during the mission period. Thus even at this early period the general principles of mission secularization had already been revealed. Secularization in itself was but a normal process in church development; but when it was attempted where conditions did not warrant a change or was prompted by unworthy motives, it was invariably the cause of disaster. This was substantiated by the events that now followed.

A new development in the secularization movement occurred when a general law was published in 1749 ordering the transfer of all parishes and missions in the Americas from the care of the religious orders to the secular clergy. There had been long developing on the part of the Spanish rulers a marked coolness towards missionary expansion and a certain hostility towards the religious orders. After the period of the two great Catholic kings, Charles I and Philip II, under whom the Church had made its greatest advances in the new world, the Hapsburg dynasty had begun to decline. For more than a century there followed weak monarchs whose reigns were marked by favoritism, selfishness and incompetence in administration. When as a result of poor administrators the treasury became embarrassed, there developed

---

[67] Bancroft, *History of Mexico*, III, 712.

a marked coolness towards missionary enterprises. When missionaries sought funds from the government to open up new mission fields, as a rule "their appeals went unnoticed save when foreign aggressions carried a threat that could not be ignored." [68] In 1701 with the death of the last Hapsburg, Charles II, Spain was given a Bourbon dynasty in the person of Philip V, the grandson of Louis XIV of France. But although Philip and his successors with the energy of the French injected new life and efficiency into Spanish administration, reorganizing the army and navy and recuperating the government's financial system, their more watchful economic policy reacted against the missions. The support of the missions was regarded as an unnecessary burden. But what was perhaps of greater consequence, the coming of the Bourbons introduced into Catholic Spain the principles of Voltaireanism and Jansenism which were then so prevalent in France,[69] and which served as the basis of a spirit of hostility and opposition which was being manifested at that time towards the Church in general and in particular towards religious orders.

It was under these circumstances that on October 4, 1749, Ferdinand VI issued a general law secularizing all churches and missions in the new world. The acting Viceroy of New Spain, Revillagigedo, in an instruction prepared for his successor, recounted the details of this important change as follows:

> The King, after consulting a *junta* composed of the principal ministers, certain prelates and other worthy persons, by a royal cedula of October 4, 1749, decreed the removal of the regulars in the Indies from the *curas* and *doctrinas,* which they had held since the beginning of those dominions while a fit clergy was being formed to exercise the ministry of souls. . . . He sent the order secretly to the viceroys and governors of the provinces who exercise the *Patronato Real* . . . and ordered that it should be executed at first in the archdioceses of Lima, Mexico and Santa Fe in order that its success in these might prepare the way for its execution in all the other churches and establish the rules which were to be followed. . . . And he desired that I should instruct them as to the manner in which they ought to

---

[68] Priestley, *op. cit.,* 32.
[69] Chapman, Charles E., *A history of Spain* (New York, 1918), 428.

execute it, in order that in its execution there might be no occasion for scandal, confusion or disturbance.[70]

The law of 1749 has a twofold relation with the question of mission secularization in New Spain. On the one hand it marked the first attempt at universal secularization on the part of the government, and on the other it was the occasion of a commentary by the viceroy, in which was revealed both the changed attitude of the official classes towards the missions and the source of the belief that there existed from the beginning a law which decreed the secularization of the missions after a period of ten years. Turning first to the latter, the viceroy's commentary was as follows:

The missions should in conformity with the law have been reduced to *doctrinas* long ago, and the Treasury would have been freed of the increased expenses which have been and are being occasioned by the *sínodos* with which the missionaries are maintained; because it is more than a hundred and thirty and a hundred and twenty years since some of these missions were established and subjected completely to the direction of their respective missionaries. During so long a time none of them have been restored [to the bishops], *as should have been done after ten years,* in virtue of the provisions of the law. As a result of this, the Royal Treasury has been injured not only by the expenses which the missions occasion it as long as they continue to exist, but also by the fact that it is deprived of the tributes which the Indians would have contributed if the missions had been given to their diocesan bishops in the stated time; and the damage goes further still because the Indians have no property in common in their missions nor liberty since they live with great servitude and subjection, depending on and subject to the will of the missionary fathers. So great is this that it might be said without fear of mistake that the missionaries, under the pretext of their being neophytes and other pretexts advanced, want to perpetuate their despotic rule over them. As a result, if the governors of the provinces and their subalterns attempt to enforce the municipal laws of the kingdom for the sake of good government and in order that the pueblos of the Indians might be ruled in conformity to them

---

[70] "Officio del Conde de Revillagigedo sobre secularización de curatos y separar de ellos a los Regulares," *Instrucciones que los vireyes de Nueva España dejaron a sus sucesores* (México, 1867), 41.

and in opposition to that which the missionaries have established and ordered in their own form of government, then the wrath of the missionaries conspires against these just provisions, so that the governors in order to escape this anger and avoid an inexorable persecution find themselves obliged to yield to the policy of the missionaries. The Viceroy, perplexed by the fights and quarrels and in danger of being accused of disloyalty, impiety and stubbornness towards the religious order in charge of the particular missions, cannot make a decision since his position demands that he avoid the inconveniences and ill consequences that would follow, with injury to the reputation of his employees and his own person. . . .

The source of all this evil comes from the fact that under the pretext of a misinterpreted and misconceived law, Spaniards have been excluded from the Indian community villages at the missions. But the damage of this was recognized too late for the evils which I have already specified were permitted to arise and we suffered revolts of the Indians. If, on the contrary, the congregation and population of Spaniards had not been hindered, those evils would not have occurred. The Indians would now be better disciplined and advanced in the spiritual as well as the temporal, and imbued with a greater spirit of subordination and obedience; in a few years the missions would have been abolished and the Indians would be enjoying freedom and the fruits of their labors, while the King would be enjoying the payment of tribute; the dominion would have been more populated and its most distant provinces developed, provinces that are very rich in fruits and mines; and finally, with the Indians instructed and accustomed to everything pertaining to their Christian, political, civil and social life, there would be no fear of the danger of their insurrection.[71]

An analysis of Revillagigedo's *instrucción* shows that a new meaning had been given to the term, secularization. According to the viceroy secularization meant the turning of the missions over to the bishops, the replacing of the regulars by diocesan priests, the distribution of the mission lands and properties to the Indians, the transfer of the Indians from the control of the missions to a form of pueblo government and laws, and finally, a two-

---

[71] "Instrucción del Sr. Conde de Revillagigedo al Sr. Marqués de las Amarillas," *op. cit.*, 31–32.

fold boon to the treasury in the form of tributes to be paid by the Indians and of *sínodos* no longer to be paid by the government to missionaries, the new diocesan priests now being obliged to look to their Indian parishioners for support. It was a novel definition of secularization, one which it would seem arose from the double error of extending in an unwarranted manner the meaning of the decree of 1749 and of identifying with it the cedula of 1607.

As has been already noted, secularization according to the decree of 1749 simply meant the substitution of seculars for regulars in the parishes and missions of the new world. However, from Revillagigedo's *instrucción*, it would seem that among certain officials, at least in New Spain, more than this had been hoped for. There was the desire to remove the Indians from the control of the missionaries and place them under civil officials in a pueblo form of government; there was also a feeling of dissatisfaction over the royal order which prohibited white settlers from intermingling with mission neophytes; and finally, there was a need for the added revenue which the payment of taxes by the Indians would give to the treasury, this latter being particularly desirable in view of the new reforms which had been introduced into the Spanish financial system and of the more stringent demands which had been sent as a result to the viceroys and governors of the colonies. Moved by the desire for these changes and probably by other motives that cannot be determined, Revillagigedo, perhaps unconsciously, read them into the law of 1749. But he did not stop here. As has been already noted, the law of 1607 was at this time being broadly interpreted to mean the exemption of regulars and their missions from episcopal jurisdiction for a period of ten years. The viceroy easily confused episcopal jurisdiction with the substitution of diocesan or the bishop's priests for the priests of the religious orders, and accordingly identified the cedula of 1607 with the decree of 1749, and thereby through his double error gave rise to a new theory of secularization.

This, it seems, is the explanation of the present day belief that from the beginning there existed a law which ordered that after ten years the missionaries should be replaced by diocesan priests, the mission changed into a parish, the mission lands and goods distributed to the Indians, and the natives themselves organized in pueblos and raised to the status of citizens.[72]   But while the later significance of this new definition of secularization is quite clear, its immediate consequences cannot be so easily determined. However, from a later California governor's reference in 1796 to a law reducing the missions to *doctrinas* after ten years,[73] as well as from the specification of a ten year time limit in the secularization decree of the Spanish *Cortes* in 1813,[74] it would seem that it was gradually accepted.   What is of more immediate interest, it probably influenced the widespread application of secularization which was now attempted in New Spain.

Although the decree of 1749 ordered secularization throughout both Americas, it seems that when an attempt was made to apply it many difficulties arose to prevent its execution.   This is suggested by the following description by Revillagigedo of the first attempts to apply the law:

> The cedula was sent to all the bishops and in all parts their provisions were executed with equal success, although in some parts it was applied with more vigor than in others, depending on the greater or less activity of the prelates, the supply of suitable clergy, or the necessity of having some consideration for the religious.[75]

Several cedulas which were issued within the next few years emphasize these latter difficulties which the law met.   Thus, shortly after publishing the law the viceroy found himself obliged

---

[72] From present day writers this view may be traced back chronologically as follows: Blackmar, *Spanish colonization in the southwest* (Baltimore, 1890), 130; Bancroft, *History of California* (San Francisco, 1884), I, 580; Tuthill, Franklin, *The history of California* (San Francisco, 1866), 108; Dwinelle, *The colonial history of the city of San Francisco* (San Francisco, 1863), 20; Jones, *Report on the subject of land titles in California* (Washington, D. C., 1850), 13. Jones spent several months doing archival work in Mexico and there possibly learned of this view either from the reference to it in the secularization law passed by the Spanish *Cortes* in 1813, from hearsay, or through his own reading of the archival copy of Revillagigedo's *instrucción*.

[73] Bancroft, *History of California*, I, 580.

[74] Cf. Engelhardt, *op. cit.*, III, 96.

[75] "Officio del Conde de Revillagigedo, sobre secularización de curatos y separar de ellos a los Regulares," *op. cit.*, 42.

to issue an order restricting its application to those *doctrinas* which were "held illegally by the religious who had been appointed by their superiors without title or royal presentation or the authorization of the bishop, this against the form provided by the laws of the Indies and commanded by the Council of Trent." A royal cedula of February 1, 1753, placed a further restriction on the law by ordering that it should be applied only as parishes were left vacant by the death of the regulars, the secular clergy being then appointed to succeed them.[76] As Revillagigedo remarked in another *instrucción:*

Because there could not be found a sufficient number of diocesan priests well versed in the different Indian dialects to take over the *doctrinas* and because the religious, deprived of their curacies and the income attached to them, would be without any means of support, it was necessary to execute the law more slowly. The seculars were to take over the parishes of the religious only as they were made vacant by the death of the incumbents.[77]

Finally a cedula from the king, dated June 30, 1754, acknowledged these difficulties by ordering that a knowledge of the principal Indian dialects should be required at the University of Mexico as a prerequisite for a theological degree, and that the religious orders should be allowed to retain a number of large parishes in order that they might thereby possess a means of support.[78] The immediate application of general secularization had proved to be impracticable and it was apparently resolved to execute it only gradually as conditions warranted. Consequently, little more is heard of secularization during the next decade.

But the secularization movement received a new impetus in 1767 "when like a bolt from a clear sky there came a royal order expelling the Society of Jesus from the dominions of Spain and its colonies in America and in the Philippines." [79] It would seem that

---

[76] *Ibid.,* 42.

[77] "Instrucción del Sr. Conde de Revillagigedo al Sr. Marqués de las Amarillas," *op. cit.,* 30–31.

[78] *Instrucciones que los vireyes . . .,* 98–99.

[79] Engelhardt, *op. cit.,* I, 304.

Charles III, when he passed from the throne of Naples to that of Spain, had brought with him a number of foreign ministers whose nationality made the government unpopular. In 1766 its exactions led to severe outbreaks throughout the kingdom which for a time assumed the proportions of a rebellion. An extraordinary council was appointed to investigate the matter with the result that it charged the Jesuits with responsibility for the outbreaks and recommended their expulsion from Spain. Although its proceedings and motives were kept secret:

> A document of Campomanes is at hand summing up some of the charges made at the meeting of the *Consejo*. They were the following: responsibility for the Squillace riots; the diffusion of maxims contrary to the royal and the canon law; a spirit of sedition; treasonable relations with the English in the Philippine Islands; monopolization of commerce and excess of power in the Americas; a too great pride, leading them to support the doctrines of Rome against the king; advocacy by many Jesuit writers of the right of tyrannicide; political intrigues against the king; and aspiration for universal monarchy. While the evidence in support of these charges is no longer available, it is clear that they were exaggerated, or even without foundation, . . .[80]

On February 27, 1767, the king signed a decree for the expulsion of the Jesuits and its execution was ordered to be carried out with great secrecy and dispatch, so that the blow should fall simultaneously and without warning in all parts of Spain's dominions. It was published in Mexico City on June 24, and immediately over four hundred members of the Order in New Spain were removed from their missions, colleges and churches and banished to the Papal States.[81] It was one of the greatest tragedies in the history of the Church not only in America but throughout the world.

The suppression of the Jesuits precipitated a disastrous wave of secularization which dealt a heavy blow to the work of evangelization in New Spain. Of the fifty or more Jesuit missions along the west coast, over half were transferred to the secular clergy of

---

[80] Chapman, *History of Spain*, 450–451.
[81] Engelhardt, *op. cit.*, I, 310.

the Diocese of Durango while the rest were placed under the Franciscans.[82] From the Jesuit missions secularization spread to those of the Franciscans, four of their establishments in the Santa Fe district being secularized in 1767,[83] and a large number in the Sierra Gorde region, where Father Serra of later California fame was laboring, being transferred to the Archbishop of Mexico City.[84] But what is more significant, this widespread movement was accompanied by the official sanction of a type of secularization which had formerly existed only as an abuse. Since the mission lands and properties, due to the general confiscation of Jesuit properties which had been ordered, were considered as having belonged not to the Indians but to the Jesuits, military officials were everywhere placed in charge of the temporal administration of the missions, the clergy whether diocesan or regular being restricted to spiritual jurisdiction.[85] The following description of this new type of secularization as applied to the Lower California Missions holds true for those of Sonora and Pimeria as well:

> Not only was the government of the province forever removed from mission control, but also the temporalities of the missions,—that is, the flocks, crops, and economic resources in general,—were left in the hands of military commissioners. Only the church properties and spiritual authority were to be in charge of the Franciscans.[86]

While possibly not directly influenced by it, this corresponded to Revillagigedo's conception of secularization,—not only a replacement of the religious by diocesan priests, but especially the removal of the administration of the mission temporalities from the charge of the clergy.

But it soon became evident that this broad definition of secularization meant simply the destruction of the missions and their neophytes. When the clergy found themselves deprived of all finan-

---

[82] Priestley, Herbert I., *José de Gálvez, visitor-general of New Spain* (Berkeley, 1916), 285.

[83] Bancroft, Hubert H., *History of Arizona and New Mexico* (San Francisco, 1889), 274.

[84] Engelhardt, *op. cit.*, I, 394–396.

[85] Priestley, *op. cit.*, 285.

[86] Chapman, *History of California: the Spanish period*, 185.

cial assistance by the withdrawal of the government *sinodos* and their removal from the administration of temporalities, they were unable to carry on their work. The Indians scattered and the missions declined and in certain cases had to be abandoned.[87] But what was a greater cause of disaster, the military commissioners proved to be dishonest and inefficient in their administration of the temporalities with the result that the material prosperity of the various missions came to an end. In Sonora the accounts of their stewardship were muddled and incomplete,[88] and in Lower California "the military men proved to be self-seeking or else incompetent. They gave very little thought to the Indians and very much to the search for the vast treasure which the Jesuits were reputed to have accumulated. As a result the missions were nearly ruined, and the Indians were left in sad straits, while little or no treasure was found." [89] It was evident that this new type of secularization could end only in failure. For the Church it meant an inevitable decline of evangelization; for the Indian it meant the confiscation of his lands and his subjection to the exploitation of greedy officials; it was a success only for those who enriched themselves with the confiscated property. The government soon learned that secularization served but little to increase its revenues and it therefore took steps to suspend it.

That the reaction against secularization set in almost immediately seems to be quite certain. Thus when the visitor-general, José de Gálvez, visited Lower California in 1768, he was appalled at the destruction which had been wrought by secularization and immediately ordered that the administration of mission temporalities should be transferred to the charge of the Franciscans. In like manner in 1771, six secularized missions in the El Paso district were found to be in such a sad state of decline that to save them from complete ruin it was found advisable to place them once again under the care of the Franciscans.[90] Although it cannot be determined whether other missions were similarly returned to the religious orders, extant evidence reveals that the govern-

---

[87] Priestley, *op. cit.*, 286.
[88] *Ibid.*, 285.
[89] Chapman, *op. cit.*, 184–185.
[90] Bancroft, *History of Arizona and New Mexico*, 274.

ment refrained from all further attempts to apply its secularization law. This was reflected in the following statement which was written in 1790 by Hipólito Villarroel, the leading political writer in New Spain at that period:

> The religious through their humility and poverty . . . , are better fitted for educating and governing the Indians than are secular ecclesiastics, because of the petulance, conceit and cupidity of the latter. The Indians look on the seculars with loathing and horror because they are accustomed to the kindly but respectable treatment of the regulars. This repugnance is enough to keep the Indians from making progress favorable to themselves and to society, while they are subordinate to the seculars.[91]

This new policy was even more clearly made manifest in 1793, when a new viceroy, Juan Vicente de Revillagigedo, the second of that name, admitted the failure of secularization and sent a lengthy report to the crown in which he strongly advised a return to the old policy of leaving the missions in the hands of the religious.[92] This advice was apparently followed for thenceforth, until the coming of the radicals into power, the Spanish crown took no further steps to secularize the missions. Government initiative in secularization had proved itself to be the occasion for too many abuses.

While this latter determination came after the California Missions had been begun, it may be said that before their establishment every phase of mission history had been fully revealed. Spain, Catholic and intimately associated in the government of the Church, had chosen the missionaries, after *encomenderos* had failed, to act as the instructors and protectors of its new wards, the Indians. Soon after, it began its vast program of defensive expansion, and again turned to the missionaries to serve as its agents of colonization. To achieve this end, the religious orders developed during the course of nearly three centuries an efficient and well organized mission system. Its methods and the length

---

[91] Quoted by Fisher, *Viceregal administration in the Spanish-American colonies,* 198.

[92] Priestley, *The coming of the white man,* 184.

of duration of its individual units were determined not by pre-established principles or laws but by actual conditions as they were met. Among the more advanced peoples of the Aztec Confederacy its organization was simple and the time required for the achievement of its end, comparatively short. But among the nomadic, less civilized tribes of the *tierra de guerra,* where the missionaries had to begin at the bottom of the cultural ladder, a more highly organized system was needed and a greater length of time required before the purpose of the mission could be accomplished. Normally, it was only when this was realized, and then only as the development of a diocese or the need for laborers in a new mission field prompted it, that the missions were secularized. But even under these conditions, secularization was a risky thing and open to many abuses. Its dangers were fully revealed when the government attempted to enforce a law of general secularization. It produced so many evils that the work of the missions would have been completely ruined and the Indians eventually destroyed had not a stop been brought to it by suspending the application of the law. When, therefore, the first of a new chain of missions was established in Upper California in 1769, the experience of over two centuries directed its methods of organization and prepared it for the dangers that would threaten it.

CHAPTER II

BEGINNINGS OF MISSION SECULARIZATION
IN CALIFORNIA: 1769–1821

When the first of the California Missions was founded in 1769, its establishment contradicted the general trend of opposition which was manifesting itself in Spain and its colonies towards the missions. Only three decades before, the Spanish crown had sought to secularize all the missions in the New World; while two years previous the suppression of the Jesuits had given the secularization movement the greatest impulse it had received in the course of more than two centuries. It was only because an emergency demanded it, that a new chain of missions was begun in California; and it was only because special circumstances arose to forestall all attempts to bring it to an early end, that the California Missions were allowed to develop into one of the most perfect examples of the mission system. But once these circumstances were removed, the forces behind the movement of secularization reappeared and threatened the Missions with destruction. It was this strange cycle of events which marked the beginnings of secularization in California.

I

The Spanish occupation of California had been planned since the days of Cortés. At first, in the century of remunerative conquest, it was for the purpose of finding the rich kingdom of Quivera or the strait of Anián and the treasures of the Orient to which it led. Later it was for the purpose of protecting the Manila Galleon against buccaneers or of forestalling French and English advances. But whatever the motive, the spread of the Faith was always the accepted corollary. Had the projects initiated by Rodríguez Cermenho in 1593 or by Sebastián Vizcaíno in 1602 been carried out, the story of California would have been rather like that of New Mexico. But as is always the case with defensive colonization, each succeeding project was allowed to lapse when the danger became less imminent. With the passing of the buccaneers, the Pacific came to be looked upon as a comfortable Spanish lake. As a viceroy wrote in 1607, "the greatest strength of the royal dominions in the Pacific is that of the difficulty the king's enemies have in getting there or in remaining, after they have arrived." [1] Spain felt secure in her New World possessions and California was doomed to peaceful obscurity for another century and a half.

But when in 1765 there was sent, as visitor-general to New Spain, a man endowed with the energy and administrative capacity necessary to make the occupation of California a reality, the defensive were destined to overshadow the religious motives. José de Gálvez's purpose was to reform the administrative system in the government, increase revenues and, if possible, win personal distinction for himself. He early saw in California the promise of all three. Its exposure to foreign occupation, particularly since the publication of the *Noticia de la California* in Europe in 1757,[2] was a weakness in the system of defenses, its occupation offered the possibility of rich returns to the Crown, and success where so many others had failed would mean much in the way of personal glory. He discussed the project with the viceroy, Croix, and in 1768 sent four lengthy reports to the king exposing the danger of foreign occupation. Recent reports showed that the Russians were encroaching upon the California coasts, while since Anson's capture of the Galleon and its secret chart in 1742, the English and the Dutch were over-interested in the Pacific. "Any one of these three peoples," said Gálvez, "might easily plant a colony in Monterey, a port with excellent facilities for a settlement. Thus Spain's possessions in the Pacific might be invaded and exploited as those of the Atlantic (from Virginia to Georgia) had been." [3] Gálvez's chance came in 1768. While he was on his way to Lower California for the purpose of effecting a reform

---

[1] Chapman, Charles E., *A history of California: the Spanish period* (New York, 1921), 141.

[2] *Ibid.*, 199.

[3] *Ibid.*, 214.

in the frontier government there,[4] he received a dispatch through the viceroy from the Spanish minister, Grimaldi, informing him that the Spanish ambassador to Russia had reported new developments in the Russian occupation of the Pacific Coast from Alaska southward, and ordering him to "instruct the governor appointed for California—concerning the vigilance and care which he should exercise in order to observe the attempts which the Russians might make, frustrating them as much as possible. . . ."[5] Gálvez grasped the opportunity. While the letter did not order an expedition to Monterey, it gave him all the authority he needed. On May 20, he informed the viceroy that he intended to send an expedition to occupy Monterey and on May 24, before Croix could have had time to reply to him, he embarked for Lower California.[6]

In the first plans for the California expedition there is no evidence that Gálvez intended to use missionaries as his colonization agents. From the harsh methods that described his part in the expulsion of the Jesuits[7] as well as his prominence in the movement of mission secularization that followed,[8] it would seem that he shared in the general lack of sympathy for them. If his program of frontier reform can be taken as an indication, California was to be occupied by armed colonists who, settled in towns and living off the land, would supply the necessary defense and at the same time make the project self-supporting.[9] Finally, his hopes to find vast stores of wealth concealed, according to the popular belief, by the Jesuits in the Peninsula,[10] indicates his plan for the financing of the expedition.

But the conditions he met on his arrival in Lower California, soon forced him to abandon this scheme. Of wealth he found little, while the civilians were the least promising of materials for a colony. Their administration of the missions had reduced them

---

[4] Priestley, Herbert I., *José de Gálvez, visitor-general of New Spain* (Berkeley, 1916), 239 ss.

[5] Engelhardt, *The missions and missionaries of California*, II, 4.

[6] Chapman, *op. cit.*, 218–219.

[7] Priestley, *op. cit.*, 211 ss.

[8] *Ibid.*, 285.

[9] *Ibid.*, 241.

[10] Chapman, *op. cit.*, 220.

to such a wretched state, that he was obliged on the contrary to restore the management of the temporalities to the Franciscans.[11] This concrete proof of the superiority of the mission system as a means of colonization impressed him with the desirability of using the missions as the instrument for the occupation of Upper California, an alternative made more imperative by the necessity for haste. Without prior inquiry or chance for his refusal, he commissioned Father Junípero Serra, who had only recently arrived to take over the former Jesuit missions, to establish a chain of missions in the new territory. To assure their foundation the old missions were requisitioned to supply from their scanty means the necessary agricultural implements, seeds and cattle. And finally as the means of defraying the general expenses of the expedition the Pious Fund was called upon to bear the burden.[12] In his final instruction to the expedition, Gálvez declared that the object of the conquest was "to establish the Catholic Faith, to extend the Spanish domain, and to check the ambitious schemes of a foreign nation." [13]   Circumstances had indeed led Gálvez to espouse the cause of the missions, but it was a secondary motive compared with the necessity for defense and his desire for personal distinction.

When on April 11, 1769, the first band of friars and soldiers landed at San Diego, there began a work of conquest that was noteworthy particularly for its difficulties. A small band of priests and soldiers, less than fifty in all, faced over two hundred thousand Indians; [14] and as the teachers of Christian civilization they found as their material one of the lowest type of the American Indian. The evangelization of California was to be a most difficult task. Even at that early date, peoples from the north, the south and the east had converged upon it with the result that there were at least twenty-two distinct and unrelated groups of languages.[15] Besides the barrier of idioms, there was little of the

[11] Priestley, *op. cit.*, 251.

[12] Engelhardt, *op. cit.*, II, 5-7.

[13] *Ibid.*, II, 5.

[14] Kroeber, Alfred L., *Handbook of the Indians of California* (Washington, 1925), 880.

[15] Radin, Paul, *The story of the American Indian* (New York, 1927), 354.

picturesqueness and dignity of other Indian groups to inspire the missionary. The primitive Californian stood low in the scale of civilization. His home was a temporary hut formed by the boughs of trees and covered with reeds; clothing was limited to a girdle of reeds for the women and a head-dress of feathers and shells for the men; while for food his nomadic life made him depend on the fruits of the chase and the spontaneous produce of the soil. His art he confined to basketry and beadwork and his craftsmanship to the making of bows and arrows and the construction of rude rafts of bullrushes. Social organization was simple and loose, limited to the family and tribe and devoid of all concepts of confederacy and communal pueblos. Finally, the religion of the California Indian was even weaker and more rudimentary. Its dogma consisted of a few myths and legends; its gods were without definite character; its priesthood consisted of medicine men; and its ceremonies were only slightly ritualistic. In this he differed markedly from the rest of the American Indians.[16] The conversion and civilization of so low a people could be looked for only through the agency of the highest type of mission organization and then only after a lengthy period of time.

The other problem that confronted the little band of *conquistadores* was an economic one. Unlike earlier groups, their chief means of communication with the base of supplies was by sea. The voyage made in small, frail vessels and requiring over two months, was so perilous that it had already cost the lives of one-fourth of those who started. Should the supply ships fail to appear on time they were doomed to want and famine, for there was little in California in its natural state upon which they could live. Thus, as it has been remarked, they "occupied a position resembling that of the Robinson Crusoe of literature. They were set down in a land that was rich in potentialities, but lacking in the immediate requirements of civilized life." [17] On one occasion, in 1772, when the supply ship was late in coming the situation was saved by a bear hunt, now quite famous in California history. But if the Spanish occupation of California was to be given any

---

[16] Cf. Kroeber, "Types of Indian culture in California," *University of California Publications; American Archaeology and Ethnology,* II, 81–86.

[17] Chapman, *op. cit.,* 249.

stability it could not depend on bear hunts; there was need of a vigorous agricultural program, an introduction of farming and a knowledge of the possibilities and needs of the soil.

To meet these problems Father Serra established his missions on the agricultural and stock-raising basis, that had already been perfected in the earlier missions of New Spain. The sites were chosen where the Indian population was numerous, where good land and water abounded, and where a sufficient supply of timber was within reach. After a cross had been erected and a temporary chapel dedicated, the work of conversion was begun. The simple Indians, attracted by curiosity and more often by gifts of goods or clothing, came to the mission. In time some of them remained, built their rude huts near the chapel and formed the beginnings of a mission community. This was the story of the five missions which Serra founded during the first three years of the California occupation. Located at strategic points up and down the coast, from San Diego to Monterey, he saw in them the first links of a great chain that would embrace the whole territory, gather the thousands of natives under its civilizing influence and transform the unproductive land into one of the most fertile regions of New Spain.

But unfortunately the early development of these infant establishments was retarded by a series of disputes that arose between the Father President and the military commander. Serra took Gálvez's words literally that the conquest was for the sake of evangelization, and brooked no interference in mission affairs. The commander, Fages, on the other hand, viewed the statement of the visitor-general more from the standpoint of utility. Influenced no doubt by the recent trends of political and military supremacy over the religious, he insisted on exercising a definite authority over the missions. When Serra sought the removal of certain mission guards, who by their undue familiarity with the Indian women had caused much of the work of the missionaries to be undone, Fages insisted on their freedom from mission jurisdiction. Likewise, when new missions were established, Fages overrode Serra's objections and insisted on determining the time and place of their founding. "As neither Fages nor Serra was of a yielding disposition" their lack of harmony soon assumed the proportions of a break which threatened the very existence of the enterprise.[18] The climax was reached when on October 12, 1772, the religious received an order from the viceroy in Mexico directing them to submit to Fages. It seemed that a policy of mission domination by the military was about to prevail, and accordingly on October 20, Serra set out for Mexico City to fight it.[19]

Happily, when he came to his journey's end, he found that he was to deal with a man quite different from Gálvez. The new viceroy, Antonio Bucareli, was undoubtedly one of the greatest viceroys ever sent to New Spain. "Far from being a narrow bureaucrat, he was capable of a broad point of view which grasped both the patent and the underlying problems of the whole viceroyalty. He was simple, straightforward, unselfish, clear-thinking, and sincerely religious, without a shadow of conceit or pretense, and even without great personal ambition, except to perform his duty in full." [20] More significant still, he was in sympathy with the missions. In 1773, as governor of Havana, he, alone of all Spanish high officials, had offered a temporary haven to the Jesuits and eased the hardships of their exile.[21] In like manner, he received Serra's complaints with understanding and responded with a series of legislative decrees and active measures that gave the missions a definite place in the California program.

From an analysis of the *Reglamento Provisional* and the two sets of instructions to the California governors which Bucareli issued between 1773 and 1776, it seems that the viceroy envisioned a twofold program of development; the conversion and civilization of the natives, and the colonization of the territory by white settlers.

The first phase, the training and development of the natives, was to be the work of the missions. As Palou in his *Noticias* describes it:

---

18 Chapman, *op. cit.*, 244.
19 Engelhardt, *op. cit.*, II, 105–106.
20 Chapman, *op. cit.*, 270.
21 Engelhardt, *op. cit.*, I, 310.

Concerning the petition that the government, control, and education of the baptized Indians should belong exclusively to the missionaries, it was declared that it should be carried out in all economic affairs pertaining to the father of a family regarding the care of his household, and the education and correction of his children; and the governor shall be instructed to preserve harmony and to cooperate with the said missionary fathers.[22]

In conformity with this policy, every effort was to be made on the part of the government to assist the work of the missions. Bells, vestments, agricultural implements, seeds, cattle and various other supplies were to be furnished each new mission on its foundation and double rations were to be allowed it for a period of five years to further the first struggle for permanency. Laborers, blacksmiths and carpenters were to be supplied at government expense to lay the foundations of the mission and instruct the Indians in agriculture and the various crafts. And finally, the property and rights of the missionaries were to be respected, and soldiers, guilty of misconduct and bad example, were to be removed from the mission guard.[23]   Such an arrangement was intended to have far-reaching effects.   As he pointed out in his instruction to the newly appointed governor of California, Rivera:

The first object is of course the conversion of the natives; but next in importance is their gathering in mission towns for the purposes of civilization.   These little towns may become great cities; hence the necessity of avoiding defects in the beginning, of care in the selection of sites, in the assignment of lands, laying out of streets, etc.   The missions may be converted into pueblos as soon as they are sufficiently advanced.[24]

Although his plans for the rapid assimilation of the natives were impracticable because they were based on a false idea of the California Indian, Bucareli's mission legislation would have insured a steady advancement and eventual completion of the work of Indian conversion and civilization.   And what was more perti-

[22] Quoted by Engelhardt, *op. cit.*, II, 119.
[23] Bancroft, *History of California*, I, 209-210.
[24] *Ibid.*, I, 217.

nent to the immediate present, it gave the missionaries that security which they needed if success was to be gained. Thenceforth, as the viceroy put it, they were commissioned "to exert all
their energies for the benefit of the missions, the erection of others,
and to spare no pains to attract the immense number of pagans
to the knowledge of the true Religion, and to the benign subjection to their August Sovereign." [25]

Equally wise were the measures which the viceroy drew up
for the colonization of California by white settlers. If Spanish
occupation was to endure, there was needed a strong white element which by developing the resources of the land and promoting commerce would make the province self-supporting. Bucareli
realized this and in his instruction to Rivera ordered him to make
a start towards white settlement by taking with him to California
a number of soldiers and their families.[26] Accordingly, the new
governor got together in Sinaloa fifty-one persons of all ages and
both sexes. After crossing to Lower California where he found
much difficulty in supplying his small expedition, he directed that
they should take the overland route up the Peninsula to the new
territory. When finally, on September 26, 1774, they reached
San Diego the beginnings of real colonization had been made,
white women for the first time having set foot in the province.[27]

More promising still was the Anza colony which Bucareli sent
to Upper California in 1775. The hardships encountered by the
Rivera colony on the Lower California route as well as earlier
experiences on the route by water had showed the necessity of
an overland route from Sonora by way of the Colorado. Bucareli
attacked the problem with his usual energy. In September, 1773,
he commissioned the young captain, Juan Bautista de Anza, to
open the route to California. When at the end of the next year
he returned and reported the practicability of the route, the viceroy drew up plans for the largest colonization project yet attempted in California. On October 23, 1775, there set out from
Tubac (in what is now Arizona) a company of 240 settlers, which
when it arrived at Mission San Gabriel on the following January

[25] Quoted by Engelhardt, op. cit., II, 138.
[26] Bancroft, op. cit., I, 217.
[27] Chapman, op. cit., 302–303.

4, and then at the number of 244, not only placed the province for the first time on a permanent basis but opened the way for great possibilities in the future development of colonization and commerce.   If Bucareli's far-visioned program had been carried out, California would have become as thoroughly Hispanic as the older provinces of New Spain.[28]

But Bucareli's program was never allowed to prove itself.   A reorganization of the government in 1776 removed California from his jurisdiction, while in 1777 a new governor, Philip de Neve, was appointed.   By his failure to heed the viceroy's injunction to preserve harmony, he did much to hinder the progress of the Missions.   By such petty acts as the stopping of the double rations, forbidding the mission guards to care for the few horses of the Missions along with their own, and preventing Serra from exercising his right to confirm, Neve clearly manifested his hostility to the Missions.   His opportunity for inflicting harm of a more serious nature came when in June, 1778, he was asked to make suggestions for a proposed reorganization of frontier presidios.   He submitted his recommendations before the end of the year and then, of his own initiative, set about to draw up a plan of reform for California.   Issued on June 1, 1779, and approved by the king on October 24, 1781, Neve's "Regulation and instruction for the presidios of the peninsula of California, the erection of new missions, the encouragement of colonization, and the extension of the establishments of Monterey," annulled Bucareli's beneficent legislation and threatened the future progress of the Missions.[29]   Instead of an equal and harmonious development of Indian conversion and civilization at the hands of the missionaries and of white settlement of the territory through colonization, it proposed to remove the Indian, except in what concerned his religious instruction, from the charge of the missionaries, and place him for the purpose of his civilization and assimilation under the influence of the white settlers who were to be introduced through large scale colonization.

It cannot be denied that the proposals for colonization were wise and well adapted to the needs of the country.   They did away

---

[28] *Ibid.*, 294 ss.
[29] Bancroft, *op. cit.*, I, 317-318; Engelhardt, *op. cit.*, II, 327-328.

with the necessity of bringing food supplies for the presidios over the expensive and uncertain sea route from San Blas and made the province self-supporting. As the *reglamento* decreed, settlers were to be obtained from the older provinces and established in pueblos. Given a house-lot and tract of land for cultivation, supplied with the necessary live-stock, implements, and seed, and supported by the government for five years, the *pobladores* in return were to sell to the presidios exclusively the surplus products of their land, and be ready to serve as militia for the defense of the territory.[30] Unfortunately, as will be presently noted, the program was never to be fully carried out, and its chief importance lies in the fact that it was to serve as a model for later secularization projects.

But less wise were the *reglamento's* provisions concerning the Missions. Under the pretext of providing for the establishment of three new missions along with a presidio in the Santa Barbara Channel region, Neve changed entirely the nature of the mission system and the policy of the government towards it. Briefly, he proposed that in addition to the three new establishments a second line of missions should be located further inland from fourteen to twenty leagues east of the existing chain. But more noteworthy, each new establishment was to be provided with only $1000 as a foundation endowment from the Pious Fund, while the necessary cattle, implements and seed were to be supplied by the older missions. Still more significant, the mission was to consist merely of a church and a priest's dwelling and, finally, at each there was to be only one friar instead of the customary two. In time, after death or retirement had reduced the surplus numbers, the same limitation was to apply to the older missions.[31]

According to these provisions, the governmental and economic phases of mission life were to be abandoned and the task of the friars limited to religious instruction:

There was to be no more agriculture, no stockraising, and no teaching of mechanical arts for the benefit of the neophytes. The Indians were to be permitted to live as they pleased, to come to the instructions if they pleased, and to execute the

[30] Bancroft, *op. cit.*, I, 336–337.
[31] Engelhardt, *op. cit.*, II, 331.

lessons imparted or laugh them to scorn, which was more probable since the missionary could neither clothe nor feed, neither divert nor protect them.[32]

Since after assembling the savages for instruction, the missionary would have to dismiss them to their hovels, whatever elements of civilization they were to receive would come from their contact with the white settlers. According to the evidences of earlier mission history, this meant not the elevation but the degradation of the natives.

Before turning to the application of the *reglamento,* it must be stated that Neve missed a glorious opportunity to stabilize later California history. The crying needs of the province were the Christianization and assimilation of the native population and the introduction of a strong Spanish element to serve as the economic backbone of the new society. Bucareli had found the answer by making the missions the instruments for the advancement of the Indians and by outlining a definite program for colonization. This latter Neve completed with a set of regulations that revealed his powers of organization in their fullest. But like so many of the new type of Spanish official that he represented, through hostility to the religious he impaired that necessary adjunct of white colonization, the mission system. He closed his eyes to the lesson of the two centuries previous, to the fact that whether in New Spain or New France or New England, the Indian left without the protection of religious teachers always fell victim to the greed and vices of the white man. Instead of the parish system which he proposed to erect, there was needed to cope with the situation created by the California Indian's low place in the scale of culture, the highest possible type of a mission system. Without acknowledging this necessity, no program of development, no matter how perfect its plan of colonization might be, could solve the California problem. Had Neve's unbalanced program been carried out, the Indian population would have been swept away by the wave of white colonization that it proposed to introduce. But within the next few years, events outside of California turned the stream of its history into a different channel.

---

[32] *Ibid.,* II, 332.

II

With the publication of the *reglamento*, Neve had put its provisions for colonization into effect at once. On December 27, 1779, he had instructed Rivera, then lieutenant-governor in Lower California, to recruit a colony of soldiers and settlers in Sinaloa and Sonora:

> They were to be married men, accompanied by their families, healthy and robust, likely to lead regular lives and to set a good example to the natives. . . . Female relatives of the *pobladores*, if unmarried, were to be encouraged to accompany the families with a view to marriage with bachelor soldiers already in California.[33]

After much difficulty Rivera succeeded in recruiting a considerable number and in the spring of 1781, they started out in two groups for Upper California, one by way of the Peninsula, the other by way of the Anza route. When in the fall of that year they finally arrived at San Gabriel, the white population in California was augmented by nearly three hundred. While insignificant in contrast to the Indian population, it heralded, as was thought, a future colonization movement that was to grow with the years.

But such hopes were brought to a premature end by a "disaster of almost unprecedented proportions in the history of Spain's conquest of the northern frontier." The section of the Rivera colony which came by the Anza route had scarcely passed the military post that had been established at the junction of the Colorado to form, as it were, the keystone of the route, when on July 17, the Yuma Indians arose and at one stroke massacred more than thirty Spanish soldiers and four friars.[34] The disaster closed California's cheapest and most practicable line of communication with the older provinces and brought to an end all projects of colonization. From time to time down to 1804 proposals were made to reopen the Anza route but the ferocity of the Yumas prevented their realization. Likewise, moves were

---

[33] Quoted by Bancroft, *op. cit.*, I, 340.
[34] Chapman, *op. cit.*, 330 ss.

later initiated to send new colonists by way of the Lower California route but the only result was a meager group of nine *pobladores* who were brought from Guadalajara in 1797 to found the new pueblo of Branciforte.[35] The closing of the Anza route settled the question of the development of Upper California under Spain. Left to its own feeble efforts, the province was to advance in a manner quite contrary to that which Neve had anticipated.

Just as the colonization projects of the *reglamento* were ended by the Yuma revolt, so was its proposed change of the mission system brought to naught by a revolt of the Franciscans. On December 7, 1780, the new viceroy, Mayorga, had asked the College of San Fernando to supply missionaries for the three new Channel missions. Fortunately for the California friars and their Indian charges, their brethren in Mexico refused to be entrapped or cajoled into accepting what amounted to a change from mission to parish organization. Numerous letters were interchanged by the viceroy and the Father Guardian, but all to no avail. The new missionaries were not seen. As the Father Guardian quite realistically explained in his letters, under the new system,

> it would not be possible to found a mission, gather the heathen savages, nor catechize, instruct and maintain those who subjected themselves to the Christian doctrine. . . . The Indians are attracted more by what they receive from the missionaries, than by what is preached to them. . . . [The material things of a mission] are only bait with which they are attracted in a shrewd and gentle manner. Once gained in the way indicated they continue this kind of mere material life until they have obtained some knowledge of spiritual things and are grounded in the doctrines of our holy faith.[36]

The arguments proved unanswerable to the viceroy, and he therefore referred the matter to the court at Madrid. Influenced no doubt by the Yuma revolt and the fate of the colonization projects, the king finally repealed the measures and left the matter of mission organization in the hands of the friars.[37]

Neve's mission regulation is important not because of its im-

35 Cf. Bancroft, *op. cit.*, I, 564–571.

36 Engelhardt, *op. cit.*, II, 372–381.

37 *Ibid.*, II, 427.

mediate effects but because of the spirit of hostility that it represented. Although the force of circumstances prevented its early
application, it really never died, neither in California nor in Mexico. Led by the same spirit, Governor Borica in 1796 wrote to
the viceroy, criticizing the mission system and urging that the
Indians be freed from the tutelage of the friars, as the law decreed, after a period of ten years.[38] With even a greater show
of hostility, a group in Mexico in 1802 petitioned the government
"to change the mission system by adopting the plan formerly
presented by Neve, of leaving the natives after conversion in
their *rancherias,* requiring only occasional visits by and to the
padres for instruction and the performance of spiritual duties." [39]
Father Lasuén, Serra's successor, immediately opposed the plan,
showing its impracticability and the disastrous results that would
follow its application. Again the arguments against it proved
unanswerable and on February 2, 1803, the viceroy, Iturriguray,
rejected the scheme.[40] Other plans were to follow Neve's and
to succeed where it had failed—in destroying the Missions and
their Indians. In the meantime they were to prosper.

With the closing of the Anza route and the abandoning of all
ambitions for the development of the province, California settled
down to enjoy what has been called its "romantic period," from
1782 to 1810. For the white population it was really a period of
quiescence. Numerically, its increase, compared to the Indian
population, was negligible, totalling about 970 in 1790, and about
1200 in 1800.[41] Socially, the white settlers provided material for
a future society that was below the ordinary. The members of
the Anza colony who contributed to the beginnings of San Francisco had been drawn from among those hopelessly submerged
in poverty in Sinaloa; [42] the forty-six people who founded Los
Angeles were in blood a strange mixture of Indian and negro
with here and there a trace of Spanish; [43] while the few citizens
of the new pueblo of Branciforte, though not convicts, were of

[38] Bancroft, *op. cit.,* I, 580.
[39] *Ibid.,* II, 6.
[40] Engelhardt, *op. cit.,* II, 585–590.
[41] Chapman, *op cit.,* 348.
[42] *Ibid.,* 304.
[43] Bancroft, *op. cit.,* I, 345.

a class deemed desirable to be gotten rid of in and around Guadalajara, whence they came.[44] Finally, the *gente de razón*, as the whites called themselves, contributed little to the economic growth of the province. The soldiers who formed the greater part of the white population abstained from industry as degrading to their profession. As a visitor in 1793 observed, to support the standing of the soldier in the eyes of the natives and to insure him their respect, it was deemed highly improper to subject him to any laborious employment.[45] In like manner, the *pobladores*, who according to the economic program were to supply the needs of the military element, "never became noted for their devotion to hard labor," [46] and produced little more than what was necessary for their own support. On the whole, the civil and military elements remained unproductive and the economic basis of Upper California continued to be that of government aid. It was indeed the "romantic period" of California history, one in which "life was one continuous round of hospitality and social amenities, tempered with vigorous outdoor sport. . . . No white man had to concern himself greatly with work, and even school books were a thing apart. Music, games, dancing, and sprightly conversation —these were the occupations of the time—these constituted education." [47] It could easily be so as long as the San Blas ships came regularly with their supplies of food and manufactured goods furnished by an indulgent government.

But if the three decades that followed the failure of the Neve *reglamento* became the "romantic period" for the secular elements of California, they were, even more, the "golden age" of the Missions. When the projects for the material development of the province had been brought to a standstill, the governors of California adopted the policy of allowing the program of mission development to go on unhampered. It was perhaps a reflection of the contemporary reaction that was taking place in Mexico, particularly under the second Revillagigedo, against the seculari-

44 *Ibid.*, I, 571.
45 Vancouver, George, *A voyage of discovery to the North Pacific Ocean and round the world, 1790–1795* (London, 1801), IV, 406.
46 Bancroft, *op. cit.*, I, 571.
47 Chapman, *op. cit.*, 390.

zation movement. Disputes between the governors and the religious indeed continued, but they were generally of a petty nature, concerned with such matters as the election of Indian alcades, the pursuit of runaway neophytes, the relations of white settlers with the Indians, the free transmittance of mail for the Missions, etc. Some were referred to the viceroy but his refusal in most instances to support the governors indicated the changed policy of the government towards the missions. More often the rough spots of church-state relations were smoothed over by the tact and diplomacy of the new president of the missions, Father Lasuén. The spirit of the times was well expressed in the following words which Governor Fages wrote in his general report to the viceroy:

> If we are to be just to all, as we ought to be, we must confess that the rapid, gratifying, and interesting progress, both spiritual and temporal, which we fortunately are able to see and enjoy in this vast new country, is the glorious effect of the apostolic zeal, activity, and indefatigable ardor of the religious.[48]

Favored by such a spirit, the mission system developed with remarkable strides. When Serra had departed for Mexico he left behind him five struggling missions. When he died in 1784 four more had been added to their number. Under his successor progress was even more rapid and by 1808 the line of missions along the coast had reached the total of nineteen, beginning at San Diego and ending at San Francisco. The maximum number of missionaries was reached in 1806 when thirty-eight regular missionaries and seven supernumeraries were attached to the nineteen establishments,[49] while the Indian population of the Missions reached the astonishing number of over thirty thousand. The glories that were those of the mission system during this its golden age have been so ably, so beautifully and so sympathetically expressed by a host of distinguished writers that any further effort would but result in an injustice to the subject. Our only observation will be that the Missions as we best know them

---

[48] Quoted by Chapman, *op. cit.*, 377.
[49] Engelhardt, *op. cit.*, II, 632.

reached the apex of their development during these years of tranquility. The simple instruction of the Indians in the elements of the Faith developed into a well formulated method that included the teaching of reading and writing, Spanish and Latin and even music. The early efforts at imparting the elements of civilization and establishing a basis of self-support were succeeded by a highly technical training in the various phases of agriculture, stockraising, craftsmanship, and even art. The broad fields, the teeming granaries and the numerous herds of cattle, the tiles, pottery, blankets and cotton goods, shoes, saddles and iron work, all produced at the Missions, were proofs of the efficacy of this training. Again, from the first step of gathering the natives around the mission center there developed a highly systematized community life. An ordered day beginning with Mass, breakfast from a community kitchen, followed by an allotment of tasks and concluding with community instructions and recreation contrasted sharply with the natives' former life of savagery.[50] And finally, keeping pace with this marvelous organization of mission life, went the develepment of the mission buildings. The rude brush huts of the natives gave way to neat adobe homes of whitewashed walls and tiled roofs, and the temporary chapels to the proud, magnificent churches which remain today the majestic monuments of this grand era. The padres the architects, the Indians the artisans, with humble materials and unskilled hands, they built strongly and simply. Yet the solid and massive buildings they erected, the broad, undecorated surfaces, the arcaded cloisters, the curved pedimented gables and terraced bell-towers, the wide spreading eaves and low sloping tiled roofs, all were so distinctive and so in keeping with their surroundings that there was evolved a type of architecture "which for the country in which it was developed has not been excelled." [51]

The romantic period was in reality the mission period. During it the padres made the greatest progress in fulfilling their God-given mission of carrying the light of the Gospel to the pagan savages. And during this period they fulfilled the commission

---

50 Cf. Engelhardt, *op. cit.,* II, 242–278.

51 Newcomb, Rexford, *The old mission churches and historic houses of California* (Philadelphia, 1925), 100.

which Spain had given them of advancing the civilization of the Indians. Finally, when these years marked the abandoning of all projects for the material development of California, the missionaries stepped into the breach and provided the province with an economic basis. Had they failed, Spanish occupation could never have endured. Because they succeeded, they were eventually to be destroyed, for in their success was contained the germ of their secularization.

III

As the growth of the California Missions had been occasioned by forces outside the province, so was their decline initiated by external political upheavals, the Hispanic-American wars of independence. Since the first days of the conquest, Spain's colonial policy had been essentially monopolistic. Commerce was controlled by the government, colonial legislation was centered in the Council of the Indies, colonial administrative offices were reserved to the Spanish-born, *Gachupines* as they were called, even the high positions in the Church were held chiefly by ecclesiastics sent over from Spain. This policy of preference to Spanish-born vassals long inspired the creoles, or American-born Spaniards, with racial embitterments which pointed unmistakably to a break between the colonies and the mother country. It first found expression in the secret plots of the eighteenth century; the new social theories of the French political school gave it form; and the successful revolutions of North American colonists and French serfs animated it. Latin America came of age, loosened the yoke of Spain's parental authority, and revolted.[52]

The immediate occasion of the revolt was, strangely enough, a political revolution in Spain, against France. In 1808, Napoleon had invaded the Spanish Peninsula, forced Ferdinand VII to abdicate, had taken his successor, Charles IV, prisoner, and placed his own brother, Joseph Bonaparte, on the throne. Without king or government of their own, the Spanish people sought to repel the invader by guerilla warfare and to rule themselves by a hastily

---

[52] Cf. Priestley, Herbert I., *The Mexican nation, a history* (New York, 1923), 194 ss.

summoned *Cortes*.[53]   These spectacular changes provided the creole leaders in America with unique opportunities for promoting revolution.   When the *Cortes* attempted to retain the old Spanish régime in the colonies, they claimed the right to set up governments of their own.   The *Cortes,* they proclaimed, was carrying on a revolution against the authority of Ferdinand VII, while they were fighting in the name of the king.   In 1810 wars broke out almost simultaneously in all parts of Spanish America, ostensibly for the cause of Ferdinand, in reality for the purpose of independence.[54]   In New Spain, the independence movement resulted in a series of wars that lasted for more than ten years. At first sponsored by a small group of politically ambitious creoles in Mexico City,[55] the movement of revolt got beyond their control and was taken up by the lower masses, the *mestizos* and the Indians.   Inspired by Miguel Hidalgo's famous *el Grito de Dolores* of September 16, 1810, and directed after his capture and execution by the more able José María Morelos and a score of lesser leaders, the cause of independence developed into a long series of race wars that tore the viceroyalty asunder throughout the entire second decade of the nineteenth century.[56]   It was these momentous changes both in Spain and in America that brought the period of mission ascendency to an end and laid the foundations for a later California upheaval.

The wars of independence had few political or military effects on California.   A few incendiary documents sent to the province from unknown sources caused the commandant at San Diego to strengthen the defences of the port,[57] while in 1818 two Buenos Aires privateers sought to win the province over to the side of independence and on its refusal sacked Monterey and looted several of the missions along the coast.[58]   But even this clash of arms failed to swerve the people in their loyalty to the king and California remained tranquil even to monotony.

---

[53] Chapman, Charles E., *History of Spain* (New York, 1919), 488 ss.

[54] Chapman, Charles E., *Colonial Hispanic America: a history* (New York, 1933), 236.

[55] Priestley, *op. cit.,* 198.

[56] *Ibid.,* 206 ss.

[57] Bancroft, *op. cit.,* II, 198.

[58] Chapman, *History of California,* 443 ss.

But more important and more far-reaching in its consequences was the economic change that the distant revolutions wrought in the province. With the outbreak of hostilities in Mexico, Spanish support was cut off and the regular supply ships failed to make their appearance in California. In 1811 the governor was informed that the activities of Morelos prevented the presidial supplies from being sent from Mexico City, while the Father President of the Missions was told that the mission drafts could not be paid because of the heavy demands of the army on the treasury. For practically the whole decade California got neither its money allowances nor its supplies.[59]

The cutting off of supplies placed the presidios in dire straits. Never established on a sound economic basis, they were now faced with the possibilities of the greatest want. For the soldiers and their families it was now a question not merely of salaries to be paid but of the actual necessities of life. Clothing was scarce, the commodities of life beyond their reach because they had not the wherewith to purchase them, and food alarmingly difficult to obtain. Commandants clamored for their men and the governor sent numerous petitions to Mexico to assist them.[60] But instead of help there came sharp replies, and, as the viceroy wrote in 1819, the governor was advised to "let them develop the rich resources of their province and talk less, and thus will they live comfortably and also be an aid instead of a burden to the government in such trying times as these." [61] This was one answer to the problems of subsistence. The governor was to choose another and an easier one.

On the other hand, the Missions did not suffer the want of the presidios. Organized on the basis of self-support, they did not find it difficult to maintain their large population of neophytes. Even the cutting off of the supplies of manufactured goods and religious articles usually sent from Mexico was offset by a commerce with foreign vessels that was developed and condoned by virtue of the necessity of the times. The only serious effect of

---

[59] Bancroft, *op. cit.*, II, 199 ss.
[60] Richman, Irving B., *California under Spain and Mexico* (Boston, 1911), 214.
[61] Quoted by Bancroft, *op. cit.*, II, 257.

the disturbances in Mexico was that friars were no longer sent to relieve the aged or retired missionaries. Not only did this prevent the establishment of a projected chain of inland missions, but it left fewer missionaries to assume the added burdens which were soon placed upon the Missions.[62]

This new burden was the demand which was made to support the provincial government and the troops. The governor had informed the Father President of this obligation in 1814. From that time on each mission was called upon regularly to furnish to the local presidios supplies of flour, clothing, blankets and shoes, and to credit the governor with large quantities of grain, tallow and hides. These were exchanged with foreign trading vessels for ammunition, weapons and other manufactured goods. In return the missionaries were given drafts on the royal treasury which, however, when presented in Mexico City were not honored. The fact that by 1820 the dues for these unpaid drafts amounted to nearly half a million dollars is a sufficient indication of what this new burden meant for the Missions.[63]

From the beginning the response of the missionaries was most satisfactory and liberal. Besides the forced contributions, they frequently made voluntary donations of money and goods that amounted to many thousands of dollars. Particularly noteworthy was the contribution made by the missionaries and neophytes at San Luis Obispo to the garrison at Monterey. A full outfit of shirts, coats, pants and hats along with eighty horses and blankets was furnished for fifty-five soldiers stationed at the presidio.[64] To furnish such supplies over so long a period of years must have been a most heavy burden and meant extraordinary sacrifices on the part of both friars and neophytes. As one of the missionaries wrote to the governor in 1816:

The Indians go barefooted in order that they may provide shoes for the troops and their families. They eat their food without butter in order that the troops may have it. They do

---

[62] *Ibid.*, II, 195–196.
[63] *Ibid.*, II, 202, 406.
[64] Engelhardt, *op. cit.*, III, 70–71.

not taste beans in order to be able to deliver them to the military store.[65]

Yet such sacrifices were often unrequited. The soldiers were inconsiderate and not content with the necessaries of life and often coupled their demands with threats. The commanders of the presidios sometimes made additional demands without consulting the governor. Finally, in 1817, Governor Sola himself manifested his ill-feeling towards the Missions by making excessive demands of tallow. At such a display of ungratefulness, the missionaries lost heart. From teachers of religion they had been forced to become taskmasters, "to overwork," as they wrote, "the unfortunate neophytes whose lot it was to go naked." [66]

This question of supplies and the disputes it engendered occupies an important place in the beginnings of California secularization. As one writer has ably put it: "Two things bring ecclesiastical institutions into disfavor. If they are poor, they become a burden and a grievance. If they are rich, they incite cupidity." [67] To the soldiers in their neglect and economic distress, the Missions appeared rich, and the sight of their crops and their herds, the fruit of long years of industry and labor, instead of inspiring them to similar efforts aroused in them a spirit of envy and covetousness. Thenceforth, the hostility of the military elements towards the Missions was to spring from their desire for the mission temporalities. As Bancroft has rightly pointed out, "here, rather than in the old-time controversies of Serra, Fages, and Neve, was laid the foundation for the bitter feeling of later years." [68] If the wars of independence did not affect California directly, they had an unhappy bearing, indirectly, on its Missions.

Meanwhile, events were transpiring in Spain and New Spain which were of equal importance in the secularization movement. On May 20, 1814, a certain naval lieutenant, Don Francisco de Paula Tamaríz, forwarded a memorial to the king, in which he

---

[65] *Ibid.*, III, 82.
[66] *Ibid.*, III, 127.
[67] Repplier, Agnes, *Junípero Serra* (New York, 1933), 291.
[68] Bancroft, *op. cit.*, II, 197.

made the most serious attack on the California Missions since the days of the Neve's *reglamento*.[69] Tamaríz, as captain of the *Activo*, had visited Upper California in 1805 and 1807, and "had noted with sorrow the contrast between the abandonment, misery and meagerness in population of the province and its rich possibilities." Combining his experience with knowledge drawn up from the account of an earlier scientific expedition which had visited the territory, probably that of the *Sutil* and *Mexicana* in 1792 the chronicler of which had been quite severe in his criticism of California institutions,[70] he presented his memorial to the king as a remedy for these evils. Summarized and topically arranged, his observations and recommendations were as follows:

The missions, perhaps the richest farms in New Spain, supported by the government and the labor of all the Indians, were engaged in a lucrative trade until stopped by the recent disturbances. Yet despite this, they are inefficient means for the spiritual and material development of the realm. Spiritually they have failed because the necessity of managing temporalities has forced the friars to neglect the principal object of their work, the spiritual conquest. The Indians are instructed through interpreters with the result that their religious knowledge is imperfect, nor has a new chain of missions been established in the interior of the country. Likewise, as civilizing agents the missions have failed because their community life and food have increased the mortality rate among the Indians.

Moreover, the missions have retarded the economic development of the province. Large sums from the Pious Fund and Royal Treasury have been expended without prospect of return. Instead of developing the whole province, the missionaries have confined their efforts to the development of the area of their missions. Instead of developing an active commerce with Mexico, they sow only enough grain for the Indians, and kill only enough cattle for their needs. What tallow they do sell, they give at ridiculously low prices because of their ignorance of its value. Likewise, because of their lack of interest, they have

[69] Richman, *op. cit.*, 224. Richman wrongly names him Pablo instead of Francisco.

[70] Bancroft, *op. cit.*, I, 506–507.

failed to develop vineyards and olive groves for which the country is adapted, and to utilize its natural resources in fish, furs and hides, trees of every kind, and minerals of gold, silver, quicksilver, and iron. The development of these would lead to a rich trade with Asia, Mexico or Lima and would more than maintain the province. Yet the contrary is the case. What products are shipped to San Blas pay only a *real* of tax to the king because the misisonaries are in league with the officials. Moreover, they falsify their reports in order to keep the government in ignorance of the wealth of their possessions.

Finally, the missions have been an obstacle to the growth of civil and military elements in the province. The religious have dominated at the expense of the civilians. Many, even of those who took part in the conquest, possess only small plots of land and then only where the missions have not located ranches. They have been deprived of the labor of the neophytes because the religious want it themselves. In like manner the absolute rule of the missionaries has prevented the use of the Indians as soldiers, with the result that new conquests have been prevented, while at the same time the artillery defenses are in poor condition because the missionaries demand pay for all services and goods rendered. All of this is proof of the lack of planning for the development of the country proportionate to the sums of money expended by the king. Yet many individuals suffer in patience, awaiting the day when they will be delivered from this cruel system.

To remedy these conditions a threefold change should be introduced. The missions should be given the status of parishes and the missionaries reduced in number to those necessary for the spiritual care of the inhabitants. On the other hand, the Indians should be organized into pueblos for the purpose of developing industry, agriculture and commerce. The native chiefs should be commissioned to allot and enforce labor among them, artisans should be introduced to teach them the various crafts, especially that of textiles, and salaried administrators should be appointed to manage the mission estates and direct the textile industries. In all of this, because of the attachment of the Indians to custom, the mission system should be followed as closely as possible. In connection with this, the government should encourage commerce by establishing a board of trade, regulating prices and by building a fleet of ships, utilizing for this purpose the materials present in the province. All of this will result in an increase of population and will pay for the expenses of the provincial government.

Finally, a vigorous effort should be made to promote colonization. First, the naval depot at San Blas should be abolished and the shipwrights and their families should be transferred to California, for the purpose of promoting ship building. Secondly, soldiers retired from service and pensioners, who at present are a burden on the government of New Spain, should be established on the land as settlers. Finally, families ruined by the revolution, exiles and convicts, particularly those skilled in textiles and other crafts, should be brought to the province at government expense and given lands as colonists. The latter, after serving their sentences, should be allowed to remain as settlers, marry wives brought from the large cities of Mexico, and become respectable citizens. Finally, these civilians by employing native labor would teach the Indians Spanish so that when the time came for their religious instruction they would be baptized with full knowledge of their religion. Thus, in conclusion, would the resources of the fertile province be developed, its natives civilized and converted more rapidly, its commerce, particularly a fur trade with Asia, fostered, and the treasury not only relieved of its burden but be given new sources of revenue.[71]

As soon as this memorial was received in Spain, the crown referred it, by a letter of July 5, 1814, to the viceroy in Mexico City, with the direction that he should appoint a *Junta* of five or seven men, acquainted with the economic, commercial and practical problems of the province, to examine the charges made by Tamaríz and correct whatever evils they found existing.[72] However, probably because of the revolutionary disturbances which

---

[71] "Memoria que presenta al Rey N. S. el teniente de navío D. Francisco de Paula Tamaríz, sobre mejorar el sistema de gobierno de la Alta California," *Las Misiones de la Alta California* (Archivo y Biblioteca de la Secretaría de Hacienda; Colección de Documentos Históricos, Tomo II, México, 1914), 89–111.
[72] *Ibid.*, 111–112.

were at that time distracting the viceroyalty, three years elapsed
before any steps were taken to organize this *Junta.*

But it was possibly during this interim that a copy of the
memorial was sent to San Fernando College with the request that
an answer should be made to its charges. The task was taken
up by one of the priests of the College, a certain Father Domingo
Rivos, who prepared a lengthy reply and sent it, undated, to the
viceroy. Briefly, its contents were as follows:

The memorial of Tamaríz is a malicious attack on the missionaries in California and on the College of San Fernando, who instead of striving to accumulate riches have expended their own
personal monies on the work of the Missions. The spiritual
neglect as charged by Tamaríz is untrue, for no adult Indian is
baptized save after a year of instruction and probation, after
which his training is continued under overseers. Moreover, many
of the Fathers are well versed in the Indian languages, while those
who do not yet know them do effective work through the use of
capable interpreters. Finally, the mission fare is not the cause
of the increased deathrate among the Indians, who were accustomed to the eating of meat before their conversion.[73]

Moreover the missionaries have not maliciously hindered the
development of the natural resources or commerce of California.
If the herds are not larger, it is because of poor pasture, the
governor himself having been obliged in 1805 to order the killing
of most of the mares at Monterey because there was not enough
pasture. In like manner the further development of grain crops,
vines, and olives is hampered by the fact that for six months of
the year there is no rainfall. Mines have not been developed because according to experts who have examined the country there
are none. Finally, if commerce were profitable, it would have
been developed long ago. The fact is that there is little wool in
the province, no market for the flour that is produced, and too
great an expense attached to the shipment of horses to Mexico.
A trade in lumber, skins, hemp and flax, sardines, salmon, and
whale oil could be developed if experts were sent to conduct it,

---

[73] "Parecer formado por el Padre Domingo Rivos a petición de D. Joaquín
Cortina, en repulsa del Informe dado a S. M. sobre mejoras de la Neuva California," *Las Misiones de la Alta California,* 175–178, 121–123, 128.

since in the case of the latter the sailors at present do not know how to salt fish and do it badly.[74]

As to the reforms which Tamaríz proposed, it would be well to transfer the naval depot to Monterey or San Francisco for it would ward off the Russians and at the same time attract settlers to the province. However, these should be settlers of proven qualities, not convicts or single women brought from the cities of Mexico. The convicts who have already been sent to the province have greatly hampered by their bad example the work of the missionaries, while the sending of single women would often lead to moral disorders. But what was particularly dangerous was the proposal to replace the missionaries by secular priests and distribute a portion of the mission lands to settlers. The religious of San Fernando College realize that their purpose is to do pioneer work, and that if relieved of the management of the temporalities they could devote more of their time and attention to the work of evangelization. Yet they feel that they should oppose such a change in view of the ruin which similar changes have produced in Lower California and Sierra Gorde, where even Archbishop Lorenzana, an ardent secularizer, was forced to admit failure. If the Missions were secularized, the danger of an Indian revolt would be increased, the Missions would go to ruin, and of the fields and vineyards distributed to the settlers nothing would remain after ten years.[75]

Finally, it would seem that this memorial is based not on fact but on the prejudices and personal motives of its author. Tamaríz on the occasion of his two visits to Upper California as captain of the *Activo* in 1805 and 1807 saw only four missions and about as many presidios. Since all that he saw of California is reduced to eight leagues of land and perhaps a little less, I conclude that he has spoken of Nueva Albión without having any knowledge of the province. Moreover, on the occasion of his visit to San Juan Capistrano he was reprimanded by the missionaries because one of the members of his crew was seducing the natives. Thereafter, he began to speak unjustly of the missionaries and so the principal motive for his memorial has been none other than to

74 *Ibid.,* 123–153.
75 *Ibid.,* 154–173.

avenge himself for the insult which he said he had received. Finally, it is said that Señor Tamaríz aspired to the governorship of Upper California. If this is true, it is no longer strange that he asked for an account of the *real hacienda* and not of the missions, because in this way all of it would accrue to the account of the governorship.[76]

While it can not be determined what reaction this letter produced, steps were finally taken in 1817 by the new viceroy, Juan Ruíz de Apodaca, to form the *Junta* which the king had ordered. Only the briefest outline of its proceedings are known. On May 28, 1817, the secretary of the *Junta* presented the viceroy with a report on Tamaríz's memorial, in which he acknowledged the necessity of developing commerce and trade by utilizing the natural resources of the province, but made no recommendations on the matter of colonization nor of the suppression of the naval depot at San Blas. As for the Indians and the Missions, he urged that the members of the *Junta* should be cautioned "to exercise great circumspection lest they alarm the religious, who, while they maintained in their reports that their sole purpose was the propagation of the faith and that the development of the temporalities of the Missions was a necessary means to this end, possibly might have hindered the development and prosperity of the country in as much as it was not their business to remedy the defects noted in the memorial." Turning then to the question of secularization, he recommended that the mission system should be replaced by a diocese. The missions should be changed into parishes, the Franciscans given the status of parish priests, and a bishop be appointed for the territory. Supported by the commerce and industry of the province, his See situated in the middle of both Californias, and himself acquainted with the territory and its inhabitants, the bishop would be able to correct abuses, promote the work of evangelization, and hasten the reduction and civilization of the natives. Without suggesting any provisions for the future administration of the mission temporalities, the report concluded with the recommendation that the Indians should be left in the charge of the religious, lest they should

---

[76] *Ibid.*, 172, 190–193.

return to their native haunts or, uniting with the gentile Indians, attack the presidios.[77]

After this report was submitted, the *Primera Junta de California* was convoked on July 5, 1817, to consider the memorial of Tamaríz and the report of its secretary and to pass judgment on both of them. However, of its proceedings only the following resolution is known. It was resolved that:

> The Father President of the Missions should be shown the laws of the Indies which determine how long the religious are to remain in charge of the missions before turning them over to the jurisdiction of the bishop, and that he should be asked: Why had they not been given up, since almost forty years had passed since their establishment? [78]

Apparently this recommendation was carried out, for on August 8, 1818, the Guardian of San Fernando College, Father Juan Calzada, sent a lengthy report to the viceroy in which he set forth the reasons why the California Missions had not been handed over to the bishop. After a lengthy introduction in which he explained the general purpose of the Franciscans and the work which they had thus far accomplished in California,[79] the Father Guardian accounted for the non-secularization of the mission as follows:

> Now, most excellent Sir, I reply to you: Why, after so many years since the establishment of the Missions of Alta California, have they not been transferred to the jurisdiction, *Real Ordinaria*, as you asked me? Sincerely, I confess that, despite many readings of the *Leyes de Indias* I have thus far been unable to find which law it is that enjoins on the religious a fixed

---

[77] *Copia del Expediente sobre la Memoria de Francisco de Paula Tamaríz, presentado en 20 de Mayo de 1814, con que se dió cuenta en la Primera Junta de California, celebrada ante el Exmo. Sor. Virrey Don Juan Ruíz de Apodaca, en 5 de Julio de 1817* (Transcript, Bancroft Library, Berkeley, California), 24–25; cf. Richman, *op. cit.*, 466, n. 35.

[78] *Ibid.*, 26.

[79] "Respuesta del R. P. Guardián Fr. Juan Calzada a Excelentisimo señor Virrey, dándole las razones por las que no han sido entregadas a las jurisdiciones Real, Ordinaria y Eclesiástica, las Misiones de la Alta California," *Las Misiones de la Alta California*, 199–230.

time in which they must transfer the Missions or the pueblos, recently converted, to the *Jurisdición Real, Ordinaria.*

Nor have I found, despite many careful searchings, any royal cedula which indicates the reported time. If we believe Pedro Parras, the *gobernadores* in the province of Paraguay have a cedula to the effect that the converted Indians remain for the first twenty years under the sole direction of their missionaries, without knowing any other. During the captivity of our beloved monarch, Ferdinand VII, I read with surprise in the *Gaceta de La Regencia* a decree of the extraordinary *Cortes* in which, answering a request of a bishop recently elected, they ordered that in conformity with the royal laws and cedulas, the religious should immediately transfer to the respective ecclesiastical ordinaries, without any excuse or pretext, all the missions in the province beyond the sea which had been in existence for more than ten years.

If that decree (which, if I may speak the truth, was given by the *Cortes* in ignorance, with haste and despotically) had been put into effect as soon as it arrived in Mexico, what lamentable results would it not have caused in the whole realm! Well did the most excellent viceroy, who was then in Mexico, and who in the time of Revillagigedo had worked so much for the cause of the missions, prudently abstain from putting it into effect even though it had been passed by the *Regencia del Reino.* From this I infer that our Catholic monarchs (whom some in the *Cortes* unjustly, but publicly, called despots) even when they despatched a cedula indicating a fixed time for the transfer of the missions, did not make it so obsolute and so general for all places as the *Cortes* had done, since they always held very different viewpoints from those of the Congress: they always sought souls before profits. And if perchance our Rulers did despatch such a general cedula (though this seems incredible to me since it has not been found) they afterwards suspended its execution, on being informed that the fruit of the immense labors of the missionaries would be lost, or to put it better, that so many souls redeemed by the Blood of Jesus Christ would perish.

That the Catholic Kings did so is clearly proved by the fact that in both Americas there are numberless missions, 100 or 200 years older than ours, which still remain under the control of the regular missionaries. This would not have happened if there had been a law or a royal cedula obliging the Regulars to transfer their missions to the *Jurisdición Real, Ordinaria . . .*

Among us, there is now in effect a statute of the *Colegios de*

Propaganda Fide, which is accepted by my whole Order, approved by the Holy See, and which, since the time of Charles II has been permitted by the *Real Consejo de las Indias* to be enforced in all the *Tribunales Reales.* This statute is as follows: 'Missionaries may remain in charge of souls recently converted to the Faith only until the bishop, in whose territory they are, wishes to designate secular priests to take over the care of these souls.' Under this supposition, we would be guilty if the most illustrious Bishop of Sonora, in whose diocese our missions are, had asked us for these missions and we had refused, or if the Government had ordered us to transfer them and we had resisted. But since neither has requested this, what guilt is ours? To whom should we transfer them if the sovereign leaves them confided to us? [80]

After this explanation, the Father Guardian then enumerated the reasons why it would at present be unwise to secularize the missions. The Bishop of Sonora did not have priests enough to take over the California Missions, for once when the missionaries had offered to surrender some of their establishments to him he had been obliged to reject their offer. Moreover, the Missions were not yet ready to be converted into parishes. There were still many gentiles to be converted, the neophytes were as yet weak in their faith, and there would be no means, once the *sínodos* were withdrawn, of suporting diocesan priests, since the Indians were too poor to do so. Finally, if the lesson may be drawn from what happened elsewhere when secularization was attempted, the proposed change would bring disaster to the work of the Missions. For the present, therefore, secularization should be deferred, though the viceroy should realize that "we are ready to transfer the Missions if the bishop or the king should ask it, provided we be allowed to defend ourselves against calumnies and to leave our posts with honor." [81]

This reply apparently satisfied the authorities at Mexico City for no further steps were taken to apply secularization or carry out the recommendations of the *Junta.*

---

[80] *Ibid.,* 230–233.
[81] *Ibid.,* 234–253.

Yet the *Primera Junta de California* is of the utmost importance, and this is the reason for the length of its treatment herein, as an indication of the various currents of opinion in California and particularly in Mexico concerning the Missions. The report of Lieutenant Tamaríz is representative of a hostile, anti-clerical element, centered in California but with sympathizers in Mexico, which first expressed itself in Neve's *reglamento*. The picture of the economic ills that afflicted the province, its backwardness in population, its lack of commerce, its miserable military forces and defences, all indicate the source of discontent. But the consequent attack on the mission system shows the spirit of jealousy and cupidity that these evils occasioned. Instead of tracing their cause to the breakdown of colonization projects that followed the closing of the Anza route, to Spain's neglect of the province, particularly since the outbreak of the wars of independence, and, finally, to their own laziness and inertia, Tamaríz and the Californians blamed the Missions. Lastly, the proposed industrialization of the Missions and their neophytes under lay administrators indicated the fond dream of every mission enemy—self-enrichment through lucrative positions as administrators, and self-ease and support by an enslaved native population.

The report of the secretary of the *Junta* was representative of the new attitude of Spanish governmental circles towards religion. The proposal of a diocese instead of the mission system showed that as liberals, yet still Catholics, they were apprehensive of Church ascendancy. Finally, the mild recommendation of the *Junta* itself revealed the forces that would finally determine government policy. The necessity of concentrating on more pressing problems, the scarcity of means for undertaking new projects, and, especially, the recognition that the Missions were the mainstay of, and that any change might endanger the hold of Spain on the province, all prompted the government to leave the well enough alone.

None of these currents of opinion were to disappear after the disbanding of the *Junta*. That the anti-clerical group was active as late as 1821 is evident from a notice which the Father Guardian of San Fernando sent to the California friars, that in Mexico "a certain Tamariz was venting his ire and fulminating accusations" against the Missions.[82]   In like manner, the reports and proceedings of the *Junta* were not to be forgotten.   Carefully preserved in the archives in accordance with Spanish administrative practice, they were to be consulted by later mission investigators with the result that the same charges were to be repeated, the same proposals for the colonization of the province by convicts, for the development of coastal trade and even of commerce with Asia were to be made and amplified in 1825; the recommended management of mission temporalities by lay administrators was to be the basis of the later secularization laws; and the proposed diocese and even the location of its episcopal see in the middle of both Californias was to become a reality in 1840. If the Tamaríz memorial did not affect the Missions immediately, it had an indisputable bearing on the movements that later led to their secularization.

More important in its immediate effects was the secularization law which was issued from Spain in 1813 and applied to California in 1821. As has been already stated, when the Spanish king was taken prisoner by Napoleon, his authority was assumed by the *Cortes* which gathered at Cádiz in 1810. This body could hardly be considered to be representative of the Spanish nation, since it consisted for the most part, not of regular deputies, the election of whom was rendered impossible by the presence of French troops in their districts, but of persons from the unrepresented regions who happened to be resident in Cádiz. University professors, ecclesiastics infected with Jansenism, and young men imbued with French Republicanism, these made the *Cortes* an extremely radical, anti-clerical and audacious one. The first manifestation of their liberalism came with the publication of the famous Constitution of 1812. Breaking sharply with all the precedents of Spanish history, it enthroned the people through their representatives and relegated the crown and the Church to secondary places in the state.[83]

---

[82] Bancroft, *op. cit.*, II, 432, note 4 ; the California President, Father Payeras, mentioned this fact in his circular to the friars, July 8, 1821 ; cf. Engelhardt, *op. cit.*, III, 103.

[83] Chapman, *History of Spain*, 492–494.

But the legislative act by which their radicalism affected California the most was a general decree of secularization which they passed on September 13, 1813. The occasion of the decree was a petition presented to the *Cortes* by the bishop-elect of Guiana, in which he asked that certain missions in his diocese be transferred from the charge of religious to his own priests. Although the details of the case are unknown, it was evidently another instance of the recurrence of the long-standing secularization controversy. But the noteworthy fact is that to settle this local dispute, the *Cortes* enacted a general decree of secularization and applied it to all missions throughout Spanish America. Briefly, the law read as follows:

1. All missions in the New World which were held by religious and had been in existence for a period of over ten years were to be turned over to the bishops.

2. These missions were to be erected into curacies and placed under the direction of suitable priests chosen from the secular clergy.

3. The religious thus affected were to move on to new mission fields.

4. If necessary, they might remain as temporary curates, though only as long as the emergency continued.

5. At least for the present, the religious may continue in charge of one or two missions in each district.

6. The government and administration of the mission temporalities were to be surrendered to the Indians, who, through their *ayuntamientos* and under the direction of the civil governor, should choose individuals to manage the temporalities and divide the lands among individual owners.[84]

Seven years elapsed, however, before the decree was applied to California. Early in 1814, Ferdinand VII was freed by Napoleon and allowed to return to Spain. Impelled "by his own inclinations, the attitude of other continental monarchs, and the overwhelming majority of the clergy, the nobles, and the people themselves of Spain," [85] the king adopted a reactionary policy and de-

---

[84] For full translation, cf. Engelhardt, *op. cit.*, III, 95–97; Bancroft, *op. cit.*, II, 399–400; Dwinelle, *op. cit.*, 39; Jones, *op. cit.*, 12–13, 54–55.

[85] Chapman, *op. cit.*, 494.

clared the Constitution of 1812 and the decrees of the *Cortes* invalid. The law of secularization of course fell under this annulment. However, the policy of Ferdinand won for him many enemies, particularly in the societies of Freemasons which were becoming quite numerous among the middle classes in Spain. The storm finally broke in 1819, when an army was assembled at Cádiz for the extremely unpopular service of the wars in the Americas. Under the leadership of Freemasons [86] the army revolted and forced the king to restore the Constitution of 1812. From the extreme of conservatism, Spain had returned once more to that of liberalism and the Church was to be the first object attacked. [87]

In New Spain the effect of the change was felt when on May 3, 1820, the viceroy proclaimed the Constitution of 1812 and on January 20, 1821, published the *Banda de la Reforma*,[88] which included as one of its provisions the secularization law of 1813. It was not long before the attempt was made to apply it in Upper California. On February 2, 1821, the viceroy instructed the Father Guardian of San Fernando College to inform the California friars of the import of the decree and of the change it would make in their missions. The Guardian obeyed and on February 7, sent a copy of the decree to the missionaries with instructions to surrender the nineteen missions, all of which had been in existence for over ten years, to the Bishop of Sonora as soon as he wished to accept them. There was nothing for the missionaries to do but comply. On July 7, therefore, the Father President notified Governor Sola of his receipt of the law. The next day he addressed a long circular to the friars, informing them of the impending change and ordering them to prepare the mission records and registers for the transfer. Finally, on July 16, he informed the Bishop of Sonora that the formal transfer of the missions could be arranged "whenever his Lordship deigned personally or through a commissioner to accept them, expressing at the same time the readiness of the missionaries to take up the

[86] Alamán, Lucas, *Historia de Méjico desde los primeros movimientos que prepararon su independencia* (Mexico, 1849–52), V, 5–6.

[87] Chapman, *op. cit.*, 495–496.

[88] Bancroft, *op. cit.*, II, 431.

work of evangelization to the north or the east." [89]   But this was as far as the attempted application of the secularization law was to go in California. While the Father President was expressing his submission to the law, a counter-movement against Spanish radicalism was taking form in Mexico. By the time the Bishop of Sonora received his letter, it had assumed the proportions of a revolution. With the country once more in the throes of war, all efforts to enforce the secularization law ceased. Accordingly, the California padres were informed by the bishop in a letter of December 20, 1821, "that secularization had not been enforced anywhere in America; that they might remain in charge of their missions; and that it would be time enough to think of new conversions when the imperial independence should be firmly established." [90]

Thus did it happen that the last year of Spanish rule in California marked the first attempt to apply secularization to its Missions. While the law of 1813 is unimportant as regards its immediate effects, there were several features connected with it which were to become quite significant in the light of later California secularization laws. The *Cortes'* decree of secularization is significant because it gave a new legal meaning to the term, secularization. Formerly, in the eyes of the law, secularization meant simply the transfer of a mission from the religious to the secular clergy with the consequent change in its ecclesiastical status. The transfer of the management, or more often the confiscation, of the mission temporalities by local military officials or individual settlers which so frequently accompanied legal secularization, was unlawful and criminal. But after 1813 it was to have the sanction of the law as one of the terms of secularization. Again, the origins of the law of 1813 are significant because the decree was used as the basis and justification for later secularization laws. The various provisions of the law seem to indicate that its authors must have consulted or were acquainted with the mission legislation of the previous century. The limitation of the missions to a ten-year period of existence reveals the influence which Revillagigedo's blunder and the tradition that sprung from it, had on the legislators. The provision allowing

---

89 Engelhardt, *op. cit.*, III, 100–103.
90 Bancroft, *op. cit.*, II, 433.

the religions to retain one or two missions in each district and to remain as temporary curates where needed, indicates that the authors of the decree were acquainted with the difficulties met with by Ferdinand VI's secularization law as well as with the reaction that set in after its failure had become evident. Yet their anti-clericalism led them to close their eyes to these lessons of the past, and, with an impetuosity that ill befits any legislative assembly, to enact a general law to meet a local problem. Later laws that used this decree as the basis of their justification stood on very poor ground.

Finally, this attempt to apply secularization in California is of interest because of the sentiments it evoked from the missionaries. Despite all implications to the contrary,[91] the missionaries were quite willing to have their missions secularized, as long as this meant simply a change of spiritual ministers and not the destruction of the Indians or the fruit of their long years of labor. With the exception of an expression of fear for the morrow, there appears in their various letters no word of protest or complaint. Rather there are present sentiments of joy as of relief from a burden which had grown heavy and unbearable because of the complications that had arisen during the past ten years. As Father Engelhardt has expressed it:

> The missionaries must have loathed a life which compelled them to assume the roles of farmers, clerks, storekeepers, and mechanics. It was bad enough to have to do this for the sake of their neophytes, but now to be engrossed in such worldly affairs merely for the sake of gratifying the indolent and unappreciative troops was worse. How they must have longed to rid themselves of the burden which robbed them of their spiritual consolations, rendered unmeasurably more difficult the religious progress of the neophytes, and made impossible the conversion of the numerous gentiles calling for priests on the other side of the sierras![92]

When later the friars took an active part in a secularization project that sought an honest solution of the California problem and

---

[91] Cf. Bancroft, *op. cit.,* II, 432.
[92] *Op. cit.,* III, 168–169.

not the confiscation of the mission temporalities, their interest was based upon the motives which they expressed at this early date. For this and the other aforementioned reasons, the secularization law of 1813 must be given a prominent place in the beginnings of the movement in California.

One further event must be noted before the chapter on the beginnings of secularization can be closed. It was the fusion that occurred between the two forces that tended to destroy the California Missions, Spanish liberalism and California cupidity. The wave of radical political doctrines that had swept over New Spain after the publication of the Constitution of 1812 and the *Banda de la Reforma* made its way to California. Newspapers and a *Catecismo Político Arreglado á la Constitución de la Monarquía Española,* which was inspired by the new principles, were welcomed by the Californians and read with the greatest avidity. As one of the friars remarked in a letter written at the time, "some at Monterey are already studying them morning and evening in order to obtain by their light the true liberty which men must enjoy in the future." [93]   Clothed with the principles of liberalism, the jealousy and cupidity of the Californians for the Missions was thenceforward to present itself to the public as a humanitarian movement.

An indication of what this new-found philosophy was to bring was manifested in the inauguration of a new policy of mission taxation by Governor Sola. As will be remembered, since the Missions and their Indians were exempt from taxation, the governor had thus far obtained supplies from the Missions by purchasing them, in theory at least, with drafts on the Royal Treasury. But when he read in newspapers brought from Mexico City that there was included in the *Banda de la Reforma* a provision abolishing all exemptions from taxation, the information was immediately used to good advantage and the missionaries were informed that thenceforth they would be subject to the general laws of taxation.[94] An occasion to apply the new law presented itself when on March 21, 1821, two of the missions exchanged their

93 *Ibid.,* III, 106.
94 *Ibid.,* III, 138–139.

grain with Russian traders for some manufactured goods. "The missions were obliged to deliver to the governor one-half of the proceeds of everything they sold to the traders, and in return to accept a note upon which they could realize nothing. Of the other half sold to the traders the missions were called upon to pay in addition six per cent tax to the governor." [95] The importance of this act is not so much the added drain which it caused on the resources of the Missions, but the fact that it demanded by law what had formerly been asked for by reason of necessity. The question of taxation immediately became a matter of bitter dispute between the civil and mission authorities and as shall be later noted became one of the immediate occasions for secularization.

When the year 1821 closed the period of Spanish rule in New Spain, the foundations had been laid for the secularization of the California Missions. The Missions had been established, at a time when officially they were out of favor, because Gálvez found in them the only means of effecting the Spanish occupation of Upper California. When within the first decade of their existence a crisis brought on by the special features of the California conquest made necessary the adoption of a definite program regarding the Missions, these two policies, the one favoring them for the sake of utility and the other opposing them because of a spirit of anti-clericalism, clashed. The latter was apparently victorious when Neve's *reglamento* replaced Bucareli's regulations and limited the work of the Missions to the spiritual care of the Indians. White colonists were to become the chief agents of the Spanish occupation, serving not only as the social, defensive and economic backbone of the province, but also as the means of civilizing the natives. But this new program came to naught when the Yuma revolt closed the Anza route. The colonization projects were abandoned and the white population entered into a period which, while romantic in its simplicity, was void of all economic or social advancement. On the other hand, the Missions, restored to their original status by a royal revocation of Neve's mission regulations, entered into the period of their greatest development.

---

[95] *Ibid.*, III, 140.

Not only were great advances made in the work of converting and civilizing the Indians, but circumstances soon made them the dominant economic factor in the province. This position thus allotted them was to react to their disadvantage. When revolutionary disturbances in the older provinces stopped the shipment of supplies to California, the military and civil elements were thrown upon the Missions for their support. This position of dependence aroused the old spirit of hostility towards the Missions, based this time on a desire for their wealth. This movement was introduced into Mexico by the memorial of Tamaríz where the foundations were laid for later opposition. Finally, the introduction of Spanish liberalism into California as well as the attempt to apply a Spanish decree of secularization clothed the spirit of hostility with high-sounding principles and gave secularization a flimsy but nevertheless a legal pretext. As the last year of Spanish rule came to its close, the result of this fusion of the two movements against the Missions was being made manifest in Sola's new policy of taxation. With the question of taxation serving as the point of attack in the next period, the movement towards the secularization of the Missions had begun.

CHAPTER III

ATTEMPTS AT SECULARIZATION IN MEXICO AND CALIFORNIA: 1822–1831

The year 1821 marked the end of Spanish rule in North America. In February of that year an uprising led by Agustín de Iturbide broke out and on August 24, with the signing of the Treaty of Córdoba, Mexican independence was proclaimed and the name "New Spain" gave way to that of "Mexico." California shared in this new freedom and was thenceforth, until its acquisition by the United States, a Mexican territory. Though the farthest removed from the central government and possessed with nativistic tendencies that served to separate it farther still, it shared in the fortunes, both good and ill, of the new nation. This was true particularly of the Missions. In Mexico the early period of independence was marked by a series of political struggles that centered around the Church and affected its position considerably. The repercussions of this struggle were felt in the distant territory to the north and, as a result, they form the basis of the story of the secularization of the Missions.

I

Independence came to Mexico as the result of a fusion, unnatural though it was, between the conservatives and the earlier insurgents against Spanish authority. The introduction of Spanish liberalism to New Spain after Ferdinand VII's submission to the *Cortes*, had led many to meet this menace to conservatism and religion by an open espousal of complete separation from the mother country. The Church, attacked, as has been already noted, by the application of anti-clerical measures and fearful of the growing influence of Freemasonry among the Spanish ruling class, soon became a leading figure in the independence movement. In Mexico City members of the higher clergy led by a canon of the Cathedral

78

were among Iturbide's chief supporters,[1] while in many sections of the land priests declared for independence from their pulpits and bishops contributed monies for the support of the rebel armies.[2] Iturbide's almost immediate and complete success was due in no small measure to the support of this influential body.

But after independence was won, this union of the various elements came to an end and the Church found the new freedom turned to its disadvantage. The variety of interests was too great to admit of continued coöperation. Under the banner of independence there had been united the conservative upper classes who sought freedom from all attacks on their privileges, the clergy who sought freedom from anti-clerical laws, the earlier insurgents who fought for equal rights to political power and position and, finally, a new group which sought freedom to determine the status of the Church in the new order. The conflict early broke out and was manifested in the struggle between Iturbide and the new congress that had been convoked in February, 1822, to draw up a constitution. Although Iturbide succeeded in having himself proclaimed emperor his position remained precarious and after a year he was forced to abdicate. While the Church was apparently entrenched during the period of the Empire, it was attacked from the outset by the radical elements that held the majority in the Congress. This body, at its wit's end for money, saw in church property the means of replenishing a depleted treasury. One of its earliest acts was to order the confiscation of the properties of the Philippine missions and the funds of the Inquisition, while later it demanded forced loans from the ecclesiastical corporations of the cities of Mexico, Puebla, Guadalajara and Vera Cruz. Finally, the rapid appearance of an anti-clerical literature and the dissemination of such pamphlets as "A Hundred Questions for Today Concerning Priests and Ecclesiastical Incomes" revealed the trend of the times. Independence had brought with it the spirit of the freethinker and the Church soon became the object of its attack.[3]

---

[1] Priestley. *The Mexican nation, a history*, 246–247.

[2] Callcott, Wilfred H., *Church and state in Mexico, 1822–1857* (Durham, North Carolina, 1926), 35.

[3] *Ibid.*, 44–45.

This effect of independence, like the news itself of Iturbide's victory, was slow in reaching California. While the former Spanish province had accepted independence on April 11, 1822, it had done so with evident reluctance. On first receiving the news of the change in Mexico, Governor Sola, representative of the older Spanish element, had characterized the notice as a document "printed in a country of dreamers, since independence is a dream," and the struggle for it a fantasy and of passing moment. As he wrote, the Californians, "aware that the immortal, incomparable Spanish nation has many and great resources with which to make herself respected, must look with contempt on such absurd views." [4] In like manner the Spanish missionaries had viewed independence with suspicion and even apprehension. The first news of independence had been accompanied both by a declaration that the province could no longer enjoy the privileges of the *Bula Cruzada* [5] and by an account of the evils which the turmoil of the revolution had visited upon the College of San Fernando by causing it to be transformed into a barracks for cavalry.[6] Father Durán was probably expressing the sentiments of his fellow missionaries as well as his own when he wrote:

> I fear much that our independence is not of good faith, but that it may be a machination of the *Illuminati* in accord with foreigners, whose purpose is disorganization and anarchy in these beautiful countries which probably are also in the scheme of the *Sect*. Time will tell.[7]

The friars might well have been cautious in their acceptance of independence for time would indeed bring disorganization and anarchy to their mission system.

It was this lack of enthusiasm on the part of the more prominent Californians that occasioned the introduction into the province of those principles of the new freedom which Father Durán feared. In Mexico, California's acceptance of independence was as yet un-

---

4 Bancroft, *History of California,* II, 450.
5 Engelhardt, *Missions and missionaries of California,* III, 160.
6 *Ibid.,* III, 165–166.
7 *Ibid.,* III, 166.

known, and rumors were current that the distant territory was becoming the center of a Spanish reactionary movement. The government, needlessly aroused by the danger, determined to send a special agent to exact the oath of allegiance. The agent chosen was a certain Agustin Fernández de San Vicente who, though a canon at the cathedral of Durango, soon showed himself a better exponent of the new independence than he was of religion.[8] On his arrival in Lower California he found that the spirit of the revolution had been already aroused by a precursor and that the natives "no longer wished to remain under the auspices of the Father Missionaries." As he informed the home government, "they have asked also that the method of control which has been observed with regard to them hitherto be abolished, a movement which may produce very fatal results." [9] But despite the danger of fatal consequences, Fernández apparently solved the problem by the application of the principles of the new freedom for a later letter relates that he forwarded "a project in regard to the management of the missions" to Mexico.[10] We are not informed whether he met a similar state of unrest among the Indians of Upper California, but it soon became evident that he was determined that they should share in the independence that had been won in Mexico. Shortly after his arrival he ordered that "those of the Indians best fitted to care for themselves might with the consent of the governor and the padres be allowed to go with their share of the property to the pueblo, or to live, under inspection, separately or in any decent family." [11] Although few accepted his proffer of freedom, the canon inaugurated a movement that was to result later in license rather than in liberty.

But more directly affecting the growth of hostility to the Missions was Fernández's choice of a native Californian, Luis Argüello, as governor. A difference had already become noticeable between the younger Californians and their more conservative

---

[8] Richman, *California under Spain and Mexico, 1533–1847*, 231.

[9] Bolton, Herbert E., "The Iturbide revolution in the Californias," *Hispanic American Historical Review*, II (1919), 233.

[10] *Ibid.*, 239.

[11] Bancroft, *op. cit.*, II, 461.

elders. A few years earlier, on the introduction of the radical decrees of the Spanish *Cortes*, they had become eager disciples of liberalism, while later when it was reported that Fernández was about to visit the province, it was written of them, that "some feel themselves already rich, others avenged, others with offices, and still more with ranchos." [12] While Fernández was prompted more by the policy of keeping native born Spaniards out of office than by a desire to satisfy these wild dreams of the Californians, the governor he chose soon manifested an attitude towards the Missions that was quite in keeping with the dreams of his compatriots. After Fernández had departed, Argüello became involved in a controversy with the Father President of the Missions over his right to establish new missions. He sought to suppress Mission San Francisco and transfer its neophytes to a new establishment in the Sonoma Valley. Rumor had it that one of his motives was the desire "to throw the few fertile ranchos south of San Francisco into the hands of settlers." [13] The Father President vigorously opposed this action as summary and illegal, stating that "the political authorities had assumed the functions of a bishop." [14] While the dispute eventually ended in a compromise, San Francisco being allowed to continue and the new mission, San Francisco Solano, established as the governor desired, it evidenced a growing spirit of hostility on the part of the Californians towards the mission system. As Argüello himself expressed it, "because the missions had hitherto been allowed to be sole owners of the lands, it was no reason why such a state of things should continue." [15]

This spirit became more open when news was received in November, 1823, that Iturbide's government had been overthrown and that the liberals had come into power. [16] Throwing off whatever restraint the reign of the conservatives in Mexico might have imposed upon him in the past, Argüello proceeded to carry out a more stringent policy towards the Missions. On January 8, 1824,

---

[12] Bancroft, *op. cit.*, II, 457.
[13] *Ibid.*, II, 496.
[14] Engelhardt, *op. cit.*, III, 183.
[15] Bancroft, *op. cit.*, II, 487, note 12.
[16] *Ibid.*, II, 485.

with the approval of the *diputación,* he instituted a new system
of taxation whereby both colonists and Missions had to contribute
twelve per cent of all their produce and live-stock, with the difference that the settlers might pay in kind, but the Missions in money.
The missionaries naturally protested against this new tax declaring that their neophytes were already over-burdened by the demands of the local authorities.   In a letter which he sent to the
Governor the Father President clearly stated their position as
follows :

> In the missions, after paying the taxes, tariff duties and
> forced loans, scarcely enough remains to furnish each man
> with a shirt, a pair of breeches, and a coarse blanket, and each
> woman with a coarse skirt of serge, in return for working
> continually. . . . On the other hand, in the town of Los An-
> geles there are already one thousand people with plenty of water
> for irrigation and abundant land which is equal to the best in
> the territory.   Single individuals there possess ranchos which
> may compete with whole missions.   Yet I ask, has the whole
> pueblo and have the ranchos contributed the least towards de-
> fraying the expenses of the troops at San Diego?   The inhabi-
> tants in that pueblo have not been molested in the least for the
> support of the military.   The same observation is true for the
> jurisdiction of the other presidios. . . . What the friars suppli-
> cate is that upon their missions the same burden be placed as
> upon the white people and nothing more ; that the same liberty
> of managing them be left to them as is given any other settler.
> The Indians will be content if they are no more molested than
> the settlers. . . .   Yet the intention seems to be to squeeze the
> very sap or substance out of the marrow.   Where in all this
> is there any consideration for the sacredness of each citizen's
> property or for the very rights of the people? [17]

But the Father President's plea for fair play went unanswered. On
the contrary, in its autumn session the *diputación* attempted a
further attack on the Missions by proposing a distribution of some
of their lands among the settlers.   Although, as one writer has
remarked, "during the Spanish and Mexican regime the supply of
land was far above the demand for it," [18] the cultivated fields of

---

[17] Engelhardt, *op. cit.,* III, 187–193.
[18] Ellison, *California and the Nation* (Berkeley, 1927), 7.

the Missions were particularly attractive to the indolent colonists. But when it was pointed out that the distribution of lands should be applied to the extensive domains of certain settlers, the measure was hastily dropped with the statement that "account should be taken of the services rendered by these families." [19]   The movement while ineffective was indicative of the attitude of certain Californians towards the "ranchos" of which they had dreamed when they first learned of independence.

The issue was defined more clearly when a new conflict arose between the authorities and the missionaries over the question of swearing allegiance to the republic which the liberals had established in Mexico. Argüello had received in February, 1825, the command that all under his jurisdiction should take the prescribed oath or else be banished from the territory. While the civil and military elements of the population did not hesitate to take the oath, their third in as many years, most of the friars refused on the ground that they were bound by their former oaths to Spain. Only when the mother country recognized Mexico's independence would they be free to swear anew. As the Father President expressed it :

> I cannot trample under foot the dictates of my conscience. . . .
> I offer to take the oath of fidelity of doing nothing against
> the established government. . . .   But I have not the courage to
> take more oaths, not out of discontent with independence nor
> for any other disagreeable motive but because I am of the
> opinion that oaths have become mere playthings.[20]

This offer was not accepted and feeling ran high against the supposed disloyalty of the friars. It finally came to a climax in April, 1825, when an extraordinary session of the *diputación* was called to discuss the means of punishing the recalcitrants. Thinking themselves now empowered to determine the fate of the missionaries, the members of the assembly immediately decreed:

> That is was for the welfare of the province that those [who
> refused to take the oath] should be entirely relieved of the

---

[19] *Legislative Records*, MS., I, 31–32; cf. Bancroft, *op cit.*, II, 513, note 3.
[20] Engelhardt, *op. cit.*, III, 217–219.

management of the property belonging to the neophytes of the missions, and should be restricted to the spiritual care; and that for the management of said property of said neophytes an upright individual should be designated for their administration.[21]

But the governor, at least, was not prepared to resort to this extreme. His instructions from Mexico had ordered exile but not secularization. Perhaps also he was fearful of the reaction which so radical a measure might create amongst the many Californians who were still devoted to the missionaries, as well as on the home government, concerning the reported liberalism of which he was as yet uncertain. He therefore cautioned the legislators to proceed with greater moderation. As he stated in the speech which he addressed to them:

> He was of the opinion that on no account was it expedient to take away the temporalities from the religious who managed them, because in the first place all would depart and leave their beloved flock without spiritual food; and in the second place because in the province it would be very difficult to find a person who could discharge the duty of managing the property. Many other reasons were set forth by the governor which it would be too tedious to relate.[22]

Sobered by this counsel, the assembly withdrew the proposal and contented itself with sending a report of the matter to Mexico.[23]

While none of these incidents which occurred during the first years of independence had an immediate effect on the status of the Missions, they nevertheless indicated the trend towards secularization. In Mexico independence had given rise to new concepts of freedom which applied in California, as Fernández had attempted to apply them, found their first object in the Missions. In like manner the same impulse provided the group of Californians who coveted the mission properties with new theories with which to cloak the real motives of their hostility. Finally, the break with

---

21 *Legislative records*, MS., I, 44.

22 *Ibid.*, 44–45.

23 Cf. Bancroft, *op. cit.*, III, 17–18; Engelhardt, *op. cit.*, III, 216–217.

Spain supplied the secularization movement with a new motive in nationalism. The fear of a Spanish reactionary movement dictated that the Spanish friars in California should be deprived of whatever power they possessed. That it was a powerful motive had been demonstrated by the *diputación's* action. New developments in Mexico indicated that it would continue to be such.

II

In Mexico the downfall of the Iturbide government which had taken place on February 19, 1823, had been due chiefly to the opposition by Freemasonry. Introduced originally from Spain and composed of "Monarchists, Centralists, and Conservatives, which in politics stood for a government by the few," [24] its exclusion by the pro-church leanings of the Iturbide group led "the order, monarchical in its principles at first, . . . to receive with favor the idea of a central republic with the reins of government under its own control." [25] As a result, by a series of secret intrigues and methods "decidedly questionable" [26] it achieved this end and established itself in power under a republican form of government which was proclaimed on October 21, 1824. The Masons dominated the government for the remainder of the decade and distinguished their régime by keeping the country in a state of ferment and guiding its policies towards the extremes of radicalism. After power had been secured, the order split into two branches, the *Escoceses* or Scottish Rite and the *Yorkinos* or York Rite, the latter organized under the influence of the United States Minister, Joel R. Poinsett. After a period of bitter rivalry and conflict, this branch finally emerged victorious and established in power a group composed of "liberals, democrats, largely creoles and mestizos, generally less well educated than the Escoceses." [27] It was under their influence that extreme radicalism was introduced into the political story of Mexico.

---

[24] Wilgus, A. Curtis, *A history of Hispanic America* (Washington, D. C., 1931), 335.

[25] Bancroft, *History of Mexico,* IV, 794.

[26] Callcott, *op. cit.,* 43.

[27] Priestley, *op. cit.,* 265.

During this period the Church, contrary to what might have been expected, did not meet with open opposition by the government. Although the position of the Church had been weakened by the mistake its leaders had made in not keeping the clergy united on political issues, it still maintained the support of the people.   It was perhaps for this reason that the new constitution, despite the Pope's refusal of recognition,[28] established Roman Catholicism as the national religion and added white to the national colors expressly to symbolize the Church's purity.[29] However, the new government was out of sympathy with the Church and did not hesitate to infringe on its rights. This was true particularly in the matter of ecclesiastical property. To meet the needs of the treasury, the government often resorted to confiscatory decrees.   Thus, in 1823, immediately after Iturbide's overthrow, it sold the remaining properties of the Jesuits, Hospitallers and the Inquisition,[30] and on August 24, 1824, it had adopted as an article of the constitution the principle that all church temporalities were to be considered as the property of the nation.[31] As a consequence of these measures the value of church property thus seized ascended by the end of 1829 to 1,880,604 *pesos.*[32]

It was under these circumstances that the next development in secularization took place, namely, a new governmental policy towards the California Missions which was arrived at by a special *Junta* created for the purpose. From the outset the new administration displayed a marked, if not favorable, interest in the Missions. On April 10, 1823, one of the higher officials, a certain General Juan José Misión made use of the Tamaríz memorial to determine, as it was stated, "the best means to be adopted to advance a matter of great importance and aggrandizement to the republic." [33] That the inquiry was for governmental purposes is indicated by the

---

[28] Bancroft, *op. cit.,* V, 47.

[29] Priestley, *op. cit.,* 260, 262.

[30] Bancroft, *op. cit.,* V, 4.

[31] Jones, *op. cit.,* 13.

[32] Callcott, *op. cit.,* 63.

[33] This incident is attested by a note attached to the *Expediente sobre la Memoria que . . .,* 26.

fact that the same Mision was later appointed as the first Mexican governor of California.[34]   The attitude of the government in this matter was more fully revealed in the following report which the Secretary of State presented to Congress on November 8, 1823. Briefly it stated that the events of the war had ruined the funds devoted to the support of the California Missions, and that the estates of the Pious Fund were entirely unproductive, so that no stipends were paid the missionaries to say nothing of the large amounts which they had advanced for the support of the troops. It was deemed advisable to sell the aforesaid properties for there was no other way of restoring their value.   A private owner, more interested in their development, would care for them better than had the administrators.

As for the funds derived from this sale, the government believed that they should not be devoted exclusively to the payment of stipends to the missionaries.   It was necessary to consider other interests such as the development of commerce, the promotion of agriculture, the building of a national navy, and the curtailment of the ambitions of certain foreign powers concerning the province.

> Although the mission system may be best suited to draw from barbarism savages who run through the woods without any idea of religion or intellectual culture, it can do no more than establish the first principles of society among them and cannot lead them to its highest perfection.   Nothing is better to accomplish this than to bind individuals to society by the powerful bond of property.   The government believes, therefore, that the distribution of lands to the converted Indians, lending them from the mission fund the means for cultivation, and the establishment of foreign colonies, which perhaps might be Asiatic, would give a great impulse to that important province.

Finally, as a further means of promoting colonization, it recommended the transportation of criminals to the province where under the supervision of the authorities they might be transformed

---

[34] Bancroft, *History of California,* II, 515; Richman, *op. cit.,* 466, note 35. Both Richman and Bancroft give the name as Miñion while the transcript has Mision.

into "farmers, useful to the nation, good fathers, good neighbors and, finally, good citizens." [35]   A final note in the general attitude of the government towards the Missions was brought out in the report of another Secretary who stated that the main obstacle to the development of republican principles in California was to be found in the "monastic-military government which had been established there in the beginning and of which vestiges still remain." [36]

From these official statements it is evident that the attitude of the government was influenced considerably by the new theories of liberty which had come into vogue with independence.   The proposals to sell the properties of the Pious Fund were indicative of the new principle of state supremacy over the Church, if not of real hostility to it.   The recommendation of a distribution of the mission properties among the neophytes pointed to the fact that thenceforth the motive for secularization was to be an ideal based more on theory than established by facts.   Finally, the reference to the Spanish background of the mission system indicated that nationalistic prejudices were to be an important factor in determining its fate.   The government was manifestly out of sympathy with the Missions and one wonders whether the reappearance of the Tamaríz memorial as well as the similarity between its proposals for the development of commerce and a navy, of agriculture and colonization and those put forward in the report of 1823, do not indicate the original source of this hostility.   However, the chief point of interest is the fact that it was this general attitude of the authorities which determined the mission policy that was presently drawn up by the special *Junta de Fomento de Californias.*

This *Junta* was established by a presidential decree on July 17, 1824, to study the means of promoting the development of California.   Numbering among its members two figures already familiar to the story of secularization, ex-governor Sola and Lieutenant Francisco de P. Tamaríz, the *Junta* held a series of sessions between January 3, 1825, and August 31, 1827, in which

---

35 *Memorias de relaciones* (México, 1823), 31–33; cf. Bancroft, *op. cit.,* II, 488, note 13; also Poinsett, Joel R., *Notes on Mexico, made in the autumn of 1822* (London, 1825), Appendix, 99.

36 *Memorias de relaciones* (México, 1826), 36–37.

it formulated plans for the colonization of the territory by Mexicans and foreigners, the organization of an Asiatic-Mexican company for the development of commerce, a new codification of general laws, and finally, a plan for the replacement of the mission system.   While none of these plans ever attained the dignity of law, they influenced later Mexican legislation respecting California.   Two of the reports directly determined the mission policy of the government both in Mexico and California and the mission legislation which they later enacted.[37]

The first two sessions of the *Junta* were devoted to a study of the California Missions and the determination of a policy towards them.   The first of these was occasioned by the appointment of a new governor for California, this office being appointive rather than elective since under the new government, California ranked only as a federal territory.   A set of instructions had been drawn up for the new governor and the newly established *Junta* was asked as its first official duty to pass judgment upon them.   The results of the discussion were published on January 3, 1825, and summarized were as follows:

As a prefatory remark it listed the various authorities consulted by the *Junta*, Vizcaíno, Venegas, the report of the *Sutil y Mexicana,* Humbolt, etc.   It disagreed with Venegas' statement that Lower California was dry and ill-suited for the support of a large population, being of the opinion that it was adapted for extensive agricultural production, the territory being greater than a mere peninsula.   As had been suspected by the Spanish government, a false impression of the climate and soil had been given by the Jesuits to protect their own interests, to hinder colonization and prevent the distribution of lands.

The new governor will necessarily meet with the same kind of opposition from those who are opposed to the dismemberment of the missions, for he will find there a system established by the Spanish government for the reduction of the natives, a system which considers the economic side as its proper object and unites it with its spiritual work to form a whole. The governor should treat with the three classes which compose the population, each in a dis-

---

[37] Bancroft, *op. cit.,* III, 3–6, 34–35.

tinct manner. The inhabitants of the pueblos and the older Indians should be ruled according to the laws of the constitution and be made independent of the missionaries except in spiritual matters; but the neophytes and the catechumens were to be kept in the missions until a more suitable system should be established. Finally, he should make a report on the state of distribution in the matter of lands, stating the number occupied by the missions, the extent and quality of unoccupied lands, and the number of *pobladores* and Indians whom he deemed capable of cultivating lands for themselves. To these he should assign, according to their ability to cultivate them, the common lands of the missions, provided there would be no danger of impairing the support of the neophytes and catechumens rendered by the missions.[38]

Three months later on April 6, the *Junta* issued a second report on the California Missions. Entitled, "A plan for the regulation of the Missions of the Upper and Lower California" and consisting of eleven pages, it developed the recommendations of the *Dictámen* and urged the abolition of the mission system. In the prefatory remarks it described the monastic-military government of the Jesuits in Lower California. This was followed by the system of the Franciscans which, first developed in their Sierra Gorde missions, embraced the administration of the mission temporalities by the missionaries. Acknowledging the progress achieved under this system and the praise which it merited, it went on to state:

> Still the *Junta* has not been able to reconcile the principles of such a system with those of our independence and our political constitution. Religion under that system could not advance beyond domination. It could be promoted only under the protection of *escoltas* and presidios. The gentiles must renounce all the rights of their natural independence to be catechumens from the moment of their baptism; they must be subject to laws almost monastic, while their ministers deemed themselves freed from the laws which forbade their engaging in temporal business; and the neophytes must continue thus without hope of ever possessing fully the civil rights of society. The *Junta*

---

[38] *Junta de fomento de Californias,* "Dictámen que dió la Junta . . . sobre las instrucciones que para el jefe superior politico," (México, 1827), 4–13.

has not been able to persuade itself that this system is the only one fitted to arouse among the gentiles a desire for civil and social life, or to teach its first rudiments, much less to carry it to perfection. It believes rather that it is positively contrary to the political aims in accordance with which it should have been organized, and still more to the true spiritual aim which should be kept in view. The conversion of the numerous gentiles who occupy the territories of the Californias is indeed an object most worthy of the attention of a nation which has made profession in its political constitution of the Catholic, Apostolic, Roman Religion, but this religion ought not to be propagated in any other form than that prescribed by Jesus Christ and His Apostles. Moreover, the holy and laudable ministry of converting the gentiles should not be limited to the members of a particular religious order, nor should the military power apply itself either directly or indirectly to this object but should confine itself to the protection of the country from all attacks and the maintenance of order. . . . The present condition of the missions does not correspond to the great progress which they made in the beginning. This decadence is very noticeable in Lower California and should suffice to prove that the system needs change and reform. But in the opinion of the *Junta* the most inexcusable abuse is the distraction from their primary ministry caused the missionaries by the necessity of caring for the temporalities and administration of each mission. Besides the harm done to the principal object of the missionaries, this latter work cannot be done without a manifest laxity in their vows, ...

The *Junta* then proposed the following plan for a change in the mission system. The direction of missionary work in California was to be transferred from the hands of the Franciscans to the supreme government. The government was to assume the administration of the Pious Fund, take charge of the mission temporalities, direct the distribution of mission lands among the neophytes as soon as they were capable of governing themselves, and enact laws for their government and the protection of life and property. Secondly, the right to engage in missionary work was not to be restricted to any particular religious order. While the present missionaries could remain as curates, provided they were approved by the provincial authorities, other priests could petition the government for permission to share in this work. To all thus authorized, the supreme government would supply the necessary stipends and travelling expenses from the Pious Fund. Thirdly, the work of conversion was to be effected by visits of priests and friars to the Indians. The mission was to serve as a center with two friars permanently attached to it, besides those temporarily residing or resting there while engaged in converting the gentiles. Finally, this arrangement was to continue until the Missions should be made formal parishes and be delivered to the bishop.[39]

A final statement of the *Junta* concerning the California Missions reveals what was probably the fundamental reason for its hostility towards them. Contained in the *Voto Final* or general recommendations which the *Junta* issued on May 13, 1827, it ran as follows:

> This is the condition in which the Mexican nation in the glorious days of its independence and liberty found it [California]: its government is levitico-monarchic; the customs introduced by the missionaries are the unwritten law which in general govern the country; in brief, the influence of these ministers called apostolic is so powerful that each missionary seems to be at the head of a small government, ... For this reason no other region in the Mexican nation has greater need of a systematized government in order that the reign of law and properity might free it from the will of the religious. Otherwise, . . . the missionaries, who are Spaniards and have a most powerful hold on the consciences of men and the administration of the missions, may effect from that immense distance the revolution which some of their compatriots attempted as the means of restoring the Mexican nation to the yoke of the tyrant whom they acknowledge.[40]

These various reports form the most complete survey that was ever undertaken by the Mexican authorities with respect to the California Missions. But unfortunately it was marred by a want of reliable information while the influence of prejudices robbed

---

[39] *Junta de fomento de Californias,* "Plan para el arreglo de las misiones de los territorios de la Alta y de la Baja California," 1–11; for a fuller summary of the *Junta's* plan cf. Bancroft, *op. cit.,* III, 21–23, note 40.

[40] *Junta de fomento de Californias,* "Iniciativa de ley que propone la Junta para el mejor arreglo del gobierno de los territorios de Californias," 40–41.

it of its value. As Bancroft, in his appreciation of the *Junta's* work, states "it is evident from the allusions to Vizcaino, Venegas, the *Sutil y Mexicana,* Humbolt's works, . . . [as well as] a noticeable confusion between the two Californias . . . that the members had no idea of the fresh and complete sources of information accessible in the form of missionary and other official reports." [41]   It failed to appreciate the historical development of the mission system and the reasons which forced the Jesuits and Franciscans to develop the material as well as the spiritual. Nor did it realize that the Missions had been forced into a position of ascendancy in California and that if at present they were declining it was because of the burden which had been placed upon them. Rather, it interpreted these facts in the light of the principles and prejudices with which it was imbued. Because of its hostility to religious orders, it regarded all reports of the missionaries with suspicion and all progress of their missions as a sign of their grasping for power. The theory of the state's supremacy over the Church led it to appropriate the mission funds for state purposes and assume the direction of missionary work, licensing priests as it would state officials. Finally, it was an idealism based on Voltairean theories rather than on facts, that led it to believe that the California Indian was capable of taking and defending his place in society. These various prejudices, surmounted by a nationalistic hostility towards the missionaries as Spaniards, so warped the judgment of the members of the *Junta* that the plan they proposed meant the destruction rather than the completion of the half-century's work of the Missions. This was made manifest as soon as an attempt was made to carry out the recommendations of the *Junta.*

III

It is not certain what effect the proposed change in the mission system had on the mind of the Mexican authorities. The fact that the Minister of Foreign and Internal Affairs requested on June 25, 1825, from the Father Guardian of San Fernando College a list of the missionaries' agents in Mexico as well as a report on the

---

[41] *Op. cit.,* III, 4.

management of the mission temporalities may indicate that the government intended to enforce the plan, at least with regard to the Pious Fund.   But the letter which the Father Guardian sent in reply disabused the government of whatever mistaken ideas the *Junta* had given it about the Missions.   As the Father Guardian pointed out, "in order that the soldiers might not suffer from want of food, the missionaries had been compelled to prefer them to their poor neophytes, lest the troops rebel for lack of provisions. We can therefore truly say that the missions alone, or the toil of the unhappy neophytes, have supported the troops since 1810, . . . the colonists being too indolent to work."   Although these supplies already furnished by the Missions amounted to over $259,151, of which not a cent had been repaid, the local authorities harassed the missionaries with new taxes and duties and excessive demands for supplies.

> As a consequence, the Indians complain bitterly for having to work hard in order that the soldiers might eat, and for receiving no pay for their toil and their pains. . . . The dissatisfaction, notwithstandnig the many means and devices employed by the friars to mitigate the hardships of the Indians, resulted in a revolt last year. . . . Such attempts to shake off the unbearable yoke may be repeated, because what the soldiers consume must be produced by the Indians.[42]

The realization that as long as the Mexican government could not send supplies, the troops in California had to depend on the Missions for their support, apparently sobered the authorities, for the plan of the *Junta* was never enacted in law.

But if the report of the *Junta* failed to have an immediate effect in Mexico, it had an unmistakable influence on the mission policy of the new governor, José María Echeandía.   While the Mexican authorities hesitated to enact a law providing the changes recommended by the *Junta,* they gave express commands to the new governor to carry out the provisions of the *Junta's Dictámen.*   On January 31, 1825, the secretary of war sent the instructions to Echeandía with the following note:

---

[42] Engelhardt, *op. cit.,* III, 208–211 ; cf. Bancroft, *op. cit.,* III, 20–21.

The enclosed relations . . . will inform you of the vexations
suffered by the inhabitants of the country at the hands of both
the missionaries and the former commandants. The President
desires that these evils should be remedied. But this reform
should be rather one of policy than of authority. It is not expedient to attack openly the system of the missionaries who if
offended might by their influence cause greater evils. Still it is
essential to proceed step by step in checking the authority with
which they oppress the people. You should teach these latter
the advantages of the liberal government, but with prudence
and moderation lest their customs degenerate into license,
which could easily happen should you proceed unwisely. As
it is not possible to give in detail the course you must follow,
it is left to your knowledge and judgment, and if you succeed
it will be to your honor. The President relies on your ability
and it is fitting that you justify his confidence in you.[43]

The mission policy of the new governor was clearly defined. In
spirit he was to oppose the mission system; in action he was to
proceed cautiously, teaching the Indians the new doctrines of
liberty; establish, according to the *Dictámen,* some of them as
private land owners; and, finally, report to the government on
the distribution of lands. As one writer has put it, "Echeandía
came to Upper California with hostility for the religious habit
and was determined to relegate it to the interior of the church
and house as soon as practicable." [44]

When the new governor arrived in Upper California in October, 1825, he faithfully followed these instructions. The first
Mexican to take charge of the former Spanish province and perhaps uncertain of the reaction this would create, he proceeded
cautiously. For the first few months he did little to arouse the
suspicions of the friars. He even gave the impression that he
favored them, for on January 1, 1826, he amended the Argüello
tax law by ordering that the contributions of the Missions should
be reduced so as to conform with those of the white inhabitants.
"The supplies furnished the presidios were to be credited as the
prescribed tax, and the balance credited to the Missions." [45] How-

---

[43] *State papers, missions and colonization,* MS., II, 42; Bancroft, *op. cit.,* III,
101, note 32, gives a summary of this letter.

[44] Engelhardt, *op. cit.,* III, 224.

[45] *Ibid.,* III, 234.

ever, this was but a gesture for "there is no evidence that any part of the balance was paid in any instance." [46]

But other acts of the governor soon revealed his real animus towards the Missions. An order restricting mission trade to the four presidio ports and thereby imposing an unnecessary hardship on the more remote establishments,[47] as well as the unfounded charge which he made to the Mexican authorities, that some of the Missions had from $70,000 to $100,000 in their coffers,[48] revealed his distrust of the missionaries. His real purpose with respect to their establishments was made manifest when an officer, whom he sent on a tour of inspection of the southern missions, "went so far as to assemble the neophytes and to make a political speech, in which he told them of the new chief who had come to the country to be their friend, and to give them equal rights with the Spaniards." [49] These "equal rights" meant the distribution of the mission properties among the Indians.

The friars unwittingly gave the Governor his first opportunity to carry out this plan. On April 28, 1826, Echeandía assembled the missionaries in the San Diego district to learn their attitude towards taking the prescribed oath. As they had done before, they offered to take the oath with the supplement, "so far as may be compatible with our religion and profession." [50] The Governor rejected this compromise and informed them of the possibility of their being deprived of the management of the mission temporalities should they fail to comply. Much to his surprise, the missionaries immediately declared themselves willing to be relieved of this office. To the friars the direction of the material things of the mission was a burden rather than, as the government regarded it, a privilege. A letter which one of the friars wrote a few months later probably expressed the sentiments of most of his confreres in the matter:

There are difficulties all around, and I am overburdened with cares which render life wearisome. There is hardly any-

---

[46] Bancroft, *op. cit.*, III, 88.
[47] Engelhardt, *op. cit.*, III, 224.
[48] Bancroft, *op. cit.*, III, 88, note 2.
[49] *Ibid.*, III, 102, note 33.
[50] *Ibid.*, III, 91.

thing of the religious in me, and I scarcely know what to do in these troublesome times. I made the vows of a Friar Minor; instead I must mañage temporalities, sow grain, raise sheep, horses, and cows, preach, baptize, bury the dead, visit the sick, direct carts, haul stones, lime, etc. These things are as disagreeable as thorns, bitter, hard, unbearable, and they rob me of time, tranquility, and health both of soul and body.[51]

As formerly noted, the necessity of supporting the troops of the province as well as the Indians of the Missions had made the burden of the missionaries unbearable. As had been the case six years before when the secularization decree of the Spanish *Cortes* had been published, they were eager to surrender this office to a government which they believed would exercise it without detriment to the neophytes.

But Echeandía was not prepared for so sudden an offer. Mindful of his instructions to proceed cautiously, he declared that as yet it would not be safe to set the neophytes free and make them provide for themselves. However, "in accordance with the policy of his government, with his own republican theories, with the spirit rapidly evolved from controversies with the friars . . . , and with the urgings of some prominent Californians who already had their eyes on the mission lands," [52] he determined to make a beginning in the matter of secularization. Accordingly, with the consent of the unsuspecting friars, he published on July 25, 1826, his "Decree of Emancipation in favor of the Neophytes."

By its terms those desiring to leave the missions might do so, provided they had been Christians from childhood or for fifteen years, were married or at least not minors, and had some means of gaining a livelihood. The Indians were to apply to the presidial commandante, who after obtaining a report from the padre was to issue through the latter a written report entitling the neophytes and his family to go wherever they pleased, like other Mexican citizens, their names being erased from the mission registers.[53]

[51] Father Arroya de la Cuesta, August 10, 1826; cf. Engelhardt, *op cit.*, III, 225–226.

[52] Bancroft, *op. cit.*, III, 101–102.

[53] *Ibid.*, III, 102–103.

The decree bore a striking resemblance to that issued by Fernández a few years before and naturally so, for both were based on the same principles of liberty and equality which had come into vogue with independence. However, the application of these principles soon showed that they were better in theory than in practice.

The Englishman, Beechey, who visited California in November, 1827, has supplied the chief account of the effect of the decree of emancipation:

> A feeling of discontent pervaded the missions, in consequence of some new regulations of the republican government, liberating all those converted Indians from the missions who bore good characters. This philanthropic system at first sight appeared to be a very excellent one and every friend of the rights of man would naturally join in a wish for its prosperity. But after a few months' trial, much to his [the governor's] surprise, he found that these people who had always been accustomed to the care and discipline of school boys, finding themselves their own masters, indulged freely in all those excesses which it had been the endeavor of their tutors to repress, and that many having gambled away their clothing, implements, and even their lands, were compelled to beg or plunder in order to support life. They at length became so obnoxious to the peaceable inhabitants that the padres were requested to take some of them back to the missions, while others who had been guilty of misdemeanors, were loaded with shackles and put to hard work, and when we arrived were employed transporting enormous stones to the beach to improve the landing place.[54]

Emancipation not only meant the demoralization and degradation of the neophytes but it also ended in many cases their contentment with mission life. As a contemporary remarked, "the ideas instilled into the minds of the neophytes made a great change in them. They were not as contented nor as obedient as before." [55] Several incidents that followed the publication of the decree served but to confirm this view. At Los Angeles a former mission Indian

---

[54] Beechey, Frederick W., *Narrative of a voyage to the Pacific and Beering's Strait* (London, 1831), II, 320.

[55] Mrs. Ord, *Ocurrencias*, MS., 52; quoted by Bancroft, *op. cit.*, III, 104, note 38.

in a fit of drunkenness publicly abused the alcade and the governor and declared that the whites were only fit to be killed, while shortly afterwards at San Luis Rey and San Juan Capistrano many of the neophytes refused to work and, until the guards had been increased, threatened a serious outbreak.[56] "In truth," to adopt Beechey's conclusion, "the decay of these establishments, for want of laborers, began with Echeandía's interference." [57]

It is not certain how fully the missionaries appreciated this fact for there is little evidence to reveal their immediate reaction to emancipation. But according to Father Durán's comments on the experiment, which he wrote four years later, the friars were now quite certain of the incompatibility that existed between the theories of liberty and equality and the actual state of the Indians. If formerly they had hesitated to oppose the application of these high-sounding principles to the lives of their neophytes, half believing that they were ready to take their place in society, they were now firmly convinced that "the neophytes were almost without exception and during their whole life like school children . . . whom the winning of honors does not impress, the advantage of gain from their personal labors does not interest, and who have no inclination save for an absolute independence without rational limits." [58] Echeandía's attempt at emancipation really marks the beginning of a policy of opposition on the part of the friars to all experiments at secularization. Formerly they had welcomed it as a means of relief from an unbearable burden. Thenceforth they opposed it, not out of self interest, as so many have presumed, but because any sudden change in the mission system meant the degradation of the neophytes and the destruction of the fruits of over half a century of labor and sacrifice. Their attitude towards the question of adapting the Missions and their Indians to new conditions was set forth by Father Durán when, in the same letter, he wrote:

The governors should be enjoined not to undertake any innovation of importance until they have gone over the whole territory under their command and have seen it with their own

[56] Engelhardt, op. cit., III, 241.
[57] Op. cit., II, 13.
[58] Engelhardt, op. cit., III, 339.

eyes. To do otherwise is to act like blind men with the risk
of having to regret it afterwards, as was the case with the premature emancipation of a certain class of Indians which has
produced nothing but disorder and vice among the so privi-
leged and insubordination among the rest.[59]

As will be later noticed, when an earnest effort, divorced of all
nationalistic prejudices and covetous motives, was made to effect a
gradual transformation in the mission system, the California friars
were foremost in sponsoring the move.

Meanwhile it had become evident that the experiment in emancipation could not be continued. Beechey was probably but reflect-
ing the minds of a number of Californians when, in connection
with his observations on the effects of the decree, he wrote:

> The missions have hitherto been of the highest importance
> to California and the government cannot be too careful to
> promote their welfare, as the prosperity of the country in great
> measure is dependent upon them, and must continue to be so
> until settlers from the mother country can be induced to resort
> thither. The neglect of the missions would not long precede
> the ruin of the pueblos and of the whole district; thus, while
> the missions furnish the means of subsistence to the presidios,
> the body of men they contain keeps the wild Indians in check,
> and prevents their making incursions on the settlers.[60]

Protests from the missionaries that they could not meet the demands for supplies as well as an increasing number of complaints
from the destitute troops at the neglect of Mexico in the matter of
their support,[61] forced the governor to realize this same truth, that
emancipation, if continued, "would ruin the territory by cutting off
its chief resources and exposing its people to the raids of hostile
Indians."[62]   The experiment was therefore dropped and for the
next four years California was freed of all further attacks on the
mission system.   The only good that the emancipation decree had
produced was the realization which it brought to the missionaries
and, as one of them rather significantly remarked, "to all who had

---

[59] *Ibid.*, 343.
[60] *Op. cit.*, II, 14–15.
[61] Bancroft, *op. cit.*, III, 57–58.
[62] *Ibid.*, III, 90.

no eye on a share in the spoliation," that schemes evolved in distant Mexico by theorists and anti-clericals, when applied in California, meant the degradation of the Indians and the destruction of whatever progress had been thus far made. It had taken a disaster to awaken the friars, themselves too often idealists, to this danger.

But while the failure of this first experiment forced Echeandía to desist for a time from all active measures against the Missions, it did not lessen his hostility towards them. On December 6, 1826, almost in the face of facts that belied his statement, he sent a most unfair report to the authorities in Mexico in which he spoke "of the monopoly by the friars of all the land, labor, and products of the territory; of their hatred for the present system of government; and of the desirability of making at least a partial distribution of mission property among the best of the neophytes." [63]   Indeed, a demand which he made in October of the next year for a detailed report of the lands held by the various missions [64] seems to indicate that he still had in mind the instructions which the *Junta* had given him in its *Dictámen* and that he was determined to effect eventually the complete secularization of the Missions. This purpose finally manifested itself when the governor drew up a "Plan for the conversion of the Missions of the two Californias into pueblos" and on December 14, 1828, sent it secretly to Mexico for the approval of the authorities there.

In a letter which accompanied this document Echeandía explained that he had drawn up the plan as the best means of removing the Indians from the rule of the religious in accordance with the principles of humanity, the republican form of government, and for the prosperity of the country. The Indians had been enslaved under the mission system for a time longer than necessary for their conversion and removal from savagery. They had been clamoring for liberty and had been quieted only by the use of armed force and by his promise of the plan. Since they awaited the result, he therefore asked that it be approved as soon as possible. [65]

---

[63] *Ibid.*, III, 104, note 37.

[64] *Ibid.*, 104.

[65] Tays, George, *Revolutionary California: the political history of California during the Mexican Period*, 381.

If in the past there had been outbreaks on the part of the neophytes, they had arisen not because of the life in the missions but because of the oppressions and excessive demands of the troops.[66] Instead of acknowledging this as the cause of unrest and devising another method for supporting the troops, Echeandía proposed as the solution a plan which meant the end of the mission system. Briefly, it provided that:

1. All the missions both in Upper and Lower California, with the exception of the two on the northern frontier, should be converted into pueblos within five years, the beginning to be made with those nearest the presidios.

2. Each pueblo was to consist of the neophytes and such other Mexican citizens as should choose to join them, would possess as its property the lands of the missions and all appurtenant chattels, and would be governed according to the provisions of the law.

3. Each family in the pueblo was to be given a building lot, a field for cultivation, and a share of the mission livestock and agricultural implements, with the provision that these properties should remain individable and inalienable for five years.

4. Other land to the extent of a square league for every five hundred families was to be used as a public common, while the mission buildings, with the exception of the church and rectory, were to be devoted to public use.

5. After this first distribution of property, all that remained over was to be placed under the care of administrators, and out of the net proceeds and profits of these effects there were to be paid the salaries of the public officials and the upkeep of public institutions.

6. Finally, the missionaries could remain as parish priests or, if they chose, move on to found new missions in the Tulare country or in any other place in the interior of the territory.[67]

As its contents indicate, Echeandía's plan was the most definite and comprehensive scheme thus far proposed for the secularization

---

[66] Bancroft, *op. cit.*, III, 110, note 51.

[67] Echeandía, "Plan para convertir en peublos las Misiones de las dos Californias," *Departmental records,* MS., VI, 243–251; for a complete summary of the plan cf. Hittell, Theodore, *History of California* (San Francisco, 1885), II, 93–95. Bancroft, *op. cit.,* III, 106, evidently was not certain of the existence of a plan at this date.

of the Missions. Indeed it was to serve as the model of all later secularization laws, and, therefore, must be considered as the most important factor in the determination of the ultimate fate of the mission system. Because of this fact, it is a matter of special interest to identify the sources and contributing factors that led to its formation.

It is quite improbable that the materials for the plan were obtained from Mexico. *The Junta de Fomento* had indeed proposed definite changes in the mission system, but none of these found their way into Echeandía's plan. The *Junta's Plan para el arreglo de las Misiones* was in all probability as yet unknown to the California governor, for had he known of its existence he would have likely made use of its comprehensive provisions for the regulation of religious affairs in the place of the brief ruling his own plan gave this matter. Indeed, the existing evidence indicates that the *Dictamen* was the only one of the many reports made by the *Junta* which was known in California at this time. The general policy of opposition to the Missions which it enjoined was, therefore, the sole element in Echeandía's plan that had its origin in Mexico. But, on the other hand, in California there had been developing a definite program of secularization. Neve's *Reglamento* on colonization had suggested a method for the distribution of the mission lands and properties; the secularization decree of the Spanish *Cortes* had proposed the idea of administrators; and both of these had been incorporated in the secularization scheme which the *diputación* had proposed to Argüello. Evidently, the project had not been abandoned but had now reappeared in Echeandía's plan.

This fact seems to be indicated by the elements that compose the plan. The incorporation of the neophytes into the pueblo system, the procedure to be followed in the distribution of mission lands and goods, even the conditional five-year period, are traceable to the Neve *Reglamento,* as is the proposal for administrators, to the *Cortes'* decree. Moreover, it would seem that the small coterie of Californians who formed the nucleus of local opposition to the Missions, were instrumental in having these provisions incorporated into an official plan. The lack of evidence to substantiate Echeandía's assertion that the plan had been promised to the discontented neophytes as the means of placating them indicates that his statement was more of a pretext than a serious motive.   From the remarks of several contemporaries, it would seem that the plan was drawn up as a result of other influences that had been brought to bear on the governor,—that "he aimed only to enrich himself by despoiling the missions" and sought to remove the neophytes from the supervision of the friars in order that "his own particular friends might appropriate their services for their own use." [68]   In all probability, while the plan was quite in keeping with Echeandía's attitude toward the Missions, its form-ation was due primarily to "the urgings of some prominent Cali-fornians who already had their eyes on the mission lands." [69]   This was the reason for its secrecy and importance.   It united the two groups which had so long been aiming at the destruction of the Missions.   Once it was approved in Mexico the full force of their opposition would be revealed.   The mission system as such would come to an end, satisfying thereby every prejudice that had ever made itself felt in Mexico City and every covetous ambition that had ever been harbored by Californians.   Echeandía's plan fore-doomed the Missions and their Indians.

But the expected approval did not come from Mexico.   On the contrary, a new series of events occurred which put the question of secularization in the background and forced Echeandía for the next year and a half to desist in his attack on the Missions. Curiously, this remarkable change was occasioned by the passage of several laws in Mexico which aimed at the expulsion of all Spaniards from the Republic.   Since the break with Spain the position of Spaniards had been rendered quite precarious by creole and *mestizo* hostility.   When finally a plot to restore Spanish rule was uncovered in January, 1827, the pent up rage of nationalism was unloosed upon the heads of these unfortunates.   Under the encouragement of the *Yorkinos* who seized it as an opportunity for destroying the power of the more conservative *Escoceses,* the National Congress ordered all Spaniards, except certain exempted

---

[68] Fernández, *Cosas de California,* MS., 45; Dr. Marsh, *Letter to Com. Jones,* MS., 2, quoted by Bancroft, *op. cit.,* III, 107, note 46.

[69] Bancroft, *op. cit.,* III, 102.

classes, to leave the country within six months. This was followed by other more stringent laws until finally every Spaniard of any consequence had been driven from the country and, incidentally, large amounts of capital and a rich foreign trade.[70] The laws included California within their scope and the Mexican authorities, in keeping with their general attitude of suspicion, took definite steps to apply them, particularly to the Spanish missionaries. An agreement was made with the Franciscan College of Nuestra Señora de Guadalupe de Zacatecas to send its Mexican religious to California,[71] and instructions were sent to Governor Echeandía to expel the Spanish friars immediately.

But it was easier to send orders from Mexico than to enforce them in California. While Echeandía took steps to apply the law, threatening those friars with exile who refused to take the prescribed oath of allegiance,[72] several events soon forced him to abandon such stringent measures. Shortly after his publication of the expulsion laws the governor received strong protests from the town assemblies of San Jose, Monterey and other places which, pointing to "the evils that must result from such expulsions, expressing for the missionaries the deepest love and veneration, and pleading eloquently that the people might not be deprived of their spiritual guardians," [73] awakened him to the position of esteem which the missionaries held in the popular mind. More important still, two serious revolts broke out among the troops in 1828 and 1829 which, caused by destitution and the non-receipt of salaries from Mexico, impressed the governor with the consequences that would inevitably follow the destruction of the only existing source of supplies, the Missions.[74] Under these circumstances he deemed it more prudent to delay the application of the expulsion laws and to send instead a list of the Spanish friars to Mexico.[75] With it, on June 30, 1829, he sent the following letter explaining his reasons for not applying the law:

---

[70] Bancroft, *History of Mexico*, V, 54–61, 76.
[71] Tays, *ut supra*, 376.
[72] Bancroft, *History of California*, III, 51–53.
[73] *Ibid.*, III, 97; Engelhardt, *op. cit.*, III, 274–277.
[74] Bancroft, *op. cit.*, III, 66 ss.
[75] Engelhardt, *op. cit.*, III, 268–269.

There are twenty-one missions but only three Mexican friars; the others are Spaniards, who by their industry have placed the missions in a state of actual wealth. If unhappily the missions should be deprived of these fathers, we should see the population in a lamentable condition for want of subsistence. The neophytes would give themselves to idleness and pillage, and other disorders would ruin the missions, and they would resume the savage life from which the greater number or nearly all have come; then after they had settled down in the mountains, all agricultural and mechanical industry would cease, and the rest of the inhabitants and troops would perish.[76]

The presence of danger had at last forced Echeandía to abandon the theories and prejudices which had prompted his earlier secularization projects, to see conditions as they actually existed, and to acknowledge, as Beechey had done before him, the great service which the Missions rendered the territory. After this admission of defeat it appeared that the mission system would be freed from all further threats of secularization. The governor, probably in a feeling of disgust or, as Bancroft puts it, "not in robust health," [77] tendered his resignation to the authorities in Mexico [78] and while awaiting the arrival of a successor did nothing further against the friars. Had not a new set of circumstances arisen, the mission system would have probably been allowed to continue undisturbed and Echeandía would have escaped the opprobrium of being "largely responsible for many of the troubles which Alta California suffered in the ensuing years." [79]

IV

This new series of events had begun in Mexico with the ousting of the Masons from the control of the government. A reaction had set in against the radical wing of the Order which had violated the constitution by seizing the presidency through armed force. A new political party composed of more conservative elements appeared and on January 1, 1830, brought an end to Masonic

---

[76] Quoted by Tays, *ut supra*, 378; cf. Bancroft, *op. cit.*, III, 96.

[77] Bancroft, *op. cit.*, III, 32.

[78] *Ibid.*, III, 53, note 47.

[79] Chapman, *History of California*, 458.

control and declared the vice-president, Anastasio Bustamente, acting President. Bustamente, a man "possessed of much presence of mind, courage, and sound judgment . . . a lover of civilization and enlightenment, and apparently a disinterested patriot," [80] gave the country an efficiency and financial stability in government that it had not known during the distracted years of liberalism.[81] What was of greater significance, his administration was favorable to the Church, which was "virtually restored to its former influence." [82]

When the new President shortly after his accession to power addressed a very friendly letter to one of the California friars, it became evident that the reaction would make itself felt in that distant territory.[83]   On March 8, 1830, the President, after receiving reports of Echeandía's unpopularity and complaints of plunder which had been raised against him, appointed a new governor in the person of Lieutenant Colonel Manuel Victoria.   It was hoped that Victoria, active and conscientious, well acquainted with the California situation through several years residence in the Peninsula, and favoring a more conservative mission policy, would put an end to the radical tendencies which had manifested themselves of late in the territory.[84]

The final significant event was the arrival in Upper California on July 1, 1830, of the man who had been originally named by the Masonic government to succeed Echeandía, José María Padrés.   As governor-elect Padrés had openly manifested his hostility to the missionaries.   In a letter which he had addressed to the Secretary of State on March 30, 1829, he had described how

the Californians, bred and educated by Spanish missionaries and officials, thought as they did and were submerged in a most crass ignorance.   Their fanaticism and lack of a broad education made him fear for some sort of a catastrophe. . . . To avoid the evils that beset the country, he proposed two reme-

[80] Bancroft, *History of Mexico,* V, 94.
[81] Callcott, *op. cit.,* 68–72.
[82] Bancroft, *op. cit.,* V, 105.
[83] Engelhardt, *op. cit.,* III, 328.
[84] Bancroft, *History of California,* III, 54–55.

dies. The first was sufficient armed forces to sustain the authorities; the second was to replace the missionaries by loyal Mexican clergymen.[85]

Coming now to California in the capacity of adjutant inspector, a position with which he had to content himself after Victoria had been named governor in his stead, he was naturally embittered against the conservatives and out of sympathy with the mission system which they favored. In the distant territory a man in this frame of mind could do much to offset the influence of the favorably inclined government in Mexico.

It was under these circumstances that Echeandía's secularization plan reappeared once more and after being approved by the California *diputación* became a law. The members of this body had been assembled on July 10, 1830, by the governor who wished "to justify his expulsion of Fr. Martínez," a friar who had been sent into exile for the alleged part he took in a revolt against the territorial authorities.[86] At its second session on July 14, the assembly had concerned itself with the establishment of primary schools at the various missions.[87] Six days later, on July 20, this question was re-introduced by Echeandía and replaced by the plan for the secularization of the Missions. As the incident is recorded in the secretary's minutes:

> He stated . . . that he had already taken steps in the matter of mission schools [in 1827],[88] since he considered that it was to the advantage of the country that the neophytes should be given the elements of education; and moreover [he declared] at the same time he had proposed a plan to the supreme government that the missions of Upper and Lower California should be reduced to pueblos. He then added that he wished this plan to be read and appended to the measure in order that the legislators, after calm consideration, might approve it or change it in a manner most conducive to this end.[89]

[85] Quoted by Tays, *ut supra*, 100–101.
[86] Vallejo, Mariano G., *Historia de California*, MS., II, 104.
[87] *Legislative records*, MS., I, 130.
[88] Cf. Engelhardt, *op. cit.*, III, 325.
[89] *Legislative records*, MS., I, 134–135.

Fortunately, a contemporary has left a fuller account of this important session and of the manner in which the governor introduced his plan for discussion. Summarized it is as follows :

Echeandía explained that it was of importance to the Mexican nation and more especially to the inhabitants of Upper California that a decree be issued secularizing the missions. He explained how on his arrival he had found in all its vigor the system which the Spanish government has established for the reduction of the pagan savages, a system which combined temporal administration with its spiritual work to form a whole. It was only with the greatest difficulty that he had been able to enforce the laws of congress because of the influence which the system gave the missionaries. He had been unable to adapt the missions to the new order of things because of the opposition and insurmountable obstacles which the religious had put in the way of their dismemberment. He then pointed out that all the valuable lands in Upper California belonged, not by virtue of any law but by the fact of possession, to the missionaries, and he asked them : Is it just that the twenty-one mission establishments should possess all the fertile lands while more than a thousand families of the *gente de razón* occupied only those which the missionaries wished to leave them? In proof of this injustice he quoted article 14 of the colonization *reglamento* which declared that there should be an equal distribution of lands. Reproving in strong terms the avarice of the missionaries which led them to despise strangers, he pointed out how the Mexican law of colonization had invited strangers to settle in California, that the Mexican congress had declared that lands belonging neither to individuals nor corporations could be colonized, and that the general executive power had commanded that the legislative bodies of the various states and provinces should form regulations for the colonization of their respective territories. The audience, after listening in profound silence to the reading of this message, broke out at its conclusion into noisy *vivas* which continued even after the governor had left the assembly chamber.[90]

---

[90] Vallejo, *ut supra*, II, 105–108.

After this lengthy speech, Echeandía then presented his "Plan for the conversion of the Missions into pueblos," which the members of the *diputación* after much discussion and some slight modifications finally approved in the session of August 3.[91] Finally, on August 13, an amendment was added to the plan providing for the establishment of two Franciscan monasteries at San Gabriel and Santa Clara which under governmental supervision were to supply the territory with future missionaries and the presidios and pueblos with chaplains and pastors.[92] After the approval of the assembly, the plans were sent to Mexico and the California proponents of secularization were forced to await the approval of the supreme government.

This sudden proposal of secularization and its equally swift approval by the *diputación* were both so foreign to the usual tempo of California life that one looks almost instinctively for some great underlying motive. It would seem that pressure was brought to bear on Echeandía to forego his previous acknowledgment of the necessity of the mission system and resume his earlier attitude of hostility. The speech with which he introduced his plan was a most violent attack on the missionaries. Drawing his materials from the *Junta's Dictamen* which apparently he still possessed and from a colonization law which he had lately received from Mexico,[93] he supported his proposal with all the borrowed eloquence and specious reasoning that the well known prejudices of that famous *Junta* could lend him. And what was more, he so misinterpreted the government's colonization law, omitting all mention of the fact that mission lands were expressly exempted from the provisions of the law, that he made it appear as an official condemnation of the mission system and a justification of his own action. Such effrontery, as contrasted with the secrecy which had surrounded the earlier proposal of the plan, pointed to a new motivating force in secularization.

According to contemporary accounts this new impulse had come from the newly arrived adjutant inspector, José María Padrés.

---

[91] Cf. Bancroft, *op. cit.*, III, 302–303, note 2, where a full summary of the plan is given.

[92] Engelhardt, *op. cit.*, III, 322–325.

[93] Cf. Bancroft, *op. cit.*, III, 34–35, note 7.

Padrés was a man of considerable ability, personally mag-
netic, and moreover a most radical republican. He soon became a leading spirit among the young Californians just becoming prominent in civil life, intensified their nascent republicanism, taught them to theorize eloquently on the rights of
man, the wrongs of the neophytes, and the tyranny of the missionaries; and [to make his teachings more effective] he held
up before the eyes of the Carrillos, Osios, Vallejos, Pecos, Al-
varados, Bandinis and others, bright visions of rich estates to
be administered by them or their friends, ... [94]

Supported by these, several of whom it would seem he had converted to Freemasonry,[95] he easily "induced Echeandía to be an
instrument for carrying out the schemes which he had premedi-
tated for his private ends . . . of publishing a plan . . . so as to
change the present mission system." [96]   Thus was the publication
of a secularization plan once again the result of a conjunction,
engineered by Padrés, of California covetousness and Mexican
anti-clericalism under the guise of legalized liberalism.   In the
words of a contemporary, "Padrés [and his followers], pre-
tending to take much interest in bettering the condition of the
natives, soon commenced a work of destruction under the name
of reform." [97]

In the face of this new secularization move the missionaries did
little to oppose it.   On October 1, Father Sarria it is true pleaded
with the governor to be guided by the lessons which the evils
caused by similar measures in Europe taught, but further opposition was abandoned "because they believed that protests and
arguments addressed to the territorial authorities would be without effect," [98] and also because they hoped that the arrival of the
new governor would bring about a more conservative mission
policy.   But when governor-elect Victoria arrived at San Diego in

---

[94] Bancroft, *op. cit.,* III, 184.

[95] Tays, *ut supra,* 384.

[96] Victoria to the Minister of Relations, January 19, 1831; cf. Tays, *ut supra,* 104.

[97] Robinson, Alfred, *Life in California* (New York, 1846), 108; for other contemporary evidence, cf. Bancroft, *op. cit.,* III, 305, note 5.

[98] Bancroft, *op. cit.,* III, 108.

December, 1830, the news of his coming produced the opposite effect on the mission despoilers at Monterey.

When the day of Victoria's arrival drew near, and no approval of the plan came from Mexico, Echeandía was persuaded, probably without much difficulty to essay a *golpe de estado*. Accordingly he issued, January 6, 1831, a decree of secularization, which he took immediate steps to carry into execution before turning over the command to his successor. Victoria was known to be more a soldier than a politician, and it was hoped with the aid of the *diputación* in some way to sustain the decree and reach a result favorable to the anti-mission party.[99]

On the same day in which it was proclaimed, the decree was forwarded to the various officials throughout the territory and to the bishop and Father President of the Missions with orders that the friars should prepare for the change. Two days later, administrators, most of them the members of the *diputación* itself, were appointed to take charge of the mission temporalities and commissioned to effect the change immediately. With what success they accomplished this may be judged from the reception accorded the administrator at San Miguel.

From a cart in the mission courtyard he vividly pictured the advantages of freedom to the Indians; then requested those who wished to remain under the padre to stand on the left and those preferring freedom on the right. Nearly all immediately went to the left, where they were soon joined by the small minority who had not the courage of their convictions.[100]

This disappointing incident, as events soon proved, marked the end of the *golpe de estado*.

In proclaiming the decree of secularization Echeandía had justified his summary action on the grounds that the Indians were entitled to enjoy the rights granted all Mexicans, that due to the discontent which had arisen among them and the opposi-

---

99 *Ibid.*, III, 184.

100 Alvarado, Juan B., *Historia de California*, MS., III, 6–7; cf. Bancroft, *op. cit.*, III, 308, note 10.

tion of the friars to independence and the national government the Missions were in imminent danger of decay, and finally, that their secularization had been decreed by the Spanish *Cortes* in 1813.[101]   Yet despite this specious reasoning, "Echeandía's act was wholly illegal, uncalled for, and unwise. It was simply a trick, and an absurd one." [102]   Neither the governor nor the *diputación* possessed the authority to enact a secularization law. His instructions from Mexico did not authorize it and the force of the Spanish decree of 1813 had ceased with the establishment of the Republic.[103]   Moreover, if the Indians were entitled to full rights as Mexican citizens, they could not obtain the enjoyment of these rights through the secularization of the Missions, "inasmuch as under the regulations of the decree only a meagre portion of the land and property would go to the neophytes, whilst the bulk of the valuable temporalities would be at the disposition of the administrators." [104]   These arguments were simply meant to hide the real reason for the *golpe de estado*. Echeandía and his henchmen, faced with the loss of the rich prize upon which they had set their eyes, cast aside all caution and restraint and set themselves to the task of despoiling the Missions before the new governor could interfere.

But they had acted too late. On January 14, Victoria "by a lucky accident," as he later declared, learned of the illegal measure and immediately sent orders to Echeandía that it should be suspended. From Santa Barbara he hastened to Monterey and after relieving Echeandía of his office issued a proclamation on February 1, suspending all further execution of the decree.[105] He had seen through the pretexts of the conspirators and was determined to thwart their efforts at plunder. Writing to the authorities in Mexico he summed up the entire affair in the following expressive terms:

He [Echeandía] has committed the blunder of publishing a plan . . . . based on a decree of the Spanish Cortes and the

---

[101] Bancroft, *op. cit.*, III, 305, note 6.

[102] *Ibid.*, III, 184.

[103] Tays, *ut supra*, 384.

[104] Engelhardt, *op. cit.*, III, 353.

[105] Bancroft, *op. cit.*, III, 306, note 7.

rulings of the Legislature, and in which he inserts all his schemes and falsehoods. Among them are a number of theories apparently for the good of the neophytes, but in fact they are ridiculous and absolutely impracticable; at the same time it reveals at first glance, as Your Excellency will notice, the object of his wicked aims. He would give the Indians only a small and useless share, leaving all the wealth at the command of the administrators.

It all amounts to this: that said individual has generously given offers of protection to a number of thieves, with whom he has become party, that they may find lodgment in such a wicked monopoly. At this time he doubtlessly resolved to get control of the twenty-one missions, by employing his favorites; thus very easily acquiring a fortune of hundreds of thousands while his satellites devoured and acquired the belongings of the neophytes, earned by the labor and sweat of their brow, and preserved by the zeal of the missionaries.[106]

Thus, with this indictment of its underlying motives, was the first attempt at secularization brought to a close.

Though the first decade of independence had ended with the defeat of secularization, it had brought into clear relief the motives which underlay the movement. Republican theories, nationalistic hostility and anti-religious prejudices had thus far been the chief reasons for the attack on the padres and their Missions. The Calfornians under Argüello had used the first two to cloak their cupidity and strengthen their demands for secularization. In like manner the efforts of the *Junta de Fomento* had been perverted by these same prejudices. When an attempt was made to apply its program, the evils it produced made evident the fallacies into which it had fallen. Yet the final attempt to effect secularization revealed that when a crisis produced a union of these various forces, reality and truth were forgotten and the secularization of the Missions was demanded even though it meant their destruction. Though the timely intervention of Victoria had prevented such an outcome, it did not put an end to the forces that prompted the movement. Should they again unite, the secularization of the Missions would be an accomplished fact.

---

[106] Victoria to the Minister of Relations, January 19, 1831; translated by Tays, *ut supra,* 104–105.

CHAPTER IV

ENACTMENT OF SECULARIZATION IN MEXICO AND CALIFORNIA: 1831–1834

If the first decade of independence brought into clear relief the motives which had thus far inspired the movement towards secularization, it also revealed, though perhaps less clearly, the need there was of a readjustment of the mission system. Since the break with Spain, California had changed profoundly. It was no longer an isolated Spanish outpost where the saving of souls overshadowed the saving of territory for the king of Spain. Commerce had brought it into closer contact with the world and its material interests; the introduction of new governmental principles had made it politically minded; and the talk of colonization had made more ardent the desire for an increase of its *gente de razón*. It was no longer the California that had existed when the Missions were first established. If they were to endure, it was necessary that they adapt themselves to their new environment. From their willingness to accept the experiments of Fernández and Echeandía, it would seem that the missionaries had realized this. They felt the need for a change, yet they were confused as to the method which should be followed. The attempts at complete secularization had at least revealed an extreme that was to be avoided. By arousing their opposition it had taught the friars the lesson that, while new methods might be adopted, the aims and principles of the mission system could not be changed. The Indian must be safeguarded, both in soul and body, against himself and his white neighbors. Because secularization, due to the motives on which it was based, did not guarantee this, the padres had been forced thus far to oppose it. But now, for the first time since independence, circumstances were such as to favor a solution of this problem. With a conservative government in Mexico and a sympathetic ruler in California, an effort was to be made by both civil and religious authorities to adapt the Missions to the changed

116

conditions. The story of the next four years is centered around this effort, the fair promise of success that it gave, and finally the defeat it met when the old forces of secularization again united and wrought the destruction rather than the salvation of the Missions.

I

As has already been noted, Bustamente's government in Mexico was in principle conservative. Yet from the outset, due perhaps to the various reports of the *Junta de Fomento* and, more probably, to the attempts at secularization which had already been made in California, the government early manifested a deep interest in the question of a change in the mission system. On April 3, 1830, shortly after his accession to power, Bustamente addressed a letter to the Father President in which he asked for "his opinion regarding the stipends of the missionaries from the Pious Fund; what could be done to improve the natives materially and induce them to become private owners of land and cultivate the same; whether or not some of the Indians could be sent to Mexico to learn trades or devote themselves to various arts; information on the commerce of the country." [1] The same purpose was manifested in the instructions which the Mexican Secretary of State drew up and delivered to Victoria before his departure for California. Among other things,

> he was to pay particular attention to statistics, the public lands, and the Indians, and especially to the enfranchisement, education, and civilization of the neophytes of the missions. In view of these last named objects, it was suggested that some of the most promising Indian youths should be selected and, at the expense of the richest missions, sent to Mexico for education as teachers of various branches, including the most useful arts. [2]

The similarity between the two documents would seem to indicate that the new government had adopted a conservative, yet progressive, mission policy.

---

[1] Engelhardt, *op. cit.*, III, 337.
[2] Hittell, *History of California*, II, 125–126.

But when its representative, Victoria, took over the reins of government in California, his early actions pointed rather to a policy of reaction. Not only did he immediately suspend Echeandía's secularization decree but he took steps to prosecute two of the deputies, Alvarado and Castro, for the part they had taken in publishing it.[3] Shortly after, this purpose was revealed even more clearly in his refusal to convene the *diputación*. On the day before his arrival at Monterey this body had been ordered by Echeandía to convene, ostensibly in the interest of public tranquility, but more probably "to insist on carrying out the secularization scheme." [4] Obviously, the Californians and their leaders hoped to intrigue the new governor into carrying out their selfish project. But Victoria frustrated their plans by refusing to convoke the *diputación*. When a storm of protest was raised by his opponents, he issued a public *manifiesto* in which

> he alluded to the criminal motives and seditious plans of the opposing faction, whom he accused of being moved 'by personal interests disguised in the habiliments of philanthropy,' and declared his intentions of thwarting the schemes of Echeandía. He further stated that a majority of the diputados had been illegally elected, and that he had reported everything to the National Government, without whose orders he would not convoke the assembly.[5]

From his uncompromising opposition to secularization as projected by the Californians, it seemed that Victoria had adopted a reactionary policy, opposed to all changes in the mission system. Yet events soon revealed him in a different light.

After Victoria's departure for California, the Mexican authorities had received the Father President's reply to Bustamente's inquiries. In a lengthy letter, Father Durán revealed the attitude of the missionaries with respect to a change in the mission system. Concerning the first point, the Missions have no need of assistance from the Pious Fund, for they produce their own food and clothing

---

[3] Bancroft, *op. cit.*, III, 186, note 10.
[4] *Ibid.*, III, 187.
[5] Engelhardt, *op. cit.*, III, 355.

and obtain the other necessaries through the sale of their products to trading vessels. The government should rather give its attention to paying the destitute troops who "for twenty years have lacked the necessaries and clothing for themselves and their families."

"On the second point, regarding the improvement of the neophytes, . . . this has been the rock which has shipwrecked the best political talents and those most desirous of promoting the happiness of these poor people." Throughout their lives, the neophytes display a repugnance for civilization and an invincible inclination for a savage mode of life. Like children they are very changeable and, although they receive Baptism voluntarily, many of them become runaways to return to a life of savagery. Echeandía made an attempt at this improvement by emancipating a certain class of neophytes but failed because they gave themselves up to indolence and drunkenness, having no appreciation of the winning of honors, of gain from personal labors but only a desire for absolute independence without rational limits. From this it may be gathered what should be feared from general emancipation. "It would amount to what I should call to plant by tearing out and to build by destroying."

From all this Your Excellency can infer what I would have to say on the third point, sending neophytes to Mexico to learn arts and sciences. I find in them no ambition or interest that would stimulate them. Moreover the displeasure and anxiety of the relatives would have to be greatly feared; for the change of climate would in some of the apprentices bring about death, or deep melancholy to which they are inclined would set in and would embitter them for being so far away from their relatives.

But there is a way which in a short time will lead to prosperity not only for the neophytes but for all the inhabitants of this territory, . . . It is very plain and simple. Let twenty young and exemplary missionaries come here, and let the troops of the four presidios receive their pay. Then let a new chain of missions and presidios be established to the east of the coast range mountains. Then let the neophytes choose between joining the new missions and receiving their share of the present mission property with all the rights of citizenship like the white people, and forming civilized towns or ranchos. Finally, let the surplus land be divided among settlers in order to encourage colonization. . . . The other thing is that provision should be made for a seminary for the education of young men who feel inclined towards the ecclesiastical state. The candidates should be recruited from the native youths of the territory, so that there be no need of having them come from abroad which is always accompanied with much hardship and little success. Only in this manner, it seems to me, can these settlements be provided with spiritual nourishment. It is plain, however, that such a seminary can not prosper save under the eye of one who is clothed with episcopal dignity. Therefore I think it is time to petition for the erection of this territory into a diocese and the appointment of a bishop to govern it. Then with the new chain of missions, and with the provisions made for the maintenance of the troops, the spiritual and temporal prosperity of the territory would be insured.[6]

The position of the missionaries as outlined by Father Durán was indeed in sharp contrast to the charges of deceit and reaction which their enemies had made against them. More than any others they were concerned with the improvement of their neophytes, and because it had come to be accepted that there must be an adjustment of the mission system to the new conditions they proposed a solution that was based on facts rather than on theories. The chief problems of the territory were the destitution of the troops and the obstacle which the necessity of supporting them placed in the way of mission expansion. Let the government pay the salaries of the troops and let new helpers be sent to the assistance of the aging friars and the mission system could be directed into new channels of expansion. The vision of a seminary and bishop was perhaps premature, yet like the entire plan it was based on the conviction that with the assistance and, what was more important, the protection of a sympathetic government, the missionaries were capable of solving whatever problems might face them. A solution would be possible if only the purpose of the government would be, as Father Durán put it, "to plant without rooting up and to build without destroying." [7]

---

[6] Father Durán to Bustamente, September 23, 1830, cf. Engelhardt, *op. cit.*, III, 337–344.

[7] *Ibid.*, III, 339.

It would seem that these recommendations were favorably received by the government and that under its direction they were intended to be gradually realized. This is indicated by the fact that early in 1831 four Zacatecan friars were sent to California to arrange for the members of their College to supply the assistance for which Father Durán had asked. After remaining in the territory for the remainder of the year, they returned to Mexico with a report that promised to give the Missions an adequate number of laborers.[8] But what was more significant, the government itself took steps to enter into details with the friars concerning a definite mission program. It forwarded instructions to Victoria to obtain from the various missonaries their opinion concerning "a scheme for emancipating the neophytes and distributing the estates on a basis to include the maintenance of religious services, the support of the padres, and the retention of community property to a certain amount with which to found new missions." [9] Unfortunately, there are extant the replies of only three friars. While all expressed their willingness to "submit to everything the Supreme Government disposes," two of them, evidently because they believed that the new move was prompted by the same motives which had inspired earlier plans, predicted that it would end in failure because of the character of the Indians, and that little would be given for the maintenance of religion because greedy officials would appropriate it for their own use. The third, however, the young Father Jimeno, was of the opinion

that the temporalities should be distributed to their legitimate owners, the Indians, and that the neophytes should be given their liberty, but that they should be obliged to work and to preserve their allotment by preventing them from becoming vagrants, running up and down as they desire, because they are very inconstant and fickle.[10]

From the lack of unanimity among the friars it is evident that the plan which the Father President had presented to the government

---

[8] *Ibid.*, III, 407–409.

[9] Bancroft, *op. cit.*, III, 308–309.

[10] Fathers Cabot, Sánchez, and Jimeno to Father Durán, cf. Engelhardt, *op. cit.*, III, 374–376.

was the product of his own mind rather than of common counsel. Yet in view of the favorable situation in Mexico, of which apparently all the friars were not aware, it seems certain that had the efforts on the part of the civil and religious authorities been allowed to continue the change demanded of the Missions would have been easily and justly effected. Unhappily, a new outbreak of mission hostility precluded its realization.

When Victoria at the outset of his administration set himself unalterably against the Californians' scheme of secularization, he made for himself a group of enemies which would be content only with his downfall. As Father Durán later remarked:

> Interested parties, among whom were some members of the territorial assembly, sure of their prey, were disappointed, and their disappointment turned into hatred for the equitable Victoria. They never forgave this just governor for having rescued the booty already within their grasp.[11]

Unmindful of this opposition, Victoria proceeded to rule California as he felt his duty dictated. "Personally brave, honest, energetic, straightforward, and devoted to what he deemed the best interests of the territory,"[12] he began a campaign against evil-doers which astonished the inhabitants, accustomed as they were to the do-nothing policy of Echeandía during the preceding five years. Several criminals were executed for stealing mission supplies, another for the outrage and murder of two children, a number of public officials were forced to resign because of their irregularities in office, and finally a number of prominent individuals, chief among them Padrés, were sent into exile for alleged conspiracies.[13] This stringent execution of justice gave his enemies the opportunity. they sought, of arousing popular opinion against him. Led by Echeandía who had tarried at San Diego on the pretext of collecting his property, they soon succeeded in picturing him as "a cruel, blood-thirsty monster, at whose hands the lives of all honest citizens were in danger."[14] By September,

---

11 *Ibid.*, III, 361.
12 Bancroft, *op. cit.*, III, 198.
13 *Ibid.*, III, 189–197.
14 *Ibid.*, III, 198.

as Victoria himself reported to the authorities in Mexico, they were secretly corresponding with one another, were ridiculing him for his observance of the laws of the Church, and were seducing the people and even the neophytes of the Missions for the purpose of driving him out of office.[15]   The storm finally broke when on November 29, the group at San Diego issued a *pronunciamiento* declaring Victoria suspended and proclaiming Echeandía temporary governor.   Victoria immediately hurried south with a small detachment of troops to meet his enemies but in the encounter which followed he was seriously wounded and forced to relinquish his command.   Thus did California lose "one of its most forceful, intelligent, and well-meaning of rulers," [16] and have thrust upon itself once again as its ruling body a group which was more concerned with the secularization of the Missions and thereby the advancement of their own personal interests than the welfare of the territory.

Only in later years did it become fully apparent that with the departure of Victoria, there went the last opportunity of effecting a just solution of the mission question.   It was probably this thought that Father Durán had in mind when in 1839 he wrote:

> If the Mexican Republic had been bred in peace, and had not at times been dominated by the spirit of Jacobinism, this California at this date might have a new chain of missions in the very heart of paganism without scarcely any expense to the Government, for the requisites to found them could have been obtained from the old establishments.[17]

There would indeed be other sympathetic administrations in Mexico and other plans would be presented by the mission authorities for a change in the system, but there would never be the same opportunity of carrying them out.   For thenceforth, as one writer has remarked:

> the Missions were to be the prize for which all the political factions in California struggled.   Much of the sectional feeling

---

15 Engelhardt, *op. cit.,* III, 356–357.

16 Tays, *ut supra,* 157.

17 Engelhardt, *op. cit.,* IV, 107.

arose over who was to control the mission properties. And it is a singular fact that feeling against Mexico flamed high only at such times as there was an administration in power in Mexico that favored leaving the Missions under the care of the friars.[18]

II

Throughout the whole of 1832 California was practically independent of Mexico, and for more than half of the period was distracted with the squabbles of the several California factions over the governorship. After the overthrow of Victoria, Echeandía had been installed as temporary governor with the understanding that the military and political commands should later be divided between two persons. When, therefore, the *diputación* convened at Los Angeles early in January, it appointed its senior member, Pio Pico, as civil governor and Echeandía as military commandant. But the latter worthy, "led by motives of personal ambition and personal resentment," [19] refused to recognize this division of power and with the troops at his command threatened the members of the assembly. The deputies, defenceless and averse to further civil dissensions, deemed it best to regard Echeandía's movement as a successful *contra-pronunciamiento* and, accordingly, on February 17, suspended all further sessions of the *diputación*.

To add to the confusion of the disinterested inhabitants, while this revolution among friends was taking place in the south, another *pronunciamiento* was issued at Monterey by a northern group which was likewise eager for power. Led by Captain Agustín V. Zamorano, the friend and former secretary of Victoria, they proclaimed the acts of the *diputación* illegal and null, declared that no governor should be chosen until the supreme government should appoint one, and, finally, proposed that in the meantime authority should be exercised by the officer of highest rank and seniority, who was none other than Zamorano. The conflict which followed was one mostly of proclamations. "The pen proved mightier than the sword, and in May both sides agreed

---

18 Tays, *ut supra*, 443.
19 Bancroft, *op. cit.*, III, 219.

to call it a draw." [20]   An arrangement was made whereby the
military command was divided between Echeandía in the south
and Zamorano in the north, while the *diputación* was left with
no authority at all. As might have been expected, such a travesty
in government augured ill for the Missions. In the *pronunciamiento* of November 29, it had indeed been promised that

> the *diputación* . . . would make no innovations whatever in the
> matter of the missions respecting their communities and prop-
> erty. . . . To the Supreme Government belongs exclusively the
> power to dictate what it may deem proper on this subject, and
> it promises to the padres to observe respect, decorum, and
> security of the property entrusted to their care.[21]

It was obviously a bid for the support of the friars, the sincerity
of which they rightly suspected. If one may judge by the lengthy
refutation of Echeandía's secularization decree which Father
Durán forwarded to Mexico a month later, "one of the ablest
documents that was ever written by a friar in California," [22] the
friars expected a renewal of the agitation for secularization.

It soon became evident that their fears were only too well
founded. When, on February 17, 1832, the *diputación* prepared
a report for Mexico on the recent revolt, it had the hardihood to
assign as the origin and cause of all the evils which afflicted the
territory, the presence of the Spanish missionaries, who possess-
ing all the wealth of the country and exercising a tremendous
influence over a large portion of the population, virtually kept
the territory and certain of its governors subject to their will.[23]
The same hostility was manifested, or more correctly, copied, in
a letter written a few days later by the leader of the Californians,
Mariano Vallejo:

> There is observed in the inhabitants generally a disinclina-
> tion for our republican ideas, and there is noticed an utter con-
> tempt for our institutions, so that the people are inclined at

---

[20] Chapman, *History of California*, 463.
[21] Bancroft, *op. cit.*, III, 203, note 39.
[22] *Ibid.*, III, 309; for full translation cf. Engelhardt, *op. cit.*, III, 379–402.
[23] Hittell, *op. cit.*, II, 148–149.

every step to act under the influence of the considerable number of Spaniards, public enemies of our system, who abound in
this territory. Favoring ignorance in the citizens, they toil
incessantly to stupefy them, and co-operate in the destruction
of the sciences and of the enlightenment which is the fundamental, advantageous basis of countries for the preservation of
society and the source of the wealth of nations.[24]

Muddled in thought as well as in politics, such a mind deemed
itself empowered to decide the fate of the Missions. Of a similar
vein was the final report which the members of the assembly sent
the supreme government on May 15. As they put it, the recent
revolt was due "to the detestable and anti-republican mission system, and to the presence and intrigues of the friars who sought
a restoration of Spanish institutions." [25] Such statements belied
the sincerity of the promise of immunity which had been given
the padres and portended a renewed effort to secularize their
Missions.

However, the political anarchy which disturbed the first half of
the year of "home rule" made impossible any concerted action in
the matter of secularization. Yet the Missions were not left un-
molested. The military campaigns of the two local chieftains
caused a heavy drain on their resources and were the cause for
further restlessness on the part of the neophytes. When the army
of Zamorano was known to be on its way south, Echeandía called
upon the Missions for troops and supplies. As an eyewitness
described it:

Echeandía retreated to St. Juan Capistrano, where he sought
the co-operation of the Indians. His promises of liberty and
land were sufficient to entice all from their labors, and caused
the subsequent abandonment of their former pursuits. Rapine,
murder and drunkenness were the result; and, in the midst,
revelled the Mexican chieftain.[26]

---

[24] Engelhardt, op. cit., III, 370–373.

[25] Bancroft, op. cit., III, 229; for full translation cf. Engelhardt, op. cit., III,
368–369.

[26] Robinson, op. cit., 132.

Even after peace had been established this despoiler of the Missions continued his demands for supplies and by his pernicious example excited the Indians to still greater excesses.

> Echeandía and his party . . . were draining St. Juan and the splendid Mission of St. Luis of their richest possessions. Daily reports were received of robberies and murders committed by the Indians of San Diego, who were in a wretched state. At the mission below that place, which is called St. Miguel, they revolted and attempted to kill the priest, but he defended himself within his house with the assistance of two soldiers, and finally drove them off. They subsequently united with Echeandía's party. Stabbings were frequent at St. Juan and St. Luis, and the drunken Indian as he staggered along from his scene of debauch ejaculated, 'Soy libre!' 'I am free!' [27]

Eventually, the "freedom" of the neophytes became so unrestrained that Echeandía, through fear of an Indian uprising,[28] was forced to send them back to their missions, with the provision, however, that the friars were to be held responsible for all their excesses.[29]

But the fire which he had kindled could not be smothered so easily. He had promised the Indians "liberty and land" and now found himself obliged, by the threat of an uprising, to keep his word. It would seem that as early as May 20, he had found it safer to turn over the management of the temporalities at San Diego to the natives, with the result, as the friar stationed there wrote, that "the waste in the management was notorious." [30] But such consequences did not deter Echeandía. Possessed with supreme authority in the south, he had the assurance to meditate the enforcement of his earlier decree by forwarding to the missionaries under his jurisdiction a supplementary decree of November 18, "as if the events of the past months had been but a mere temporary interruption of his plans." [31]

---

[27] *Ibid.*, 135.
[28] Cf. Bancroft, *op. cit.*, III, 227.
[29] Engelhardt, *op. cit.*, III , 416–417.
[30] *Ibid.*, III, 419.
[31] Bancroft, *op. cit.*, III, 314.

The decree was prefaced with an argument on the necessity of secularization under superior laws and instructions, a statement of the enthusiasm with which the Indians had welcomed the author's efforts, a presentment of their complaints of injustice and a general discontent under the padres' management which threatened serious consequences, a mention of good results at San Juan Capistrano, where the padres were said to have voluntarily given up the temporalities, and a plea to the missionaries to accept their duties as parish priests.[32]

The plan itself was brief and to the point, its chief provisions being as follows:

1. Freedom and a distribution of property were to be made to all neophytes of ten years' standing. Organized in peublos, they were to choose their own alcades and police officers, though the government would appoint a commissioner to act as general supervisor and, incidentally, as administrator of the remaining properties.

2. The other neophytes, until they could fulfill the conditions prescribed for detachment, were to continue to work in community, the commissioner regulating all relating to their food, raiment, wages, labor and punishments.

3. Out of the community property should be paid all public expenses, and it is understood that at a proper time a part will be used for the foundation of new missions among the neighboring gentiles.

4. The missionaries now in charge will be considered as parish priests and as depositaries of the community property, signing the account to be rendered annually by the chief steward.[33]

Despite the cunning designation of the friars as depositaries of community property with the power of signing reports and the ready promise of future aid for the establishment of new missions, the decree contained the essential features of every scheme for secularization—the removal of the Missions and their Indians from the control of the friars, the distribution of a cer-

---

[32] *Ibid.,* III, 315.
[33] For the full translation cf. *ibid.,* III, 314, note 23.

tain portion of the properties to the neophytes, and the management of the rest by civilian administrators. It was a scheme on the part of Echeandía to quiet the Indians, whom he was beginning to fear, and to satisfy his friends, whose support he needed, but the missionaries refused to be taken in by it.

On the receipt of the proposed plan, the friars of the four southern missions were practically unanimous in their opposition to its enactment. Their stand, as contrasted with their previous coöperation with Victoria, in itself gave evidence of the motives of the author. Two of the friars, the former superior, Father Sánchez, and the President, Father Durán, drew up lengthy replies in which they ably exposed the faults and inconsistencies of the plan. Since both were similar in argument and expression, a composite summary might be presented as follows:

If obedience to the law required the secularization of the Missions, the suggestion would come with better grace from one who had given a better example of such obedience than Echeandía. The fact of the matter is that there is no legal foundation for secularization in the decree of the Spanish *Cortes* of September 13, 1813, for if in the nineteen years that have elapsed the executive power made no effort to put it into effect, "it is an evident sign of the untimeliness of the law as to the letter and its construction." Let the supreme government order secularization and it will be obeyed.

If the neophytes welcomed Echeandía's efforts with enthusiasm, it was because there are several ways of winning popularity among school-boys, one of the most successful being to let them do as they please. If the Indians in the south were assuming a threatening attitude, it was due to the license they had enjoyed under Echeandía, and to his unwise act of having put arms in their hands. Having promised them liberty in return for their support, he is now obliged to redeem his word. In order to give his transaction a decent appearance in the eyes of the world and the supreme government, and in order to put method into the reform, as he calls it, he was compelled to accumulate slanders against the well-known honor of the missionaries. This is the key which opens and explains all the political phenomena of

Señor Echeandía.[34]   But all such protests were to no avail.
Echeandía was determined to secularize the four missions no
matter what the consequences might be. After a short delay he
appointed four of his associates as administrators,[35] and was
about to begin the application of his plan when the arrival of a
new governor once again brought his scheme to an abrupt halt,
though this time not to an end.

III

In Mexico the news of the troubles in California had been received with the greatest dissatisfaction. Shortly after his overthrow, Victoria had sent his account to the authorities with the
pertinent observation that the uprising would inevitably result
not only in the ruin of the Missions but in a break on the part
of the Californians with Mexico. Alarmed at the thought, the
first impulse of the government was to send Victoria back to
California with a large armed force to bring the rebellious territory to order. But eventually, a more moderate course was
adopted, and a new governor was appointed in the person of
José Figueroa, the former commandant-general of Sonora and
Sinaloa. Already acquainted with the California situation, it
was hoped that he would restore order by more peaceful means.[36]

The appointment of a new governor required that a mission
policy be formulated once again, and, if one may judge by the
events which had occurred since such a policy had been drawn
up for Victoria, it was not to be as favorable as the previous one.
During the year which had elapsed since the first declaration of
the government's attitude towards the Missions, a bitter fight
had taken place in Congress over the Pious Fund. It was proposed that the properties should be disposed of by emphyteutic
sale, evidently for the purpose of putting "in the hands of the

---

[34] Sánchez, *Notas al reglamento de secularización, 1832*, MS.; for summary
cf. Bancroft, *op. cit.*, III, 315–317; Durán, *Notas á una circular ó bando in-
timado por El Sr. D. José María Echeandía á las cuatro Misiones, 1832*, MS.;
for translation cf. Engelhardt, *op. cit.*, III, 422–441.

[35] Bancroft, *op. cit.*, III, 326, note 44.

[36] *Ibid.*, III, 232–234.

government a large amount of ready money." [37]   The proposition
was opposed by a group led by the California deputy, Carlos Carrillo, who favored the renting of the estates for short periods
and the application of the revenues to the work of the Missions.
Carrillo prepared a lengthy report on the services which the Missions had rendered the nation.   With full justice to the truth,
he wrote:

> During the troubles of the past twenty years, the missions
> have been not only self-supporting, but have contributed the
> amount of half a million dollars for the maintenance of the
> troops.   In addition they offered the only encouragement to a
> growing and profitable commerce.   In other words, California
> has been sustained and saved for Mexico by the earnings of the
> Indians under the mission system; and but for the missions the
> territory today would be in possession of savages or in the
> hands of a foreign power.[38]

Although threatened with defeat when one of their number, after
being commissioned to deliver these arguments in the hall of Congress, made his speech for the other side, the friends of the Missions were finally victorious.   On May 25, 1832, a law was passed
by which the estates of the Pious Fund were to be rented for
terms not exceeding seven years, and the revenues devoted exclusively to the Missions.   The opposition which had been manifested gave evidence that Bustamente's government was not without its opposition party, at least in matters pertaining to the
Missions.

It is this incident which perhaps can best explain the strange
fact that when, on May 17, 1832, instructions were issued to
Figueroa before his departure for California, they were found
to be contradictory in the matter of a mission policy.   On the
one hand the new governor received from the Minister of Relations, Lucas Alamán, a set of instructions which, disapproving
Echeandía's decree of 1831, both because he had gone far beyond
his authority in issuing the decree without the approval of the
supreme government, and because some of its provisions were

[37] *Ibid.*, III, 311.
[38] Engelhardt, *op. cit.*, III, 405.

not in accord with the law of 1813 on which it purported to be founded, stated:

> If on your arrival in Upper California you find this decree in force, you should immediately restore the missions to the condition in which they were before its publication, for this purpose enacting such measures as your prudence may deem most fitting. At the same time you will study the condition of the missions, ascertain which establishments are ready to be transferred to the bishop in accordance with the decree of September 13, 1813, and formulate a suitable plan for this, based on reports and first-hand information obtained by visits to these establishments.[39]

This instruction was evidently based on the lengthy report which Father Durán had over a year earlier forwarded to the Mexican authorities criticizing article by article the decree of 1831. Its directions were favorable towards the Missions and on the whole in accord with the policy previously adopted by the government. As Bancroft has remarked:

> it emanated from the same administration which had appointed Victoria and was similar in spirit probably to those given that officer, . . . The necessity for a change was recognized, and the duty of the new ruler, as of his predecessors, was to ascertain and report the best practical methods.[40]

But another set of instructions was given Figueroa by Minister Ortíz Monasterio which apparently "authorized him to go practically much further toward secularization than did the document just mentioned." [41] Its provisions concerning the Missions were as follows:

1. Echeandía's instructions not having been carried out, they were to be put into effect at the earliest time possible.
2. It being a matter of the greatest necessity that the neophytes rise from the state of abasement to which they find them-

---

[39] *State papers, missions and colonization*, MS., II, 34–35; cf. Bancroft, *op. cit.*, III, 235, 324–325; Engelhardt, *op. cit.*, III, 468–469.
[40] *Op. cit.*, III, 324–325.
[41] *Ibid.*, III, 325.

selves reduced, you will cause to be distributed to such as are
fitted for it such fields of the mission lands as they may be
capable of cultivating, in order that they may thus become fond
of labor and may go on acquiring property ; but the lands necessary for the support·of divine worship, schools, and other· objects of common utility must be kept undisturbed. By this
means, another system more adapted to the interests of the territory may be substituted for that of the missions, the influence of
the missionaries be lessened until they retain only the spiritual
administration, and thus in fact the missions may be secularized.
Yet for all this, it is necessary to act with prudence and tact, so
as to cause no discontent among the missionaries, with whom
care is to be taken to preserve the greatest harmony ; and to that
end are enclosed private letters written by the vice-president to
some of the most influential friars.

3. From among the Indian youths a number of the brightest
should be selected and sent to Mexico to train for the ministry.[42]

From an analysis of the two sets of instructions it would seem
that they were inspired by the two distinct mission policies which
had thus far prevailed in Mexico. The document drawn up by
Alamán represented the more recent and conservative view,
namely, that there was need of a change, that a study of the Missions should be made with this end in view, and that a report
should be made as to the most practical method of carrying it
out. It was the same policy of cautious procedure which had
been outlined for Victoria two years before. On the other hand,
the instructions prepared by Monasterio represented the older,
the more radical view. The Missions were not to be restored to
their former state to await a more judicious plan. Rather the
experiments prescribed for Echeandía in the *Dictámen* of the
Junta de Fomento were to be begun or, if already in force, continued. The events which had occurred and the lessons which
had been learned since 1825 were to have no bearing on the
matter. Apparently, the prejudices which had nullified the efforts
of the famous *junta* still swayed some of the members of even
Bustamente's cabinet.

The confusion in the government's instructions was particularly

---

[42] Figueroa, *Instrucciones generales*, MS., 33–34 ; cf. Tays, *ut supra*, 396–397 ;
Bancroft, *op. cit.*, III, 325–326.

unfortunate in view of Figueroa's personal leanings. It is true that in a letter sent from Acapulco on July 7, 1832, he promised:

> As soon as I arrive in Upper California, I shall punctually suspend the decree which Echeandía published in order to abolish the missions. I shall restore those which have been suppressed and shall report on those which according to their condition and the provisions of the law of September, 1813, can be secularized and placed under the control of the bishop.[43]

Yet, personally, he was inclined to follow the instructions which ordered an immediate change. Politically, he was not a conservative, his appointment by Bustamente having been dictated rather by necessity than by motives of generosity.[44] Nor was he in sympathy with the Missions as is indicated by a communication which as governor of Sonora he had forwarded to Echeandía in 1826, urging him to "protect those unfortunates [the neophytes] who from necessity have to bear all the rigors of those friars." [45] While it may perhaps be too severe to say that "his own ideas . . . agreed with those current among irreligious Mexican politicians, who appear to have accepted as axioms the vaporings of French atheistic philosophers," [46] it is safe to say that his personal sympathies, despite the contradiction thereby implied, led him to obey both instructions,—to undertake a study of those missions which might be secularized, and to initiate immediately a series of experiments in emancipation. The events that followed showed this.

But when the new governor arrived at Monterey on January 14, 1833, he was joyfully welcomed by the missionaries. To them he was the representative of a sympathetic home government who had come to suppress the disorders which were destroying the Missions. Their confidence was perhaps inspired by the fact that with the governor there had come the long-expected missionary reënforcement of ten Zacatecan friars. Under the leadership of their superior, Father Francisco Garcia Diego, they took over

---

[43] *State papers, missions and colonization*, MS., II, 36–37.
[44] Bancroft, *op. cit.*, III, 234.
[45] *Ibid.*, III, 325, note 42.
[46] Engelhardt, *op. cit.*, III, 471.

the eight missions north of Soledad.[47]   This timely aid undoubtedly raised the spirits of the older friars. Not only did they plan to send some of their number to the relief of their beloved San Fernando College, which was in danger of extinction for want of resident friars, but, assisted by the younger missionaries and supported by the new governor, they looked forward to a period of peace in their own lives and of development in the Missions. It was in this spirit that Father Durán on February 5, extended to Figueroa the welcome of the missionaries:

> I believe and declare that Your Honor has come to us as a generous protector, who will dry our tears which with so much bitterness we have shed in the days of our affliction, and that you will be the staff and support of our old age, whilst years and labors lead us to the grave.[48]

But this confidence in the new administration was destined to meet with a bitter disappointment.

In contrast to this warm welcome by the friars was the rivalry which took place between the various political factions for the favor of the new governor. Since Figueroa had landed at Monterey, he first came under the influence of Zamorano and the northern party. Swayed by their protestations of innocence, he forwarded to the authorities in Mexico a most severe condemnation of Echeandía's usurpation and at the same time informed the former governor that he was ordered to report immediately to his superiors at Mexico City.[49]   But Echeandía was not to be caught napping by his northern rivals. As early as October 17, 1832, before Figueroa's departure for California, he had sent a lengthy letter to the new governor in which he had expressed his submission to the national authorities, justified his political activities as done out of love of country, and defended his mission policy "by dwelling on the powerful and baneful influence of the missionaries, all of whom with two exceptions he denounced as *apologistas* of Spain and all that was Spanish." [50]   In

---

47 Engelhardt, *op. cit.*, III, 452–463.
48 *Ibid.*, III, 447.
49 Bancroft, *op. cit.*, III, 243.
50 *Ibid.*, III, 239, note 34.

like manner after the arrival of Figueroa, he sent him a second letter on February 7, in which he explained the new steps which he had taken in the matter of secularization, told him how he had suspended all action in the matter as soon as he had heard of his coming, and, finally, urged that strict measures be adopted in favor of the Indians. These proposals met a ready response from the governor whose "views [in this matter, at least] were for the most part identical with those of Echeandía . . . . He announced February 18th to Echeandía his policy and his general approval of the latter's views, stating that he hoped to begin the distribution of lands at San Diego in April." [51]   Apparently, Echeandía had found favor with the governor and his action in the matter of secularization was to have an unmistakable influence on the latter's policy. When he finally sailed from San Diego on May 14, it might have been said that his hostility towards the Missions continued after him. The first to attempt the secularization of the Missions, through his influence he was to have no small part in their final destruction. It was with justice that Robinson wrote of his departure:

> What a scourge he had been to California! What an instigator of vice! 'Hombre de vicio' as he was called. The seeds of dishonor sown by him will never be extirpated so long as there remains a mission to rob or a treasury to plunder. If Mexico in her zeal for the welfare of her territories had been more circumspect in the choice of officers for California, she would not have experienced the humiliation that she has borne, nor incurred the expense of so many expeditions to reconquer it. [52]

Having established his authority and restored the insurgents to the good graces of the government, Figueroa soon turned his attention to the Missions. Mindful of Alamán's instructions to determine the condition of the Missions, he set out in the latter part of June on a tour of investigation in the south. But it soon became evident that he intended to follow Monasterio's instructions as well by making a distribution of the mission lands to

---

[51] *Ibid.*, III, 326–327.
[52] *Life in California*, 149–150.

certain of the neophytes. This is revealed in a letter which
Father Durán addressed to the governor on July 3. Having
learned that he was formulating a regulation for emancipation,
he felt it his duty to expose to the governor certain abuses which
indicated the dangers of emancipation:

> I have seen with the greatest amazement that [the Indians
> who dwell in the pueblo of Los Angeles] . . . live far more
> wretched and oppressed than those in the missions. There is
> not one who has a garden of his own, or a yoke of oxen, a horse,
> or a house fit for a rational being. The equality with the white
> people, which is preached to them, consists in this, that these
> Indians are subject to a white comisionado, and are the only
> ones who do the menial work. I saw with mine eyes on Corpus
> Christi Day the poor Indians sweeping the street through which
> the procession wended its way. . . . For offenses which the white
> people consider small, or as nothing among themselves, those
> Indians are placed over a cannon and given one hundred blows
> on the naked body. . . . All in reality are slaves, or servants of
> white men who know well the manner of securing their services
> by binding them a whole year for an advanced trifle. . . . I have
> seen these things and have asked myself, what will be the result
> of a general or partial division of their lands or goods, and of a
> partial or general emancipation of the individual? . . . The
> benevolent ideas of the Government will never be realized, be-
> cause the Indian evinces no other ambition than to possess a
> little more savage license, even though it involved a thousand
> oppressions of servitude.[53]

Good Father Durán's warning was too late, for the governor
did not receive it until July 22, whereas on July 15, he committed
himself to secularization by the publication of a decree entitled,
"Provisional regulations for the emancipation of the mission Indians." Briefly, it provided that at each mission the more advanced Indians, who had been Christians for at least twelve years,
possessed a trade or a knowledge of agriculture, and were dili-
gent in their application to work, should be selected by commissioners in conjunction with the friars. The neophytes thus
emancipated were to be given lands, cattle, implements, and seed,
and were to be settled in pueblos where under the supervision

[53] Engelhardt, *op. cit.*, III, 477–479.

of the authorities they were to enjoy full civil rights. Should they neglect their work, or lose their live stock, or abandon their homes to give themselves up to vagabondage, idleness and vice, they were to be returned immediately to the supervision of the friars.[54]

The motives which inspired this move may be learned from a letter which Figueroa addressed to Mexico five days later. In it he described the difficulties that faced secularization. The neophytes were as children, still inclined to savagery, possessed an imperfect knowledge of agriculture and stock-raising, and, in fact, had been kept in the most abject ignorance by the padres. If given complete freedom at once, they would barter their possessions for liquor, become beggars and eventually return to the wilderness.[55] His provisional regulations for emancipation were evidently a sincere attempt to meet these difficulties, although it would seem that they were prompted in no small measure by a lack of understanding and a feeling of hostility towards the friars. But despite this underlying motive, the religious offered no opposition to the measure. When sent a copy of the plan, Father Durán replied by offering the submission and coöperation of the missionaries. But that he doubted its success may be drawn from the following significant statement which he attached to his letter:

> May God grant his blessing, which is so necessary, because the ideas of the Indians and those who are not Indians and those of the Government are very different. The latter wants the Indians to be private owners of lands and of other property; this is just. The Indians, however, want the freedom of vagabonds. The others want the absolute liberation and emancipation of the neophytes without the command to form civilized towns, in order that they may avail themselves of their lands and other property as well as of their persons. I do not see how these opposing interests can be harmonized.[56]

Evidently, the friars were as anxious as the government for the improvement of their neophytes but it was becoming more and more apparent that this would never be realized until measures

---

[54] Bancroft, op. cit., III, 328, note 50, gives the plan in full.

[55] Ibid., III, 328, note 49.

[56] Engelhardt, op. cit., III, 481.

should be taken to protect the Indians from their own weaknesses and the greed of the *gente de razón*.

This attitude of the friars was more fully revealed in the next step which Figueroa took towards secularization. On August 2, before he could have determined the outcome of his experiment in emancipation, the governor called upon the superiors of the two missionary bands to state "what missions were in a condition to be secularized under the law of 1813; what objections to secularization existed; and what would be the best means to be employed?" [57] Both superiors sent lengthy replies in which they clearly revealed their stand in the matter of secularization. Father Diego's letter, containing the views of the Zacatecans, was dated September 24, 1833, and was briefly as follows:

While it was true that the law of 1813 included all the missions, with the exception of one, within its scope, it could not be applied without disaster. Once emancipated, the Indians, addicted to gambling, stealing, drunkenness and vice, would return to a life of nakedness and savagery. "When the Cortes passed this decree they were not aware of the character, vices, ignorance, frailty, and needs of these wretched Indians, otherwise the legislators, two thousand leagues away, would not have enacted the law or included California." Indeed the law can not be applied to California, for "a law that ceases to be useful and beneficial to the community, ceases to have binding force. This is the idea of the legislators themselves, for they do not intend that a law should be enforced when it produces harm and no good." Some would say that the native alcades would guard the Indians against their native vices. Yet, "it is certain that they would not choose the best men for alcades. Even the alcades are often guilty themselves and must be punished." Finally, with regard to the measure that should be taken to raise these wretched people from their low condition, "I would omit flogging, and would permit the neophytes to cultivate some fields for themselves." [58] Their eight months' experience with the California Indians had already convinced the Zacatecans, who as Mexicans were presumed to favor

---

[57] Bancroft, *op. cit.*, III, 333.
[58] Engelhardt, *op. cit.*, III, 487–488.

liberal policies, that the Missions were not yet ready to be completely secularized. The same fact was to be even more clearly revealed in the reply which the superior of the Fernandinos submitted.

Sent on October 3, Father Durán's letter, based on long years of experience and earnest thought on the matter, was an exhaustive treatment of the secularization question. Briefly, its main points were as follows:

Any plan to secularize the Missions must face two great obstacles: first, the natural apathy, indolence, and incompetency of the neophytes; and, secondly, the question of supporting the troops after the Missions had been suppressed. The Indians would do nothing for the support of the troops after secularization, and if any of their property were taken by force, they would find means to do away with the rest of it and escape to the wilderness and a life of savagery. Therefore, before effecting any radical change, the government must be sure respecting resources for the future.

Concerning the method to be followed, Father Durán suggested three plans. The first was to establish a new line of missions and presidios east of the old line, change the old missions into Indian pueblos, and give the Indians their choice between remaining in the pueblos or being attached to the new missions. This would effectually prevent them from escaping from civilization, and would also free the territory from the danger of attack and outrage by renegade neophytes, hostile gentiles, and ambitious foreigners. This plan, though best, was probably impracticable, because the national government could not be induced to bear the expense.

The second plan, though not so expeditious, was sure and would lead to the same result. It was to have a bishop appointed for California, an energetic man, not bent on leading a life of ease, and to give him the exclusive control of all tithes under the protection but not the direction of the governor. With these means placed at his disposal, the bishop could in a few years have in operation a seminary "for the ecclesiastical education of the sufficiently numerous sons of decent and honorable families, who have no goal or suitable career in this limited society," a college of missionaries, a cathedral, and all the necessary agencies for converting gentiles and furnishing curates.   Then the Missions might be secularized without risk.

The third expedient, less desirable than the others, was a partial and experimental secularization of certain of the older missions, where the neophytes had been Christians for a long period.   A portion of the property might be distributed, and the rest kept as a community fund, administered by stewards of their own choice, free from tithes, and devoted to the support of Religion. The missionary should have for a time a fatherly control, and the alcades and majordomos should be responsible for losses and evils resulting from a failure to follow his advice.   The neophytes should be made to understand that if they neglect their privileges they will again be put under the padres.   "At the same time, the government should see that similar results are observed in the white people, so that the natives may receive practical lessons through the eyes, which is the shortest way to progress.   With these precautions the difficulties and drawbacks following the secularization of the missions may partly be overcome." [59]

Father Durán's reply to Figueroa was a development of the plan which he had submitted to the government three years before.   As was then noted, the friars, aware of the demand for a change in the mission system, had been long striving to discover a plan which would accomplish this and yet preserve the advances that had been already made during the six decades of mission history.   The present plan might be considered as the final product evolved from these serious endeavors.   Before the change should be attempted, it proposed the creation of a diocese to serve as the basis of stability while the transformation was being effected. Then, gradually, the Missions could be converted into parishes and the more advanced of the neophytes incorporated into civil society.   The mission system as such, lest it hinder the change, would move on with the less advanced neophytes to establish itself without expense to the government among the pagan tribes to the east.   It was a practical plan and depended for success on but three conditions: Let the troops, and therefore the territorial government, be made to look to themselves rather than to the

---

[59] For summary cf. Bancroft, *op. cit.*, III, 333–335; for full translation cf. Engelhardt, *op. cit.*, III, 488–495.

Missions and their neophytes for support; let the Mexican government and its California representatives, moved by motives entirely unselfish, protect the Missions, their neophytes, and their property, from the designs of greedy despoilers; and, finally, let vigorous efforts be made to improve not only the Indians but also the *gente de razón*, making them industrious, law-abiding, and educated, in order that they might provide the necessary example. Let these conditions be fulfilled, and the emancipation of the Indians would succeed. Father Durán's plan was based on actual conditions, as they existed in California, and not on theories or prejudices, as they existed in Mexico, and for a brief moment it looked as though it would be tried.

When Figueroa received the replies of the two missionary superiors he regarded them with favor. This was due, perhaps, to the fact that his experiment in emancipation was forcing him to view the California situation more realistically. After issuing the decree of emancipation, he had "made an earnest effort to give the Indians the civil liberty . . . so valuable in the eyes of Mexican theorists." [60] He had visited the southern missions in person, exhorted the assembled neophytes, and explained to them the advantages of the proffered freedom. Yet the results had been disheartening. On the one hand few of the white population praised it, while on the other the Indians little prized it. At San Juan Capistrano, where the experiment was tried on a large scale, the neophytes had been unwilling to leave the mission and had accepted emancipation only when they had been given lands at the mission proper. At San Luis Rey, out of one hundred and eight families qualified to be emancipated, only four had accepted their freedom and then only with some hesitancy. Finally, at San Diego out of fifty-nine heads of families, all with the exception of two refused emancipation unless the property would be given to them to do with it as they pleased. On all sides emancipation seemed unsatisfactory.

It was only passively approved by the *gente de razón*, who saw in it no direct avenue to the mission lands and herds and servants, while the neophytes themselves were ambitious only

60 Bancroft, *op. cit.*, III, 331.

to have the property to dispose of as they pleased, and could see little that was attractive in pueblo life under authority, in a living that was to be earned, in having fields that must be tilled, and cattle that could not be bartered.[61]

Such a rude awakening from his cherished dreams made the governor realize the truth of what the friars had written him, and he therefore accepted their reports with favor.   Accordingly, when, about the same time the replies of the two superiors were received, word came from Mexico that plans were being formulated in Congress for the complete secularization of the California missions, Figueroa immediately sent the Mexican authorities copies of the friars' replies as well as a lengthy report of his own, in which he strongly protested against so drastic a move:

> I believe that the measure for a general secularization is premature.   It must be effected by degrees, partially, and with some tact.   For the mission system, another system adapted to the character and circumstances of our natives should be substituted in a way that would hardly be noticed.   Otherwise with one blow the labor of many years will be destroyed.   An absolute and sudden change must of necessity cause general confusion and irreparable havoc.[62]

To confirm this, the governor pointed out the immaturity of the Indians, the necessity of leading them, as it were by hand, to civilization, the efforts which he himself had made in the matter of experimental emancipation and the failure which had thus far attended its application.   However, with patience and perseverance it could eventually be made to succeed, and in the same manner the older missions, in the manner proposed by Father Durán, could be gradually secularized.[63]   He then concluded with the following criticism of the proposal by Congress to divide the mission property among the Indians, the troops, and the inhabitants, natives as well as foreigners:

> The mission properties are the exclusive fruit of the labor of the neophytes.   They alone sacrificed themselves for the acqui-

---

[61] *Ibid.,* III, 331–332, note 54.
[62] Engelhardt, *op. cit.,* III, 496–497.
[63] *Ibid.,* III, 497–498.

sition of such property. From this property every passer-by has been succored and aided, . . . the troops of the territory have been supported . . . the expenses for Divine Worship and its ministers paid. . . . From it, in short, the inhabitants of California in various ways are maintained. . . . It would be much to the point to find out for what reason they [the neophytes] should be despoiled of it, or by what right it should be enjoyed by other people whom it cost nothing.[64]

Evidently, Figueroa's opposition to complete secularization was prompted, not by sympathy for the Missions, against which he was personally prejudiced, but by a realization of their economic value to the territory. This in itself marked a step towards an equitable solution of the mission problem, for once the authorities appreciated the services rendered by the mission system to the territory, they would proceed more carefully in their attempts to change it. But, unhappily, just as the promising movement begun under Victoria had been brought to naught by a political upheaval, so also was this favorable change on the part of Figueroa of no account, for when his strong denunciation of secularization reached Mexico, it was found that it had arrived too late.

IV

The secularization movement which had been rumored in California was but the manifestation of a larger political upheaval which had taken place in Mexico in the fall of 1832. Despite the great benefits which it had brought the nation, the Bustamente government had met with the bitter opposition of the liberals. They based their opposition on the fact that Gómez Pedraza, who had been elected in January, 1829, and whom, it should be noted, they themselves had ousted, was still legally the president. An opportunity for revolt was offered when a proposal was made by the government to have the Church aid the State by contributing to its support. Immediately, Bustamente's enemies appeared as champions of the Church and, combining their legal stand with a skilful appeal to the faithful, they succeeded in overthrowing the conservatives in September, 1832, and in installing Pedraza

---

[64] *Ibid.*, III, 499.

as *ad interim* president.[65]   But soon the new government forgot
its pledges of respect for the law and security to the Church.
In January, 1833, a new congress, dominated by the radicals of
the day and referred to as the "reddest Congress Mexico had
had up to that time," [66] chose Santa Anna, the leader of the
revolt, as president, and Gómez Farías, an ardent anti-clerical,
as vice-president. Santa Anna, possibly to escape the demands
for anti-clerical legislation, absented himself from the Capital,
leaving the executive power in the hands of his vice-president.
Once at the head of the government, Farías with the assistance
of Congress immediately began his attack on the Church.

Striking at the privileges of the clergy, the Congress voted
first of all to remove its monopoly over the intellectuality of the
nation by providing that education should be made free, lay,
and obligatory. This move connoted the suppression of the
church schools, which were doing the only valuable educational
work in the Republic, and closing the University, which was
now in an advanced stage of decrepitude. To carry out a program of national education a Direction of Instruction was provided. A still more vital blow was struck at the domination of
the Church when the Congress pretended to assume the old
royal prerogative of the patronato. That is, it took upon itself,
as repository of the exercise of sovereignty, the appointment of
the officers of the church. Even more radically, it suppressed
the legal collection of church tithes, and annulled the civil
obligation of monastic oaths.[67]

It was under these circumstances that the proposal to secularize the Missions had been brought once again to the fore. Padrés,
the arch-enemy of the friars, who on leaving California had
vowed "to return with full powers to carry out his proposed
reforms",[68] had been biding his time in Mexico until the liberals
should return to power. When his friend, Gómez Farías, became
vice-president, his opportunity came and he took advantage of

---

[65] Callcott, *op. cit.*, 73, 78; Priestley, *op. cit.*, 269.

[66] Callcott, *op. cit.*, 89.

[67] Priestley, *op. cit.*, 270; cf. Callcott, *op. cit.*, 90–96, for a detailed treatment
of these measures.

[68] Bancroft, *op. cit.*, III, 259.

it. He became the chief promoter of a colonization project for California based on the idea of utilizing the mission wealth to finance it. He succeeded in interesting a number of influential men chief among them being a certain José María Híjar and his friend, vice-president Farías. Among these, it would seem,

> there was undoubtedly a perfect understanding . . . that such a condition of things should be created that the Supreme Government might absorb the Pious Fund under the pretence that it was no longer needed for missionary purposes, and thus had reverted to the State as a quasi escheat; while the co-actors in California should appropriate the local wealth of the Missions, by the rapid and sure process of 'administering' their temporalities.[69]

Whether or not the agreement was so explicit, the trio had a colonization project adopted by the government which spelled the doom of the Missions. When word was received in the latter part of June that Figueroa was ill and wished to resign, arrangements were made on July 15, for Padrés to succeed him as military commander, and Híjar as civil governor. The next step was to have a law passed secularizing the Missions. Juan Bandini, the California deputy and one of Padrés' northern disciples, identified himself with the scheme and proposed the law in Congress. Accordingly, on August 17, 1833, Mexico for the first time enacted a law of secularization for the California Missions.[70]

Unlike the secularization decrees issued in California, the law was concerned solely with the replacement of the friars by secular priests. With a great amount of detail, it provided that the Missions should be converted into parishes, the friars replaced by members of the secular clergy, a vicar-general, as representative of the bishop, be installed in the place of the Father President, and finally that all expenses incurred in the change should be paid from the Pious Fund.[71] As a general secularization law,

---

[69] Dwinelle, John W., *The colonial history of the city of San Francisco*, 54.

[70] Bancroft, *op. cit.*, III, 259–261.

[71] *Ibid.*, III, 336–337, note 61; for full translation cf. Dwinelle, *op. cit.*, Addenda, No. XV, 26–27.

the law of August 17, was incomplete for it made no provision respecting the real difficulties of secularization, the disposition to be made of the mission property and the treatment to be accorded the neophyte population. It was a proof of the carelessness arising from haste that marked the enactment of the law.

Evidently, this defect was noticed for supplementary regulations were soon enacted. On November 26, a more general decree was issued authorizing the government:

> to adopt all measures to insure the colonization, and make effective the secularization of the missions of Alta and Baja California, using for that purpose in the most convenient manner the estates of the pious fund of those territories, in order to furnish resources to the commission and families now in this capital and intending to go there.[72]

Finally, all doubt concerning the purpose of the secularization law was removed when on April 23, 1834, instructions were issued to Híjar for the care of the colony which was being organized in Mexico at the time. Briefly, they were:

1. He was to begin by taking possession of all the property belonging to the Missions of both Californias, the military commander assisting him if necessary.
2. The colonists were to be transported to California and supported for one year at the government's expense, the funds coming from the Pious Fund.
3. The colonists were to be located in new settlements, given full ownership of lands, and provided with live-stock and implements from the Missions. The Indians were to be attached to these settlements, being mixed with the other inhabitants rather than allowed to form exclusive Indian communities.
4. After the distribution of the movable mission property had been made, one half of what remained was to be sold to the best advantage, and the remaining half kept for the purpose of paying the expenses of Divine Worship, the support of the missionaries, education, and the purchase of implements for the colonists.[73]

---

[72] Bancroft, *op. cit.*, III, 337.

[73] For full translation cf. Engelhardt, *op. cit.*, III, 508–509; Bancroft, *op. cit.*, III, 344, note 5.

This series of laws secularizing the Missions for the purpose of promoting the colonization of the territory was on the whole quite unsatisfactory. Among the various provisions were found contradictions and lacunae which left much to the discretion of the directors of the colony. That this would have been the cause of the greatest destruction and injustice is evident from the fact that to entice native Mexicans to join the colony the directors were liberal in their "promises to distribute the mission wealth, including the neophytes as servants." [74] When the colony finally set out for California in April, 1834, there was every indication that in the plans of its directors the looting of the Missions was to be the price for the increase of the white population of the territory.

In the meantime news of what was taking place in Mexico reached California and led to a counter-movement in secularization. The leanings towards secularization became evident when the *diputación* assembled at Monterey in the spring of 1834. At the opening session on May 1, Figueroa delivered a lengthy speech in which he indicated that despite his former opposition to secularization, he was beginning to view it more favorably. He introduced the subject by declaring that the Missions were intrenchments of monastic despotism and were in need of a reform to make them correspond to the republican system. The supreme government, sincerely desirous as it had always been to ameliorate the condition of the unfortunate natives, had conferred upon his predecessors the necessary powers to secure for them the advantages of the independence of the country; but nothing had been accomplished. Echeandía had professed to carry out the dispositions of the government; but he had done so only in name. By imprudently exciting the Indians with ideas of liberty without securing for them the substance of it, he had instead of producing favorable results only brought on symptoms of disorganization. The supreme government had highly disapproved of this conduct and "commanded me that if I found the edict of secularization in operation, I should order it to be suspended, restoring the Missions to their former condi-

---

[74] Bancroft, *op. cit.*, III, 262.

tion. Yet I was to report whether or not they were in a state
to be secularized, and also I was to go on gradually dividing the
lands of the missions among thte neophytes in order to convert
them into private property." In accordance with this injunction,
he himself had projected and put into execution a plan of emancipation, which, he thought, after a few years would restore the
unhappy neophytes to the enjoyment of their inalienable rights.
Already the three pueblos established in accordance with this
plan had progressed regularly and rapidly. Within a very short
time a great difference became noticeable between the Indians
who were emancipated and those who remained at the Missions.
He therefore believed himself justified in predicting not only the
preservation of the Indian race, instead of the annihilation which
was inevitable under the mission system, but also its elevation
to the dignity of a free people. But the continued development
of this project had been interrupted by the arrival of a secularization law from Mexico, dated August 17, 1833, which compelled
him to await further instructions. In the meanwhile he wished
to submit the matter to the *diputación* and desired to be enlight-
ened as to whether any immediate action ought to be taken,
and, if so, what it should be.[75] There is no evidence to support
Figueroa's picture of the success of emancipation, but if one may
judge by the failure that marked its first application, it would
seem that the governor's enthusiasm was motivated not so
much by facts as by a desire to have secularization applied
immediately.

This desire on the part of both Figueroa and the Californians
was manifested more plainly in the sessions of the *diputación*
during the next two months. An analysis of the proceedings
reveals a curious change from submission to the provisions made
in Mexico for secularization to a determination to take the initiative in the application of the law. For the first month the members of the assembly seemed to be undecided in their attitude
towards the Mexican secularization law. Thus, when at the sec-

75 Figueroa, *Discurso de apertura*, 1834, MS.; cf. Hittell, *op. cit.*, II, 183–185;
Langston, Kathryn L., *The secularization of the California Missions, 1813–1846*
(MS., Library, University of California), 9; Engelhardt, *op. cit.*, III, 502–
504; Bancroft, *op. cit.*, III, 249–251, 339–340.

ond session on May 2, the governor submitted copies of his original instructions for the consideration of the *diputación,* the members referred them to a committee on the Missions.[76] In like manner, when he asked on May 15, whether the secularization law of August 17, 1833, should go into effect immediately, the question was again referred to the committee.[77] Similarly, when proposals were made that the mission lands should be surveyed and inventories taken of the mission properties, action was again delayed.[78] The policy which prompted this delay was revealed when the committee on the Missions made its report on May 24. It did not believe that the governor was authorized to execute the secularization law, for he had received no instructions to this effect from the supreme government. Rather he should await the arrival of the commission which the government was sending to carry secularization into effect and determine all questions relating to mission lands and property. However, it was allowable to make suggestions to the authorities in Mexico on the various measures of the law, and for this purpose it submitted a number of recommendations.[79] Thus far the *diputación* had been scrupulous in its observance of legal formalities.

However, a change of mind was soon made manifest among the members. This became clear when a debate took place at the session of June 3, on the right of the *diputación* to proceed with the secularization of the Missions. Carrillo, the former deputy to Mexico, opposed it on the grounds that this was exclusively the right of the national government and that a special commission was being sent by it to exercise its power. Castro, on the other hand, countered with the view that secularization should be applied as circumstances demanded. The matter was finally settled, when Figueroa declared that he had in his possession documents which had been sent to Echeandía and which invested him with the direction of all colonization in the territory. He felt that by the same authority the *diputación* as well

[76] *Legislative records,* MS., II, 51.

[77] *Ibid.,* II, 71–72.

[78] Bancroft, *op. cit.,* III, 249, note 18.

[79] *Legislative records,* MS., II, 93–94.

as himself was empowered to take such measures in the matter of secularization as circumstances demanded.[80] It would seem that this argument satisfied the consciences of the members, for during the next month the *diputación* busied itself with the preparation of a set of regulations for secularization.[81] Finally, on July 19, Carlos Carrillo, won over now to the scheme "for some reason, doubtless satisfactory to himself," [82] proposed the enactment of a law for the provisional secularization of the Missions. The proposal was willingly accepted and acted upon. The secularization regulations which had been already drawn up were approved article by article in the secret sessions of July 30 and 31, re-read and finally approved on August 2, and officially promulgated by the governor on August 9 under the title: "Provisional Regulations for the Secularization of the Missions of Upper California." [83]

The plan was a lengthy one, being in reality a collection of the various regulations drawn up in previous secularization laws. The final product of a cumulative effort of over two decades, it was to be the instrument which governed the actual secularization of the Missions. Special importance, then, must be attached to its various provisions. Summarized, they were as follows:

1. The civil governor, according to the spirit of the law of August 17, 1833, and his instructions from the supreme government, was to immediately convert into pueblos ten missions and continue with the others successively.

2. The friars were to be relieved of the administration of temporalities but were to continue exercising their spiritual

---

80 *Ibid.,* II, 98–100.

81 Hittell, *op. cit.,* II, 185, states that this determination of the *diputación* to act on secularization was caused by the arrival from Mexico of a general law of April 16, 1834, which ordered the secularization of all missions throughout the nation. However, he gives no references in support of this view. On the other hand, Bancroft, *op. cit.,* III, 341, note 3, maintains that "this law seems never to have been mentioned in Californian discussions, and was probably not understood to apply to California, as very likely . . . it was not intended to apply."

82 Bancroft, *op. cit.,* III, 342.

83 For a complete chronicle of the sessions of the *diputación,* cf. Bancroft, *op. cit.,* III, 249–250, note 18.

ministry until such time as a formal division of parishes should be made and secular priests be appointed by the bishop. At each mission a suitable building would be provided for their use and the library, sacred vessels, church furniture, etc., placed under their care.

3. The territorial government would assume the administration of the temporalities, appointing commissioners for this purpose. The commissioners were to present their credentials to the friars, with whom they were to preserve harmony, politeness and due respect, explain to the Indians the regulations and the change to be effected, make an inventory of the properties, and assume general control of the mission.

4. To each family and to all over twenty years of age, was to be made a distribution of the mission lands, and one half of the live-stock, existing chattels, tools, and seed for cultivation, the grain, however, remaining undisturbed and the neophytes receiving the usual rations. Finally, no one could sell or encumber his land or property, and in case an owner died without heirs, his land was to revert to the nation.

5. The remainder of the lands and other properties was to be placed in charge of the commissioner named by the governor, and was to be held by him subject to the disposition of the supreme government. But out of the proceeds of such property were to be paid the salaries of the padres, the commissioner, and other employees, and the expenses of divine worship, schools, and other objects of public order and improvement.

6. The neophytes thus emancipated were to be organized in pueblos, governed according to the existing laws, and allowed to elect their own officers. While such features of community life as the 'nunnery' were to be abolished, no change was to be made in the system of work, etc., until experience proved it to be necessary. The neophytes were to be obliged to aid in the common work which in the judgment of the governor might be deemed necessary for the cultivation of the vineyards, gardens, and fields remaining for the present undisturbed.

7. While these regulations were to go into effect at once, the approval of them was to be solicited from the supreme government as soon as possible.[84]

To these regulations should be added a supplementary decree of November 4, which, dividing the missions into first and second

---

[84] For full translation cf. Bancroft, *op. cit.*, III, 342–345, note 4; Dwinelle, *op. cit.*, Addenda, No. XIX, 31–34; for summary cf. Hittell, *op. cit.*, II, 186–187.

class parishes and asigning to their respective ministers salaries of $1,500 and $1,000, brought the legislative efforts of the *diputación* to a close and rounded out, in theory at least, its lengthy plan of secularization.[85]

It but remains to determine what motives prompted the Californians to enact so suddenly this final secularization law. A distingished visitor who happened to be in California at the time, suggests the motive in the following account:

> The provincial population made short work with the establishments—all classes of this body, as I have already indicated, being fundamentally and permanently jealous of the fathers. What fanned the smouldering ashes into flame was an abortive attempt on the part of Mexico to distribute a considerable share of lands and cattle of the missions among a colony of strangers; and, now perceiving that they had no time to lose, the Californians, as the phrase went, secularized the missions. . . . And thus the missions . . . were trodden under foot by the sons of the very men, or by the very men themselves, whom worldly wisdom had introduced into the province for their protection and assistance.[86]

That this surmise was correct is clear from the treatment accorded the Padrés-Híjar colony after it arrived in California, as well as from the manner in which the secularization law was applied from the outset. When the colony arrived at Monterey in the middle of October, 1834, Híjar immediately demanded that as director of the colony he be put in charge of the mission properties. Figueroa referred the matter to the *diputación* and although the members of that body had been a few years earlier admirers and partisans of Padrés, they refused to recognize his instructions. On October 21, a lengthy report was issued declaring that although Híjar was the director of the colony, he should have nothing to do with the mission property nor with the secularization of those establishments. The colonists would be furnished the tools and other aid called for in the instructions, but would not be allowed to settle on mission lands. Padrés

---

[85] *Ibid.*, III, 347, note 11.

[86] Simpson, Sir George, *Narrative of a journey round the world* (London, 1847), I, 302.

and his accomplices were at the mercy of the Californians and were forced to capitulate. The colony was disbanded and its members settled in various sections of the territory.[87]   As Vallejo and Alvarado later admitted, "the chief reason for this defection was the fact that Padrés had brought with him twenty-one Mexicans to become administrators of the missions, whereas, under the old plan, the Californians were to have those places."[88]   It was therefore not surprising that when administrators were appointed to carry out the secularization of the various missions, the most lucrative positions were filled by the members of the *diputación* and their friends.   The two Carillos were placed in charge of Santa Barbara and Purisima, Pico at San Diego, Castro at San Juan Bautista, Estudillo at San Francisco, and finally Vallejo at Solano, where he soon became the lord of the northern frontier and California's first millionaire. [89]   The tables had been turned on Padrés and the ideas which he had introduced were used to advantage by his former pupils.

Yet the frustration of Padrés' ambitions did not justify the Californians.   Underlying their action was the same motive of self-enrichment.   It was this desire to be the possessors of the properties of the Missions that had explained the attempt at secularization under Echeandía; and it was the same desire that explained its enactment under Figueroa.   In a keen analysis Bancroft summed up the situation in the following words:

In reality, the position of Figueroa in 1834 did not differ much from that of Echeandía in 1831.   Each desired to advance the scheme of secularization, each had instructions to that effect, each founded his action on a national law—of Spain in one case and of Mexico in the other—each expected the early arrival of a successor, each preferred from motives of personal pride and for the personal interests of friends and supporters that the change should be inaugurated by himself rather than by his successor, and each had the support of the diputación. Both knew perfectly well that they had strictly no legal right to act in the matter, and that the motives alleged, though of some weight, were not urgent for immediate action; yet both chose

---

[87] Hittell, *op. cit.*, II, 195.
[88] Bancroft, *op. cit.*, III, 274.
[89] *Ibid.*, III, 346, note 8; 353, note 16.

to assume the responsibility of such action. Figueroa's act, if somewhat less arbitrary and uncalled for than that of Echeandía, was none the less a trick. Unlike Echeandia's, but largely from accidental causes, it proved to a certain extent successful.[90]

The greatest tragedy in the history of California was this fact, that when the change in the mission system became an accomplished fact, it should have been in the form of immediate and complete secularization. In adopting this measure, Figueroa had closed his eyes to the truth and refused to accept conditions as he knew they existed. Time and again the padres, eager to sacrifice their own interests for the improvement of their neophytes, had pointed out the impossibility of transforming the Indian overnight and Figueroa himself had concurred with them. Step by step they had evolved a system of gradual emancipation which would have eventually effected the desired change in the mission system and yet protected its children from the forces that were aimed at their destruction—and again Figueroa had accepted it. Then, suddenly moved by motives that were unworthy of the great man that he was in other respects, he decreed the general secularization of the Missions—and thereby their sentence of death. As one writer has put it, "In other cases it required hundreds of years to educate savages up to the point of making them citizens, and many hundreds to make good citizens. The idea of at once transforming the idle, improvident and brutish natives of California into industrious, law-abiding and self-governing town-people was preposterous, . . . Though it required some years to finish the ruin of the missionary establishments, this was the commencement of it." [91]

---

[90] *Ibid.*, III, 341.
[91] Hittell, *op. cit.*, II, 189.

CHAPTER V

SECULARIZATION OF THE CALIFORNIA MISSIONS:
1835–1846

The enactment of secularization may be said to have come to a close with the death of Figueroa on September 29, 1835. Thenceforth it was to be a question of its application. An indication of what this was to mean for the Missions may be drawn from the tragic end of the author of secularization. In compliance with Figueroa's last wish, his remains were deposited at Mission Santa Barbara, there to await more fitting obsequies by the Mexican government. At the same time it was resolved by the members of the *diputación* to erect a monument to his memory at Monterey and to display his picture in the hall of the assembly.[1] But Mexico never sent for the remains nor did the Californians ever erect their monument. Robinson wrote ten years later:

> Days, months, years, have rolled away, and yet naught has been done to perpetuate the memory of this exalted man! This serves to show a want of sincerity in those who most deeply deplored his death, and the instability of their character.[2]

And such might have been the description of the period which now followed: inaction on the part of Mexico, and vain promises on the part of the Californians. As they forgot the memory of one who to them had been a benefactor, so also during the ten years that now remained before the American occupation, they forgot the great services which the Missions had rendered the territory, and wrought their destruction. This period was to mark the end of the mission era.

---

[1] Bancroft, *op. cit.,* III, 295-298.
[2] *Life in California,* 180.

I

At the time of Figueroa's death fifteen of the twenty-one missions had already been secularized. In accordance with the provisional regulations, the friars had been relieved of the administration of temporalities, commissioners or administrators, as they were more popularly called, installed in their place, inventories of the mission property were made, and a portion of the lands and other goods distributed to the neophytes.[3] What is especially remarkable, throughout the transfer the friars made no serious attempt to arrest the enforcement of the decree. As early as May, 1834, Father Diego had received instructions from the guardian of his college to obey the law and to refrain from all participation in politics or criticism of the government's policy. Both of these injunctions were forwarded to the Zacatecans and apparently obeyed.[4] Likewise, in January and March, 1835, Father Durán sent two lengthy letters to the Fernandinos urging them to submit patiently to the change and to send whatever complaints they might wish to make to the governor who, he was certain, "would remedy everything if the matter is placed before him in due form and with proofs."[5] Evidently the friars trusted the authorities to avoid all extremes.

But ere long the true nature of secularization became quite evident. At the time when the mission system was transferred to the care of the administrators, its monetary value was beyond all calculation. Extant records reveal that besides lands, buildings and movable goods, it possessed 140,000 head of cattle, 12,000 horses, 130,000 sheep, and an average yield in grain crops of 32,700 *fanegas* a year.[6] Within a year it was clear that these vast properties were intended to serve as a rich harvest for those entrusted with their administration. As one writer has remarked, with the exception of Figueroa and perhaps a few others, "the great mass of commissioners and other officials, whose duty it became to administer the properties of the mis-

---

[3] Bancroft, *op. cit.*, III, 353.
[4] *Ibid.*, III, 347.
[5] Engelhardt, *op. cit.*, III, 542–552.
[6] Bancroft, *op. cit.*, III, 356–357.

sions and especially their great numbers of horses, cattle, sheep and other animals, thought of little else and accomplished little else than enriching themselves." [7] As a result a wholesale slaughter of the mission cattle was begun for the purpose of selling the hides and tallow to the numerous trading vessels that now visited the coast. Despite the charge, originated by the early Californians, that "the slaughter was effected . . . by outsiders who contracted to kill the cattle and deliver half the hides to the padres," [8] it is now clear that this destruction was the work of the administrators and their henchmen. [9] The extent to which this destruction was carried on may be gathered from the following description of the slaughter of the cattle at San Gabriel:

> They were killed where they were found, in the valleys or on the hills; the hides taken off, and the carcasses left to rot. The spectacle presented was horrible. Some of the valleys were entirely covered with putrescent masses; and for years the country in the neighborhood was white with skeletons. In some places the skulls and large bones were so plentiful that long fences were built of them. [10]

But the evils of secularization were not confined to the looting of the wealth of the Missions. More than 15,000 mission Indians [11] had become subject to the administrators and it soon became evident that their destruction also had set in. Father Quíjas, in a letter of August 2, 1835, has left a graphic description of the appalling abuses at San Francisco Solano. There the administrator, Vallejo, and especially his assistant, Antonio Ortega, were undoing whatever good had been accomplished

---

[7] Hittell, *op. cit.*, II, 206.

[8] Bancroft, *op. cit.*, III, 348–349; Hittell, *op. cit.*, II, 207–208, holds the same view.

[9] Tays, *ut supra*, 426–427, has presented this view in the following words: "After several years of investigation and study of the available documents, I find myself inclined to place little reliability upon the statements of the California writers of that Era. . . . At the time the slaughters of 1834 and 1835 were in progress, the missions at which they were supposed to be taking place were in the hands of the government."

[10] Hittell, *op. cit.*, II, 208.

[11] Bancroft, *op. cit.*, III, 356.

by the friars.   Ortega in the most "unbridled and barefaced manner" had made the Indians the victims of his lust, "sparing neither young girls nor married women or widows, neither heathen nor Christian, as is affirmed by the majority of the inhabitants of San Solano."   To this pernicious example he had added words, openly encouraging the neophytes to imitate him in vice and obscenity.   Finally, he had maliciously placed every obstacle in the way of the religious instruction of the neophytes by the friars, forbidding all extra devotional practices and at times literally dragging them away from Mass in order the sooner to put them to work in the fields.   As he declared, "it did not concern him whether the Indians prayed or not; it was his business to make them work; for this had the government placed him there."   In the face of such indignities, the Indians were running away and would soon entirely abandon the mission.[12]   That such discontent was not confined to the northernmost mission is evident from the following complaint which the administrator himself, Pablo de la Portilla, sent to the governor concerning the unrest of the neophytes at San Luis Rey:

> They had absolutely refused to obey orders.   The season for sowing wheat had come on and he had prepared the necessary plows; but nothing had been done for the reason that the Indians had been unwilling to work.   They said they had at length become a free nation; and to prove it they left their houses and wandered off, abandoning the mission. . . . They would listen to no reason; it was impossible to make them understand or appreciate the advantages of industry and obedience; nothing could change their obstinacy.   They all with one voice cried out: 'We are free.   It is not our pleasure to obey.   We do not choose to work!'   It was plain, Portilla continued, that this state of affairs would have to be remedied and the Indians reduced to subordination; but he had no troops to do it with.[13]

As will be remembered, San Luis Rey was the very place where Echeandía and Pico had succeeded in filling the minds of the neophytes under the friars with insincere talk on liberty and

---

[12] For full translation cf. Engelhardt, *op. cit.*, III, 581–589.
[13] Hittell, *op. cit.*, II, 189–190.

equality, and now the demoralization that resulted was bringing them to ruin.

These evils awakened the friars to the true nature of secularization. The fact was further impressed upon them when they found themselves driven from their old living quarters to inferior rooms, insulted, and ordered about by administrators who forgot the injunction "to preserve harmony, politeness, and due respect." [14] Thus far they had stood by as witnesses and victims of the destruction and injustices of the administrators. But already one year of this management had done much to destroy the labors of three score and five, and a few more would complete the ruin. Action by the friars was demanded and accordingly in May, 1835, Father Diego went southward to Santa Barbara to confer with the superior of the Fernandinos, Father Durán. From their conference emerged a plan to carry their appeal to the authorities in Mexico, as Serra had done in a similar crisis. Father Diego was chosen to present the case in person, and accordingly on November 17, 1835, he set out from Monterey for Mexico. Upon the success of his mission, depended the future of the friars and their neophytes. [15]

When Father Diego arrived in Mexico he found that a reaction had set in against secularization. The radical reforms introduced by Gómez Farías and his "red Congress" had been met with vigorous opposition by the majority of the people. Threatened with revolt, Santa Anna had finally reassumed the presidency on April 24, 1834, and, adopting the habit of conservation, condemned the program of the radicals, dissolved the Congress, and forced Farías into exile. [16]

Then, by a series of executive decrees, he proceeded to overthrow the laws controlling ecclesiastical patronage, to restore the fugitive bishops to their seats, to lift the ban on those who had been banished, to reopen the University, and to enter on a full-fledged conservative régime. These decrees were to be

---

14 Bancroft, op. cit., III, 353, note 16.
15 Engelhardt, op. cit., III, 578–579, 605–606.
16 Priestley, op. cit., 270–271.

approved by a congress, which, it was announced, would assemble later.[17]

When this new congress met on January 4, 1835, it was found that the majority of its members were conservatives and therefore in sympathy with the Church.

As a result of these political changes, the attitude of the government towards the California Missions had become more favorable. When in July, reports were received of the evils that were taking place under Figueroa's provisional secularization law, the authorities thoroughly disapproved the course that had been taken and resolved to send a new governor to the territory.[18] What was of greater consequence, on November 7, Congress issued a decree which practically suspended all further application of the secularization laws. The law read:

> Until the curates mentioned in article 2 of the law of August 17, 1833, shall have taken possession, the government will suspend the execution of the other articles and will maintain things in the state in which they were before the said law was made.[19]

Finally, when news was received of Figueroa's death, the government immediately appointed, on December 16, a new governor in the person of Mariano Chico.[20] Instructed to enforce the decree suspending secularization, it was hoped that order would once more be restored to the territory and its Missions.

When, therefore, in June, 1836, Father Diego arrived in Mexico, apparently after a long and tedious voyage, he found the government anxious to receive his reports. He immediately presented the authorities with three lengthy memorials in which he accurately described the California situation and proposed effective remedies for its evils. In the first, dated June 26, 1836, he related how the Missions and their neophytes had been the chief

---

[17] Callcott, *op. cit.*, 101.
[18] Bancroft, *op. cit.*, III, 421, note 15.
[19] *Ibid.*, III, 355; Rockwell, John A., *A compilation of Spanish and Mexican laws* (New York, 1851), 462.
[20] Hittell, *op. cit.*, II, 217.

support of the troops since 1810 and declared that this could not be continued "because of the wretched state into which the missions have been plunged at the hands of the comisionados, who have ruined them." Moreover, he felt that he could not guarantee the continuance of the friars in California. "Their days are passed in the deepest sorrow, and they have entreated me to permit them to retire, because they can not endure so much merciless oppression." [21]

In a second memorial, dated June 27, he described the mission system and the life of industry and contentment which it had promoted among the natives. Down to 1832, 87,739 souls had been rescued from barbarism and instructed in religion according to their capacity. Moreover, great progress had been made in advancing these former savages on the road to civilization. They had been taught many trades, had transformed a wild country into well cultivated fields and profitable cattle ranges, and had erected monuments in architecture, all under the direction of the friars who aided them by their annual allowances and the alms that were given them, and "personally labored with the neophytes in order to encourage them and remove the repugnance which they have and always had for every kind of work." But now all this as well as further progress was threatened by the lack of missionaries. Death was not far distant for the thirteen aged and infirm Fernandinos, "who have sacrificed their years and their health for the welfare of the Indians." Likewise there was great probability that vacancies would soon occur among the eight Zacatecans "through death, hastened by what they have experienced in these last days, or through withdrawal to the college." An immediate remedy was necessary and to this end he had no other choice save to propose the following plan:

The only way to provide missionaries for California is the erection of a diocese whose Bishop will shoulder the labors and privations, and devote himself exclusively to the care and welfare of these souls. This prelate, protected by the Supreme Government, will have to establish a college to which all the youths of both Californias may flock, as well as many of the In-

---

[21] For full translation cf. Engelhardt, *op. cit.*, IV, 83–86.

dians of the various idioms, in order to receive the education and knowledge peculiar to the ecclesiastical state. This is the project which I venture to propose to the Supreme Government through Your Honor, as the best means to conserve Divine Worship in the missions of California, in order that the conversion of the gentiles may not be paralyzed, and in order that the white population may have spiritual assistance along with the Indians; and furthermore, in order that the Indians themselves, who hitherto have found themselves in lowliness and abjection, may commence to form an idea of the dignity of their own manhood when they behold their own elevated to the ecclesiastical state, set apart as teachers of Religion, and destined to communicate Religion to their own in their own language.[22]

Finally, on July 20, Father Diego at the request of the government presented a third report in which among other recommendations he made the following suggestions as the means of insuring permanent order in both Californias:

1. A governor who loves order, and who has given proofs of his own well-ordered conduct, who is an enemy of vice, and who would prudently strive to remove vice from among these poor people.

2. This official should take along one hundred picked men, who should go there not to still more demoralize said poor people; moreover, they should be maintained by means of the revenues of the custom-house.

3. When these soldiers have installed themselves, many of those stationed there heretofore, who on account of their vices have already proved incapable of stemming demoralization, but rather promote it, should be returned hither to Mexico.[23]

At first sight Father Diego's proposals seem more idealistic than practical and have been criticized accordingly. Yet their striking similarity to the earlier plan which Father Durán had suggested to Bustamente in 1830, and more fully developed for Figueroa in 1833, suggests their true purport. The proposals were not Diego's but Durán's and were drawn up by him at the

22 *Ibid.*, IV, 86–90.
23 *Ibid.*, IV, 72.

conference held at Santa Barbara the year before. The question of secularization was not mentioned because the decree of November 7, 1835, had temporarily suspended it. Yet the mission system was not to remain unchanged, for the proposed creation of a diocese precluded its continuation as such. On the contrary, the suggestion that the missions should be relieved of the burden of supporting the troops indicated that their properties and products were to be devoted to other purposes. It would seem that Father Durán's intention was to apply his scheme of gradual emancipation. The old missions were gradually to be converted into pueblos and part of their properties distributed among the more advanced neophytes. The remaining wealth and Indians would be devoted to the foundation of new missions among the gentiles. With them would go the missionaries, their places being taken by the secular clergy who would in time be supplied by the seminary. Finally, to insure the success of the plan, the Mexican government would have to guarantee the religious authorities its support and protection and appoint as governor of California an upright man who would suppress the forces that tended to destroy the Missions and their neophytes. It can not be determined whether Father Diego or even the government was fully aware of all the details of this plan, but, if the conjecture may be made, it seems probable that had secularization been immediately suspended and a bishop sent to the territory, this change under the guidance of Father Durán would have been eventually effected in the mission system. Nor was it too late to attempt such a change, for as yet the ravages of secularization had not advanced so far as to make a solution of the mission problem impossible.

For a moment it appeared that these proposals were to have an immediate effect. On September 19, 1836, the members of Congress adopted the following resolution:

1. The Government after hearing such parties as by law may be entitled to a hearing on the subject, and such other parties as it may think proper to hear, shall thereupon make a full report with regard to the necessity of creating a diocese for the Californias.

2. If the report should result in showing that there is such

a necessity, report should be made to the Holy See for approval and for the erection of said diocese.

3. From the three nominees proposed by the Metropolitan Council, the Government shall choose the person whom it believes most suitable, and propose him to his Holiness.

4. The person elected shall receive from the public treasury six thousand dollars per annum, whilst the diocese has not sufficient income.

5. During the continuation of the same circumstances, the public treasury shall furnish a subsidy of three thousand dollars per annum for expediting the Bulls and for traveling expenses of the bishop to his episcopal see.

6. The property belonging to the Pious Fund of the Californias shall be placed at the disposal of the bishop and of his successors, in order that they administer and expend it according to its purpose and other similar ones, always respecting the will of the founders of the Fund.[24]

Shortly afterwards, steps were taken to carry out the provisions of this decree. The Metropolitan Chapter of the Archdiocese of Mexico was apparently commissioned by the government to conduct the preliminary investigations, for on October 12, it requested Father Diego to set forth in a report the necessity of having a bishop in California. Three days later he replied with a lengthy *informe* in which he again set forth the reasons which had led him to make his proposals.[25] After such an immediate show of action on the part of the authorities, the hopes of the missionary ran high and in letter that reflected his confidence he joyfully informed his California brethren of the success of his mission:

We presented ourselves to the Supreme Government; we spoke in your behalf with the most lively interest; we energetically exposed the multitude of your necessities; and we proposed the means which to us seemed the most expedient. The precious result was the Law for the Erection of a Diocese of the Two Californias, passed on September 19, 1936.[26]

---

[24] Quoted by Engelhardt, *op. cit.*, IV, 90–91.
[25] *Ibid.*, IV, 187–189.
[26] *Ibid.*, IV, 186.

II

But once again a new series of circumstances prevented the carrying out of the plan to save the Missions. The first obstacle was the failure of Mariano Chico, the new governor whom Mexico had sent to California, to enforce the decree suspending secularization and to give that example of justice and morality which Father Diego had declared to be so imperative. After assuming the reins of government at Monterey on May 1, 1836, he soon displayed a marked coolness towards the suspension of secularization. In his speech at the opening of the *diputación* on May 27, he declared that the decree of the previous November 7, had been "issued by Congress, of which he had been a member, with the best intentions, but without practical knowledge on the subject." Since it came from the government, it had to be executed; yet "it was impossible to carry it out in every respect." He saw no way of advance or retreat, and therefore awaited the advice of the legislators which, he hoped, would "lead the government like Ariadne's thread from so strange a labyrinth." [27] But the advisors to whom he turned were of the secularization group and accordingly influenced him to protect their own interests. That their efforts were successful is evident from the following report which Chico sent to the Mexican authorities on July 22:

> I have not enforced the decree of the National Congress . . . because some of the lands once comprised in the properties of those missions have been allotted among various Indians and white persons, who have undertaken work and considerable expenses; proportionately as they were judged legitimate owners of their small endowments and of the cattle which was handed to them by lawful authority, they made them their properties. How can I manage to make them give up their possessions at once without any force? Such an attack on their properties would unite them to avenge their injury, and this command has no means of controlling them due to finding itself in need of troops.[28]

During the few short months of his rule Chico by his open immoralities, especially the public display of his mistress, had

---

[27] Bancroft, *op. cit.*, III, 424–425; IV, 44–45.
[28] Translated, Tays, *ut supra*, 437–438.

earned for himself the hatred of a large portion of the population, and by his arbitrary rule had aroused the opposition of the California politicians. Evidently, he had sought to keep himself in office by sacrificing the Missions. But this betrayal of the trust confided to him, availed him nothing. A few days after he had dispatched this report to Mexico, he had again given evidence of his high-handed methods, by arbitrarily removing from office the alcade and assessor of Monterey. Indignation was manifested on all sides and finally the popular uproar became so great that the governor, fearing for his life, took refuge on board a ship which happened to be in the harbor, and on July 31, sailed for Mexico.[29] In three months he had not only by his inaction doomed the Missions but by his misconduct had disgraced the government which he had been commissioned to represent.

The failure of Chico's administration precipitated the most serious outbreak of nativism thus far experienced in the territory. Before leaving California, he had transferred his command to Nicolás Gutiérrez, a loyal Mexican officer. But the Californians felt that it was time to have a governor of their own choosing and began to plot for the overthrow of Mexican rule. Accordingly, on November 4, 1836, a small band of insurgents led by Juan Bautista Alvarado rose in rebellion, seized Monterey and forced Gutiérrez to abdicate. Alvarado was immediately proclaimed governor and on November 7, a declaration of independence announced the creation of "the free and sovereign state of Alta California." [30]

In the face of this sudden crisis in California, a new situation arose in Mexico which prevented any action on the part of the home government. While the position of conservatism had been strengthened by the fact that the Pope had at last recognized Mexico, as well as by the fact that Bustamente had been brought back from exile and installed on April 19, 1837, as president for an eight-year term, the government was faced with many internal and external disturbances. In 1836, Texas revolted and after a bitter struggle forced an acknowledgment of her independence

---

[29] Bancroft, *op. cit.*, III, 438–440.
[30] Chapman, *History of California*, 474.

from Mexico. In 1838, France threatened the country with war unless payment was made for damages which the various disturbances had caused her nationals, in particular a French baker whose shop had been sacked by a mob, an incident which caused France's aggressive actions to be dubbed as "The Pastry War." Finally, during these disturbances, the liberals had further harassed the government by several serious attempts to overthrow its power. Successive revolts broke out in Pueblo, Sonora and Michoacan and kept the country in a state of constant turmoil.[31] As a result of these trying conditions at home, Mexico concerned itself but little with California. The project for the creation of a diocese was postponed for lack of funds, and no effort was made to send a governor to restore the territory to Mexican rule for the troops needed for such a move could not be spared. The Californians were necessarily allowed to continue their rule and, as will be noted, to pursue their spoliation of the Missions.

The next four years were one of the most turbulent periods in California history. "There was much revolutionary unrest, based largely on personal and sectional rivalries. Men fought or intrigued for office and the chance to administer the scant resources of the treasury. South fought against north, challenging its traditional predominance." [32] Alvarado found himself opposed by a succession of rivals who arose in the south, and only succeeded in maintaining his position by marching his army on four different occasions southward,—though these campaigns more often than not ended, in true California fashion, in battles of tongue and pen.

But though the period of native rule was characterized by political dissensions and rivalries, it was the signal for a united attack on the Missions. There is every indication that one of the purposes of the Californians in overthrowing Mexican rule had been to secure free rein in looting the Missions. This was revealed when Alvarado, shortly after his accession to power, rejected Father Durán's petition that he guarantee security to the Missions and their neophytes, because, as he himself admitted, "the administration of the missions and the treatment

[31] Priestley, *op. cit.*, 291–294; Callcott, *op. cit.*, 112 ss.
[32] Chapman, *op. cit.*, 455.

of the Indians did not depend on my will." [33]   As Vallejo more fully explained:

> Such guarantees it was not within the power of Governor Alvarado to grant, because in advance he had bound himself to Castro, Alviso and the other chiefs of the popular revolt to proceed at the opportune time to the secularization of all the property of the Indians in charge of the Reverend Fathers. This agreement, as yet, was not publicly known. . . .[34]

In the face of such compacts, it is small wonder that the four years of California rule, from 1836 to 1840, marked the period of real plunder and destruction of the mission system.

The chief cause for the destruction of the Missions was the fact that they were made political pawns by the several military chieftains. During the various military campaigns, the missions were heavily drawn upon to furnish funds and supplies for the troops of both sides. In purchasing military supplies from the various trading vessels that visited the territory, payment was made by giving orders on the missions for wheat, tallow, or hides, in the same fashion as checks are drawn on the treasury. After each campaign the various leaders, if not the common soldiers, were rewarded by outright gifts of mission cattle and goods. In several cases attempts were made to conceal the illegality of these acts by making the gifts of cattle in the form of loans, to be paid back to the mission later, a condition which was seldom if ever complied with.[35]

But what was even a greater cause of destruction was the fact that the positions of administrator became the plums of political patronage, to be distributed by the various leaders as rewards for political support. The result was that little attention was paid to the fitness of applicants or to the manner in which they administered the properties after their appointment. Consequently among the administrators,

> many were simply incompetent and stupid, exhausting their little energy and ability in the task of collecting their salary,

---

[33] Engelhardt, *op. cit.*, IV, 62.
[34] *Historia de California*, MS., III, 247.
[35] Bancroft, *op. cit.*, IV, 49–50.

filling the governor's orders so long as the granaries and herds held out, exercising no restraint or influence on the ex-neophytes, and allowing the affairs of their respective establishments to drift—not, as may be imagined, in the direction of general prosperity. Others were vicious as well as incompetent, always ready to sell any article of mission property, not only live-stock, but kitchen utensils, farm implements, tools from the shops, and tiles from the roofs, for money with which to gratify their propensity for gambling. Still others were dishonest and able, devoting their energies to laying the foundations of future wealth for themselves and their friends, oppressing the Indians, . . . and disposing of the mission wealth without scruple, for their own interests.[36]

After four years the effects of this rule of incompetent and dishonest administrators were appalling, comparable, as Father Durán exclaimed, to the waste and ruin "perpetrated by the most ferocious conquerors whom the world has ever produced." [37] The statistics for 1840 reveal that during the four years of spoliation the cattle decreased approximately from 180,000 to 50,000; horses from 12,000 to 10,000; and sheep from 130,000 to 50,000; while of the crops not even an estimate can be given, so insignificant had they become in comparison with the mission period.[38] Richard H. Dana who visited California during these years described the waste and ruin he saw in the following words:

In the missions, the change was complete. The priests have now no power, except in their religious character, and the great possessions of the missions are given over to be preyed upon by the harpies of the civil power, who are sent there in the capacity of administradores, to settle up the concerns; and who usually end, in a few years, by making themselves fortunes, and leaving their stewardships worse than they found them. The dynasty of the priests was much more acceptable to the people of the country, and, indeed, to everyone concerned with the country, by trade or otherwise, than that of the administradores. The priests were attached perpetually to one mission, and felt the necessity of keeping up its credit. Accordingly, their debts were regularly paid, and the people were, in the main, well treated and

---

[36] *Ibid.*, IV, 61.
[37] Engelhardt, *op. cit.*, IV, 111.
[38] Bancroft, *op. cit.*, IV, 63.

attached to those who spent their whole lives among them. But the administradores are, . . . for the most part, men of desperate fortunes—broken down politicians and soldiers—whose only object is to retrieve their condition in as short a time as possible. The change had been made but a few years before our arrival upon the coast, yet, in that short time, the trade was much diminshed, credit impaired, and the venerable missions going rapidly to decay.[39]

But even more appalling was the moral and physical ruin visited upon the mission Indians. Of the 15,000 who had dwelt under the protection of the mission system in 1834, scarcely 5,000 were left by 1840. The others had either perished or had been driven from their old homes.[40] Under the administrators, little attention was paid to the ex-neophytes. To some few lands and cattle had been distributed in accordance with the secularization provisions. But, as a contemporary observed, "left to provide for his own necessities . . . he took no thought of the morrow but lived in a state of recklessness." [41] Faced with the necessity of caring for their cattle and working their fields, the emancipated Indians, deprived of that guidance and protection which the friars had so strongly insisted upon as the condition for the success of the experiment, sold their possessions for liquor and gave themselves up to a life of idleness and thievery.[42]

Nor did the natives who remained at the missions fare any better. Under the grasping administrators they virtually became slaves, being forced to labor without fixed wages or being hired out by their masters, for the sake of personal profits, to *rancheros* or town people. The Indians indeed often protested against the injustices they suffered, especially against the sale of mission lands and goods which reduced them to starvation and nakedness, but their complaints were only met with added oppressions and rebukes.[43] Driven finally to despair, large numbers of them deserted the missions and either returned to a life of savagery

---

39 *Two years before the mast* (New York, 1840), 210–211.
40 Bancroft, *op. cit.*, IV, 62.
41 Robinson, *op. cit.*, 263.
42 Bancroft, *op. cit.*, IV, 52.
43 Engelhardt, *op. cit.*, IV, 7 ss.

or, what was more degrading, gave themselves up to vagabondage, pilfering, and vice. Among these poor unfortunates "pilfering and drunkenness increased rapidly, as did the ravages of syphilitic disease." [44] Again, Dana has left a vivid description of the moral degradation into which these conditions plunged the former neophytes:

> Of the poor Indians very little care is taken. The priests, indeed, at the missions, are said to keep them very strictly, and some rules are usually made by the alcades to punish their misconduct. Yet it all amounts to but very little. Indeed, to show the entire want of any sense of morality or domestic duty among them, I have frequently known an Indian to bring his wife, to whom he was lawfully married in the church, down to the beach, and carry her back again, dividing with her the money which she had got from the sailors. If any of the girls were discovered by the alcade to be open evil livers, they were whipped, and kept at work sweeping the square of the presidio, and carrying mud and bricks for the buildings; yet a few reals would generally buy them off. Intemperance, too, is a common vice among the Indians. [45]

Through secularization the Indian had been given not liberty but license, and because of this, "was plunged headlong into the destruction which so naturally followed." [46]

The final victims of the injustices of secularization were the missionaries themselves. They, who had sacrificed the best of their lives for the Missions and their neophytes, were now forced to take the position of mere on-lookers, powerless to interfere in the destruction that was going on around them. The majority of them endured everything with resignation and in silence. Yet from a few letters sent to their local superiors or to Mexico, we can learn what they suffered and thought. When the administrators were appointed to take charge of the missions, the friars found that men whom they had previously succored with alms, had suddenly been changed into their masters. "There were those who hesitated not to domineer in the very exercises of Religion,

[44] Bancroft, *op. cit.,* IV, 52.
[45] *Op. cit.,* 215–216.
[46] Robinson, *op. cit.,* 263.

even threatening to remove the clappers from the bells in order to prevent their ringing for the saying of the Rosary on feastdays, as is customary." [47]   But what was more unbearable they were forced to make way for the many friends and relatives whom the administrators quartered at the missions and supported from the labors of the Indians.

> The administrators who now have possession of the quarters which our brethren occupied when two religious were stationed at a mission . . . have placed in our very houses their numerous families of women, crying and turbulent children and a multitude of relatives, who all make an unbearable racket. This cannot continue thus any longer. It means being martyred with needles.[48]

Finally, the friars found that the promises of respect and decent support which had been made in the regulations of secularization were mere gestures and were never intended to be kept. They were completely at the mercy of their oppressors and forced to beg even the food they ate.

> If now we want to live apart from the administrators, we are obliged to pay for the table and for the food which we ourselves have produced. If we want to eat at their table, besides having our allowance cut down more or less, we have to conform our taste, hours and company to suit their tastes which commonly are altogether contrary to our habits, and repugnant to our character and our position. If we want to live apart, one day there will be no meat, another day will see no firewood, and on another the cook will be sick or will have run away, for the Indians do not observe regularity; and, as they see us downed, and without power to employ force, they show us little consideration. Thus we pass a life capable of tiring a saint. We have borne this for three years, but it cannot continue.[49]

Thus, in four years, secularization under the direction of the Californians destroyed the work of three score and five. The Missions that had once been so orderly and flourishing were now

---

[47] Father Durán to Hartnell, May 13, 1839; cf. Engelhardt, op cit., IV, 147.
[48] Father Durán to Father Rubio, March 19, 1839, cf. ibid., IV, 102.
[49] Ibid., IV, 115.

discarded and ruined. Of their temporal estates, nothing remained. The buildings which had sprung up as gems of beauty
in the wilderness were now lying in shambles; the golden crops
that had covered the broad vistas and filled the granaries of the
Missions were gone; and the vast herds of sheep and cattle which
had roamed their ranges were scattered and killed. Worse still,
the Indians who had been raised from the lowest depths of
savagery to a decent level of Christian civilization, were now not
only physically but spiritually dead. Hundreds of them were
dying without the sacraments and whole communities were to be
found where holy Mass had not been heard for years. Well
might one of the friars have cried out:

> All is destruction, all is misery, humiliation and despair. Only
> six years have sufficed not only to annihilate the missions but
> also to destroy in us every hope of restoring these establish-
> ments, reared at the cost of so much toil and sacrifice.[50]

The sight of this universal ruin as well as the oppressions which
they were forced to endure had already killed five of the friars.[51]
Unless relief was quickly offered, despair would overwhelm the
small band of twenty who remained.

III

This relief came in 1839, when in Mexico the government, freed
of external disturbances, turned its attention once again to California, and resumed the project of a diocese. On June 22, 1839,
the ecclesiastical authorities of Mexico City, probably at the request of the government, proposed the names of three candidates
for the new diocese. From among these President Bustamente
selected that of Father Diego as the one best qualified, and instructed the Mexican ambassador at Rome to present his name
to the Holy See along with a petition for the erection of the
new diocese.[52] The report was favorably received and on April

---

[50] Father Rubio to Father Sória, November 3, 1840; cf. Engelhardt, *op. cit.*,
IV, 214.

[51] Bancroft, *op. cit.*, IV, 62.

[52] Engelhardt, *op. cit.*, IV, 190–191.

27, 1840, Pope Gregory XVI separated both Californias from the ecclesiastical jurisdiction of Sonora, and created a distinct diocese with its episcopal see at San Diego and its bishop, Francisco Garcia Diego y Moreno. When the Bulls arrived in Mexico in the early part of September, Father Diego, who had been patiently awaiting action at the College of Guadalupe, Zacatecas, was immediately informed of his selection. After his three years of delay and disappointment, his joy must have been unbounded. He immediately proceeded to the College of San Fernando in Mexico City where he took the constitutional oath before President Bustamente and prepared for his consecration. On Sunday, October 4, 1840, the feast of St. Francis of Assisi, amid the splendor and ceremony of the famous shrine of Guadalupe and before a great concourse of bishops, clergy and faithful, this Franciscan missionary was consecrated Bishop of Both Californias by Archbishop Campo, Coadjutor Archbishop of Mexico City. As its first bishop, California had received a member of that same Order which had given it Junípero Serra.[53]

Once charged with the task of salvaging the ruin which had been caused by the secularization of the Missions, Bishop Diego drew up a well ordered plan of reconstruction. On October 4, he addressed a letter to the government in which he asked that since he could expect little assistance from the small white population of California or the Missions which were in a state of ruin, he be given charge of the Pious Fund as well as the allowances for salary and expenses provided by the decree of 1836. In a second, more lengthy petition of November 7, pointing to the ruin which had been produced by the illegal secularization of the Mission, he asked that the new missions which he hoped to establish be protected by law from a recurrence of these disorders. Likewise, he asked that the houses and gardens of the existing missions be turned over for the use of the priests; that he be given land on which to erect his cathedral, episcopal residence, a seminary, and a college for girls; that the provincials of the Dominicans and Franciscans be instructed to allow their subjects to remain in his diocese until he could obtain secular priests; and,

---

[53] *Ibid.*, IV, 195–200.

finally, that permission should be obtained from Rome to allow him to take along to his diocese as many priests as might desire to accompany him and, likewise, that a license should be obtained permitting him to establish a missionary college which would eventually supply missionaries for new missions among the gentile Indians.[54] His petitions were favorably received by the Mexican authorities and for the most part were readily granted. "On November 2, 1840, the properties of the Pious Fund were surrendered to the Bishop," who appointed a special agent for the rural estates and an attorney to receive the rents, pay the expenses and attend to all the business of the fund.[55] In like manner, in two communications of November 17 and 21, the Secretary of the Interior informed Bishop Diego that the president had instructed Governor Alvarado to restore the Missions and the management of their properties to the friars in accordance with the law of November 7, 1835, which had suspended secularization, and also that the governor had been ordered to assist him in every way in establishing his diocese.[56]

Such assurances of support augured well for the future of the Church in California. The program of reconstruction was almost identical with the plan which Father Durán had first drawn up for the solution of the mission problem. While much havoc had been wrought during the ensuing years, the new diocese, relying for its financial support not on the Missions but on the Pious Fund, could do much to repair the evils of the past. The friars, placed in charge again of the buildings and gardens of the Missions, would not only be freed of obstacles which had been placed in their way by the administrators, but would gradually reorganize both Indians and whites on the parish system. The establishment of educational institutions for both boys and girls would not only supply a long felt need but would do much to raise the moral tone of the country. Finally, the establishment of a missionary college would make possible that mission expansion which the existence of large numbers of pagan Indians de-

[54] *Ibid.*, IV, 203, 205–209.

[55] *United States house documents, Fifty-seventh Congress, No. 4442* (Washington, D. C., 1902), 293, 563.

[56] Engelhardt, *op. cit.*, IV, 209-211.

manded but which had thus far been prevented by the lack of missionaries. Based on the condition and needs of the territory, the plan of reconstruction gave fair promise of success.

More than a year passed before Bishop Diego was able to take possession of his diocese. Besides the delay caused by his dealings with the government, he spent much time in an attempt to obtain recruits for his diocese, finally securing two priests from his own College of Zacatecas, a subdeacon and five seminarians. Accompanied by these he finally set sail in November, 1841, for his distant diocese.[57] His destination was San Diego, designated by Rome as his see. Though it had but one hundred and fifty inhabitants, the episcopal town rose to the occasion and made heroic preparations for the welcome of its Chief Pastor. Indeed, "as early as September 1st the alcade had ordered the streets to be kept clear of cattle, as the Bishop might arrive any day." [58] But when the Bishop finally arrived on December 10, and took possession of his diocese, he found that San Diego was unequal to its high office. Its limited population and lack of resources, and even housing facilities, made it necessary to transfer the see to a more favorable place, and accordingly he chose Santa Barbara.[59] Santa Barbara with its nine hundred inhabitants, though surpassed politically by Monterey, was the oldest and most aristocratic of all the California settlements. Its well finished houses of whitewashed adobes "and the painted balconies and verandas formed a pleasing contrast with the overshadowing roofs blackened with bitumen, the produce of a neighboring spring." [60] The new honor conferred upon the town met with the approval of the greater part of its population and when the Bishop arrived there on January 10, 1842, he was given a welcome that was unsurpassed in the history of the place. As a witness describes it:

The whole population of the place turned out to pay homage to this first Bishop of California. All was bustle; men, women, and children hastening to the beach, banners flying, drums beating, and soldiers marching. At eleven o'clock . . . he came

57 Engelhardt, op. cit., IV, 224, 227.
58 Bancroft, op. cit., IV, 196.
59 Engelhardt, op. cit., IV, 226, 229.
60 Simpson, op. cit., I, 380.

on shore, and was welcomed by the kneeling multitude. All received his benediction, all kissed the pontifical ring. . . . The females had formed with ornamental canes, beautiful arches, through which the procession passed; and as it marched along, the heavy artillery of the presidio continued to thunder forth its noisy welcome. . . . At four o'clock the Bishop was escorted to the Mission and, when a short distance from the town, the enthusiastic inhabitants took the horses from his carriage and dragged it themselves. Halting at the small bower on the road, he alighted, went into it, and put on his pontifical robes; then resuming his place in the carriage, he continued on, amidst the sound of music and the firing of guns, till he arrived at the Church, where he addressed the multitude that followed him.[61]

Such a popular demonstration of faith and enthusiasm made the Bishop confident of success and three weeks later he published a pastoral letter in which he described to his flock "the grand projects which he had formed for the welfare, happiness, and glory of the country"—the seminary, primary schools for the children of both sexes, an academy for girls, a cathedral, and an episcopal residence.[62]   But, unhappily, a change of circumstances soon made the realization of these plans impossible.

Bishop Diego's reconstruction program had been based on financial support, not from California, but from Mexico. Now one of Mexico's recurrent political unheavals swept away this foundation, the Pious Fund. The Bustamente government, after a brief respite from internal disturbances, had been harassed again by a wave of liberal opposition. Led by Gómez Farías its enemies had succeeded in raising the standard of revolt amongst certain classes of the people who had become restless at the over-centralization of the government and a heavy burden of taxation made necessary by an embarrassed treasury. To put down the revolt, Bustamente was obliged to call the various divisions of the army to Mexico City where, once united, three of the leaders formed in their turn a military coalition against the government. On October 7, 1841, they succeeded in ousting Bustamente and in establishing Santa Anna, the instigator of the revolt, as provisional

---

61 Robinson, *op. cit.*, 203–204.

62 Engelhardt, *op. cit.*, IV, 239.

president.[63] Faced with the same financial embarrassments as his predecessor, Santa Anna had recourse to confiscation rather than to taxation. "To cover immediate and additional needs, the Archbishop was obliged to provide $200,000, surrender the inquisition building, and witness the sale of a fine estate formerly belonging to the Jesuits, and subsequently the seizure of the California pious fund." [64] This latter seizure was effected when a decree was issued on February 8, 1842, which repealed the law of 1836 and restored the administration and investment of the Pious Fund to the care of the government.[65]

A few days later on February 23, Bishop Diego's agent was obliged to turn over his accounts to the government agents, under whose direction the properties of the Fund were sold and the $600,000 obtained therefrom incorporated into the public treasury. Santa Anna made a show at compensation by ordering that the tobacco revenue should be pledged for the support of the diocese, but his pledge was never carried out.[66] In reality, Bishop Diego found himself a month after his arrival at Santa Barbara deprived of all means of support, both for himself, his dependent seminarians, and the priests of his diocese. After his bright visions of the future, it was a blow from which he never fully recovered.

For a time he hoped that the Californians would be willing to support him as enthusiastically as they had welcomed him. On January 20, 1843, he inaugurated a system of tithes whereby "all the members of his diocese, except the Indians of the missions, were to pay tithes from the products of the fields and orchards, from the yearly increase of the live-stock, and from the grape-wine, brandy, and olive oil." [67] But it soon became apparent that this measure would fail. Of the five thousand who composed the white population of the territory, the vast majority were too poor to make substantial contributions. The Californians of that day possessed "the almost universal Hispanic American proclivity

[63] Priestley, op. cit., 294; Callcott, op. cit., 122–128.
[64] Bancroft, History of Mexico, V, 239.
[65] For full translation cf. Engelhardt, op. cit., IV, 242–243.
[66] Bancroft, History of California, IV, 336–337.
[67] Engelhardt, op. cit., IV, 247.

for gambling, and drank heavily of very nearly raw liquor, as well as of fine wines when they could get them." [68] As a result of these two evils, they were "indolent, and withal had so much pride, as to make them look upon manual labor as degrading." [69] As Robinson described it: "You might as well expect a sloth to leave a tree that has an inch of bark left upon its trunk, as to expect a Californian to labor, whilst a *real* glistened in his pocket!" [70] While their enthusiastic reception of the Bishop might have indicated their willingness of spirit, their scanty means prohibited any substantial contributions to his support.

But although the poor were unable to contribute to the support of the diocese, the wealthy Californians who had been enriched by the confiscation of the mission properties and by the hide and tallow trade in which they engaged were in a position to support it. But they refused absolutely to assist Bishop Diego and his dependents. From the beginning they had shown themselves hostile to him. The spirit of their antagonism is revealed in the following comment which Vallejo made on the occasion of his arrival:

> The coming of the bishop is going to cause much trouble. The priests are beside themselves with pride, and begin to fulminate sentences of excommunication, etc., relying on that prelate. Poor crazy fools, if they think they can browbeat the leading men of California. The age of theocratic domination is past. However, Californians who have never seen bishops will now know how they dress and observe their ceremonies. If they intended to plant new missions among the savages, some good might result; but nothing is further from the minds of the priests.[71]

It had early become evident that no aid could be expected from these men who had despoiled the Missions, for when the Bishop after his arrival presented Alvarado with the government's order for the restoration of the mission buildings and gardens to the

---

[68] Chapman, *op. cit.*, 390.

[69] Wilkes, Charles, *Narrative of the United States exploring expedition* (Philadelphia, 1844), V, 181.

[70] *Op. cit.*, 150.

[71] Bancroft, *op. cit.*, IV, 196, note 13.

friars, he refused to apply it.[72]   Apparently, they were opposed
to Bishop Diego because they feared that he would deprive them
of their ill-gotten riches.   As a result, when he appealed to them
for tithes they were unanimous in their refusal, as was illustrated
by Vallejo's conduct in the north.   Haughtily referring to the
Bishop as "an Indian priest from Oaxaca," [73] he refused "to contribute a single centavo or to allow the tithes to be collected in
his district." [74]

Completely at the mercy of such scoundrels, the bishop was
faced with starvation and his diocese with ruin.   At the end of
a year the appeal for tithes produced only $1,700, and the Bishop
and his small band of seminarians were left with scarcely the
bare means of subsistence and his priests at the various missions
completely under the power of the rascally administrators.   For
a time he tried to carry out part of his plans, attempting a visitation of his diocese and the construction of a seminary.   But
though he made every effort, even joining in the labor of carrying stones and other building materials,[75] he was obliged to
abandon the project.

> Large piles of stones were heaped up in several places for
> laying the foundations of the above-named edifices, but as the
> Mexican government has seen proper to appropriate this fund
> to less pious purposes, there they will undoubtedly remain for
> some years as monuments to the frailty of human speculations.[76]

The infant diocese was undoubtedly on the verge of extinction
and in his despair Bishop Diego sent a heartrending appeal to
Mexico for assistance.   His description of the California situation reveals the sad condition to which the state of religion had
been reduced:

> Many churches have had to be closed, in other Divine Wor-
> ship is scantily maintained, and the missionaries are decreas-

---

[72] *Ibid.*, IV, 330.
[73] Vallejo, *Historia de California*, MS., IV, 91.
[74] *Ibid.*, IV, 78.
[75] Vallejo, *ut supra*, IV, 74.
[76] Robinson, *op. cit.*, 239.

ing for want of substitutes so that now they have been reduced to twenty, including the sick and aged whose resources are cut off. Instead of being able to support and civilize the savages, they are obliged to beg for their subsistence, bewail the dispersion of the neophytes, and the annihilation of the settlements they founded. . . . He found himself without even an ordinary habitation in which to live, without the means even of making a visitation of his extensive diocese, though he had twice made the attempt, but had to desist for want of funds to defray the expenses. In fact, he was without any resources whatsoever. It was much to be feared that, in the event of his death, the Holy See would decline to appoint a successor, since there was no means of subsistence.[77]

Such disheartening conditions were in strange contrast to the promising picture of the year previous.

But fortunately Bishop Diego did not have to wait for assistance from Mexico. The rule of the Californians was brought to a close by the arrival of a new governor from Mexico on August 25, 1842. The new ruler, Manuel Micheltorena, gradually put down the rivalries which had been disturbing the territory and restored once again the supremacy of law and its consequent peace.[78] To him Bishop Diego now turned and asked that the presidential order of 1840, restoring the Missions to the friars, be enforced. The governor, himself a witness of the dire straits to which the Bishop was reduced, accordingly issued a decree on March 26, 1843, restoring the Missions to the control of the friars. From an analysis of the decree, it would seem that the measure was a compromise. Its author recognized the evils which had been wrought by secularization,—the demoralization and dispersion of the neophytes, the frauds and extravagances of the administrators, the decline of agriculture and economic progress, and the impoverishment of the friars and the ruin of religion. Yet, the governor, mindful perhaps of the danger involved therein, ordered that the properties which had been alienated should be left undisturbed in the possession of their present holders. Only the remnants of the Missions, their buildings and whatever lands and live-stock still remained, were

---

[77] Engelhardt, *op. cit.*, IV, 254.
[78] Chapman, *op. cit.*, 480–481.

to be turned over to the friars.   Restored to their former position, they were to collect the scattered neophytes, provided those
of them who were in private service could get the consent of their
masters, organize them on the old basis of community life and
labor, and, what is significant, "pay to the treasury . . . for the
sustenance and clothing of the troops and the needs of the civil
officials, one-eighth part of the total annual produce and revenue
of every kind.[79]   The decree was intended to be in the interest of
the local government as well as of the diocese.

The restoration of the Missions provided the diocese with a
basis of stability which it had lost when the Pious Fund was confiscated.   The possession of the mission churches and the adjoin-
ing residences secured the friars from the attacks of the administrators while "with the small remnant of cattle and implements
left from the general wreck, with the few Indians whom past
changes had left in the communities, and with the temporary use
of such poor lands as had not yet been granted, they might now
toil to support themselves." [80]   It is true that Bishop Diego had
to abandon his ambitious program of reconstruction.   But he was
enabled to build on this new foundation that had been given him
and to organize the Church in California along diocesan lines.

During the next two years the Bishop and his priests gradually,
and it might be added, successfully, adjusted themselves to the
new arrangement.   During 1843 Bishop Diego, accompanied by
his secretary, visited and confirmed at all the southern missions
and the next year completed his visitation by journeying as far
north as San Francisco, though he was forced to avoid the Upper
Bay region because of Vallejo's hostility.   Though not the tri-
umphal march that it would have been fifteen years earlier, the
visitation of the Bishop was met with an enthusiasm that gave
evidence of a strengthening of the Church's position in the territory.   At Los Angeles Governor Micheltorena had added unusual
splendor to the Corpus Christi procession at which the Bishop
officiated.   After making a public profession of Faith, he and
his "California Battalion" had formed amid the salutes of cannon
a military escort for the Blessed Sacrament.   In like manner, when

---

[79] For full translation cf. Engelhardt, *op. cit.*, IV, 272–276.
[80] Tays, *ut supra*, 471.

the Bishop visited Monterey, all the houses were illuminated in his honor for a period of three days and the town decked out in holiday spirit. Contrasted with his first trying year in the diocese, such displays of loyalty gave him confidence in the future.[81]

But perhaps his greatest assurance for the future was the seminary which he succeeded in establishing in 1844. Since his arrival in the territory, Bishop Diego had quartered his small band of seminarians at Mission Santa Barbara under the care of Father Sánchez, who filled the double rôle of superior and professor. But this arrangement had proved unsatisfactory, as there was no guarantee for the continued existence of the theological school. Accordingly, on the occasion of his visit to Monterey, the Bishop petitioned Governor Micheltorena for a grant of land to be used for the establishment and maintenance of a diocesan seminary. The petition met with favor and resulted in a grant of eight leagues of land within the district of Mission Santa Ines. With this foundation of over 35,000 acres, the seminary was assured. The seminarians took over the buildings at the mission and on May 4, 1844, after a Pontifical High Mass, Bishop Diego read the constitutions and established the Seminary of Our Lady of Guadalupe. With its staff of three professors and a student body of seven, the infant institution served as the seed whence would spring the later Franciscan and diocesan seminaries of California. It was Bishop Diego's greatest contribution to the Church of the future.[82]

When the year 1844 drew to a close, the attempt at reconstruction seemed certain of a fair measure of success. The diocese had recovered from the first blow which the confiscation of the Pious Fund had dealt it, and now found itself on the inferior yet equally firm basis of the repossessed mission properties. The original plans and projects had been necessarily abandoned, but in their place had come an order that satisfied the simple needs of the territory and its limited population. The Diocese of Both Californias was in the pioneer stage but, like other pioneer dioceses, it gave promise of a gradual growth hand in hand with the

---

[81] Engelhardt, op. cit., IV, 259, 263–267, 280.
[82] Ibid., IV, 261–263.

development of the country. This would have been its story had not the unforeseen intervened and cast its shadow of turmoil and death over the diocese and its bishop.

This interruption in the progress of the diocese was occasioned, as had previously been the case, by a return of the Californians to power. The political leaders of the territory, ever opposed in their nativism to Mexican rule and probably dissatisfied over the removal of their henchmen from the lucrative positions of mission administrators, buried the differences which had hitherto divided them and in November, 1844, raised the standard of revolt against Micheltorena. The pretext was found in the increasing depredations of the governor's army which, composed of convicts from the jails of Mexico and Jalisco, had done much to embitter the population against the home government. After several months of marching and counter-marching, Micheltorena was defeated on February 22, 1845, and forced to resign the governorship. When, shortly afterwards, he left the country, there passed with him the last vestige of Mexican rule and, as events were to prove, the last mainstay of peace.[83]

The resumption of power by the native politicians plunged the territory once more into an imbroglio of petty intrigue and sectional strife. While harmony still existed, the leadership in the government was divided between Pío Pico as civil governor and José Castro as military commandant. But dissension between the north and the south arose when Pico removed the capital to Los Angeles, while Castro and the provincial treasurer and custom-house officials remained at Monterey. As a result, "there were constant disagreements about the division of revenues; the finances of the government became hopelessly involved; debts piled up and salaries were seldom paid." [84] Pico headed the civil government but was without revenues to support it. He therefore turned to the remnants of the mission system as the means of relief from financial embarrassment.

On March 18, 1845, only three weeks after he had assumed

---

[83] Chapman, *op. cit.,* 482–483.

[84] Hunt, Rockwell D. and Sánchez, Nellie, *Short history of California* (New York, 1929), 278.

power, the new governor informed the prefects of the two missionary bands that "the less prosperous missions would be sold,
and those having more extensive property leased . . . for the
benefit of the natives exclusively." [85]   The death sentence had
been passed and it was not long before the blow was dealt. Ignor-
ing Bishop Diego and the protests of the friars, Pico and his
legislature passed in rapid succession a series of laws for the disposal of the missions.   First appeared on April 19, a decree
ordering an inventory of "the debts and assets of each mission,
and of the resources from which the debts may be paid." Then
followed, on May 28, an order providing for the sale or leasing
of the various missions at public auction.   The legislation was
completed by a final decree of October 28, which set their sale
for the first days of December and January.[86]   The days prescribed arrived and on the fourth and fifth of December three
missions were sold for $2,330 and four others leased for a period
of nine years at the rate of $4,530 a year.   It was evident that
the mission system was at an end.[87]

The sale of the mission properties brought disaster to the diocese and its priests.   Although Pico in his various laws had
promised that the products of the rents would be divided into
three equal parts, one to be used "for the maintenance of the
Rev. Father Minister and the conservation of divine worship," [88]
these promises were soon forgotten.   At the seven missions which
had already been sold or leased, the friars found themselves deprived of their last means of support, their neophytes scattered
or hired by new masters as cheap labor, and themselves depending on the charity of strangers.   What happened under these circumstances may be inferred from a letter which the Bishop sent
Pico, informing him of the "molestation inflicted upon the priest
at San Luis Obispo" by the three purchasers of the mission, James
Scott, John Wilson, and James McKinley.   Seeking to derive as
much profit as possible from their purchase, they had ordered
the young Father Gomez, whom Bishop Diego had but recently

[85] Engelhardt, *op. cit.*, IV, 341.
[86] *Ibid.*, IV, 353, 374, 450.
[87] *Ibid.*, IV, 459–460.
[88] *Ibid.*, IV, 374.

ordained, "to surrender the parts of the buildings which he needed,
and which for some time he had been occupying." [89]

The tragedy which had occurred and the sadness which filled
the heart of the Bishop can be best set forth in his own pathetic
words:

> Four years have passed by since I began to govern this new
> diocese. During that time, what has my heart not suffered!
> San Solano, San Rafael, San Francisco, San Antonio, San Juan
> Capistrano, etc., are without priests! How can a pastor see his
> children, his beloved sheep, dying without confession, without
> the last indispensable succors? How must it not penetrate my
> vitals, and pierce my soul, to contemplate the many who die
> without Baptism, or the long time that may elapse before the
> children can be brought to where a priest lives, or before the
> priest can reach those abandoned places? Could I rest easy
> when I behold the multitude of unhappy Indians who, on ac-
> count of the ruin of the missions, have given up attending re-
> ligious instructions, holy Mass, the Sacraments and every act of
> Religion, and who, having joined the savages, already live as
> they do, or even in a worse manner; and who, demoralized as
> they are, have given themselves to robberies, drunkenness, mur-
> der, and every kind of licentiousness? Could I remain in-
> different while I think of these multitudes who die in this
> wretched state? . . . I behold this my beloved diocese in the
> same condition as a sick man who takes not the medicine and
> scoffs at the most skilful physicians. Without funds, without
> tithes, without priests, and without the hope that any may want
> to come, since they are aware how those fare who are here,
> without schools and without the means to establish them, in
> short, without anything upon which to base hope, it is impos-
> sible to advance, and so the diocese is on its way to destruction.[90]

In the face of these circumstances, the Mexican authorities
made a belated attempt to save the diocese. The reign of Santa

---

[89] *Ibid.*, IV, 513. Citizens of the United States had taken up residence in
California as early as the second decade of the nineteenth century. These early
settlers became identified with the country through business relations, friend-
ship, and marriage, a number of them even joining the Church. But the later
American immigrants were of a different mind. Trappers, vagabond sailors,
adventurers or even outlaws, "they brought with them an instinctive prejudice
against everything of Spanish origin." Cleland, Robert G., *History of California: the American period* (New York, 1922), 190.

[90] *Ibid.*, IV, 398–399.

Anna had been of short duration, for his administration had been of the most barefaced corruptness.

> He and his entourage were guilty of the most open immorality.   Graft lost all vestiges of refinement.   Huge sums expended in pleasures led to demands upon the people for still greater sums . . . In his personal dress and bearing the dictator displayed a presumptuous elegance that was irritating, and in his demands for money he aroused more than suspicion of his intention to do nothing for the country.[91]

As a result the country rose in revolt and on December 5, 1844, installed José Joaquín Herrera as chief executive.   Although the government was still in the hands of the liberals, it took no rash steps immediately and seemed to be conciliatory to the Church.[92] When therefore it was informed of the disaster that was threatening Bishop Diego and his diocese, it immediately took steps to aid him.   On April 3, 1845, President Herrera issued an executive order restoring "the assets and other properties of the Pious Fund which may remain unsold" to the Bishop and his successors.[93] Likewise, when news reached Mexico of Pico's confiscation and sale of the Missions, the government immediately forwarded an order instructing him to suspend all sales of the mission property. Dated November 14, 1845, it read as follows:

> His Excellency, the President, has received information that the Government of your Department has ordered to be put up for sale all the property pertaining to the Missions of said department which your predecessor had ordered to be returned to the respective missionaries for the management and administration of their temporalities.   Therefore, he has been pleased to direct me to say that the said Government will report on those particulars, suspending immediately all proceedings respecting the alienation of the before-mentioned property until the Supreme Government has reached a resolution.[94]

But, unhappily, neither of these measures was of any relief to the Bishop or his diocese.   The Herrera government was in its turn overthrown on December 30, 1845, by a revolt of the army

---

91 Priestley, op. cit., 296.
92 Callcott, op. cit., 137–138.
93 Engelhardt, op. cit., IV, 403–404.
94 Ibid., IV, 455.

which installed its leader, General Paredes, as the new president.[95] Paredes forgot the promises of his predecessor and neglected to restore the Pious Fund to the California diocese. "There are extant no figures to show what property if any was turned over to the bishop's agent under this decree; nor is there any record to show additional payments in 1845–6 of interest due from the government on the proceeds of past sales." [96]   In like manner, when the decree suspending the sale of the Missions arrived in California in April, 1846, Pico and his associates ignored it altogether.   Shortly afterwards, between May 4 and July 4, twelve of the remaining missions were illegally sold to private individuals for the sum of $64,937, plus the liquidation of an unknown amount of debts.[97]   The program of secularization was completed and the Missions ceased to exist.

Fortunately, a kind fate spared the two pillars of the Church in California from the pain of witnessing this final tragedy. Brokenhearted and discouraged because of the neglect of the Mexican government and weighed down with grief over the spiritual demoralization of his beloved diocese, Bishop Diego had been rapidly failing in health.   Foreseeing the end, he ordained three of his seminarians on January 1, 1846, to fill the vacancies in his diocese. By April he was confined to his bed, and finally at midnight on Thursday, April 30, after receiving the last Sacraments, he passed to his reward, four days before the final sale of the Missions was begun.[98]   A little more than four weeks later, on June 1, 1846, that other pillar of the Church, Father Durán, followed his bishop to the grave.   Both had labored courageously and had planned earnestly for the welfare of the Missions and their neophytes. By their sacrifices and untiring zeal they had defended them when enemies sought their destruction.   But now, quite symbolically, when these two sturdy columns were removed by death, "the whole mission structure collapsed and buried them in its dust.   The missionaries and the missions had now become extinct." [99]

But although secularization brought destruction and death to

---

95 Bancroft, *History of Mexico*, V, 290–292.

96 Bancroft, *History of California*, IV, 554.

97 Engelhardt, *op. cit.*, IV, 507–508.

98 *Ibid.*, IV, 516–518.

99 Tays, *ut supra*, 494.

the Missions, it did not crush the Church in California. Five weeks after Father Durán's death a new series of events began which changed the entire course of California history, both civil and religious. On July 7, 1846, American forces occupied Monterey and annexed California to the United States; and two years later the discovery of gold in one of the cañons of the Sierras started a migration from all corners of the world which increased almost at a stroke the population of the territory to over 100,000 and transformed it overnight into a modern American State. "The quiet, dreamy life of the old Mission days was at an end; a new California, born of full age and armed for every enterprise, had taken its place." [100]   The diocesan organization which Bishop Diego had established on the ruins of the mission system gave the Church a basis of stability in the midst of these revolutionary changes and enabled it to grow hand in hand with the new order. From the germ of life that it preserved there sprang a new and more numerous diocesan clergy to continue the glorious traditions of the Franciscan missionaries; in the place of the lost mission congregations there arose well organized parishes of a new generation of Catholics; from the See of San Diego there eventually grew an archdiocese with three suffragan sees in California; and, finally, with the assistance of a government which was established on the basis of law and freedom, the Church regained what it had lost,—its cherished Missions and the Pious Fund. [101]

---

[100] Eldredge, Zoeth S., *History of California* (New York, 1915), III, 320.

[101] Cf. Geary, Gerald J., "The transfer of ecclesiastical jurisdiction in California, 1840–1853", *Historical Records and Studies: The United States Catholic Historical Society*, XXII (1932), 137 ss.

BIBLIOGRAPHY

I. BIBLIOGRAPHICAL AIDS

California Mission history is but a segment of the great field of Hispanic American history. A valuable bibliography of the bibliographies of this general field will be found in Cecil K. Jones, *Hispanic American bibliographies, including collective biographies, histories of literature and selected general works . . ., with critical notes on sources by José Toribio Medina* (Baltimore, 1922). Of practical value to the graduate student, for its discussion and evaluation of the noteworthy general books and the special volumes on each region, is A. Curtis Wilgus, *The histories of Hispanic America, in Bibliographical series,* no. 9 (Pan American Union, Washington, D. C., 1932). A valuable guide to the general field of mission history in Hispanic America will be found in volumes II and III (*Americanische missionsliteratur*) of Rob. Streit's, O. M. I. monumental *Bibliotheca Missionum* (Munster, 7 vols., 1916–1931).

The unpublished documentation for the particular field of California Mission history is listed in: Herbert E. Bolton, *Guide to materials for the history of the United States in the principal archives of Mexico* (Washington, D. C., 1913), and Charles E. Chapman, *Catalogue of materials in the Archivo General de Indias for the history of the Pacific Coast and the American Southwest* (Berkeley, 1919). The supplement to these two guides is James A. Robertson, *List of documents in Spanish archives relating to the history of the United States which have been printed or of which transcripts are preserved in American libraries* (Washington, D. C., 1907). To control the many documents and transcripts which have been added since 1907, recourse should be had to the individual catalogues of the various American libraries.

Ambrose P. Dietz, *Biblioteca Californiae* (Sacramento, 2 vols., 1870–1871; revised, 1930), and University of California, *Spain and Spanish America in the libraries of the University of California* (Berkeley, 2 vols., 1928–1930), serve both as catalogues for documentary sources housed in the State and University libraries, and also as bibliographies of printed Californiana. The latter is particularly valuable for its title and topically arranged subject index. A more recent bibliography and "unquestionably one of the most valuable tools in existence for students of California history" is Robert Ernest and Robert Grannis Cowan, *A bibliography of the history of California, 1510–1930* (San Francisco, 3 vols., 1933). As supplements to these general bibliographies the following descriptive lists are of special value: J. Lloyd Mecham, "The northern expansion of New Spain, 1522–1822: a selected descriptive bibliographical list," *The Hispanic American Historical Review,* VII (1927), 233–276; Henry R. Wagner, *The Spanish southwest, 1542–1794: an annotated bibliography* (Berkeley, 1924) ; Willard O. Waters, "California bibliographies," *California Historical Society Quarterly,* III (1924), 245–259. Finally, a general catalogue of periodical articles will be found in the following series of theses written for the degree of Master of Arts at the University of California: Doris W. Bepler, *Descriptive catalogue of western historical materials in California periodicals, 1854–1890;* Esther H. Jensen, *A history of California periodical literature from 1891–1898, together with a descriptive catalogue of materials for western history in the most important magazines of the period;* Olive F. Smith, *A history of California periodical literature from 1899–1906, together with etc.;* Mary H. Tobin, *A history of California periodical literature, from 1907–1914, together with etc.* Unfortunately, none of these catalogues have been published. The manuscript copies, however, can easily be had at the library of the University of California.

II. MANUSCRIPT SOURCES

The chief source of archival material for California mission history was the *Archivo de Californias,* MS., 273 vols. This collection was kept in the United States Surveyor-General's Office at San Francisco with the result that, at the time of the fire in 1906, many of the documents were destroyed. However, many of the more important materials in this collection had been previously copied by Hubert Howe Bancroft and his associates, and are at present preserved in the Bancroft Library of the University of California. These materials are catalogued in volume II of *Spain and Spanish America in the libraries of the University of California.* A useful guide will also be found in Tays, *Revolutionary California,* MS. 790–795. The two other important depots of manuscript materials for mission history are the Franciscan Archives at Mission Santa Barbara and the Cathedral Archives of San Francisco, at which latter the collection entitled, *Archivo del Arzobispado de San Francisco,* MS., 5 vols., was consulted. In the Bancroft Library the following manuscript sources were of special value in the study of the secularization of the California missions:

Alvarado, Juan Bautista, *Historia de California,* 5 vols.
Copia del expediente con que se dió cuenta en la primera junta de California, celebrada ante el Exmo. Sr. Virrey Don Juan Ruiz de Apodaca, en 5 de Julio de 1817.
Guerra y Noriega, Jose de la, *Documentos para la historia de California,* MS., 6 vols.
Legislative records, MS., 4 vols.
Ord, Mrs. Augustias de la Guerra, *Ocurrencias en California,* MS.
Pico, Pio, *Documentos para la historia de California,* MS., 2 vols.
State papers, missions and colonization, MS., 2 vols.
Vallejo, Mariano Guadalupe, *Historia de California,* MS., 5 vols.

III. PRINTED SOURCES

It would be beyond the purpose of this work to attempt a survey of the numerous collections of printed sources containing materials for a general history of the missions in Hispanic America. For the brief sketch which forms the introductory chapter of the present volume an important printed source was *Instrucciones que los virreyes de Nueva España dejaron a sus sucesores* (México, 1867). Containing the advice of one viceroy to another for a period of over two centuries, it is of particular value in the study of secularization. Of equal importance is the *Recopilación de leyes de los reinos de las Indias* (Madrid, 1681). A compilation of Spanish colonial legislation, it contains much material for a general history of the missions. The writer also made use of materials found in the two following collections of sources: Nels A. Clevens, *Readings in Hispanic American history* (Boston, 1927); and Charles W. Hackett, ed., *Historical documents relating to New Mexico, Nueva Vizcaya, and approaches thereto, to 1773, collected by Adolph F. and Fanny R. Bandelier* (Washington, D. C., 2 vols., 1923–1926).

For the Mexican approach to the question of secularization in California an important collection of printed sources is *Las misiones de la Alta California*. (Archivo y biblioteca de la Secretaría de Hacienda: colección de documentos históricos, tomo II, Mexico City, 1914). This collection, published by the Mexican government, contains several hitherto unprinted sources of primary importance for the study of the Tamariz Memorial and the *Primera Junta* which it occasioned. Of equal importance are the printed reports of the second *Junta* assembled in the volume entitled: *Junta de fomento de Californias: Colección de los principales trabajos en que se ha ocupado la junta nombrada para meditar y proponer al supremo gobierno los medios mas necesarios para promover el progreso de la cultura y civilización de los territorios de la Alta y de la Baja California* (Mexico City, 1827). Of the seven reports which compose this volume, three of them are concerned with the secularization of the California Missions. The Mexican government's attitude towards the Missions is also revealed in the *Memorias de relaciones* (Mexico City, 1822–). Containing the annual reports of this cabinet officer to Congress, the *Memorias* frequently make mention of the California Missions. Those of 1823 and 1826 are of special importance to the study of secularization. Finally, mention must be made of Herbert E. Bolton, "The Iturbide revolution in the Californias," *The Hispanic American Historical Review,* II (1919), 182–242. Containing the reports and instructions which passed between Canon Fernández and the government at Mexico City on the occasion of the former's mission to the Californias, it throws new light on independent Mexico's attitude towards the Spanish missions.

While there is much printed material of a primary nature which treats of the Missions from the California viewpoint, the writer must confine his treatment to the printed sources which deal specifically with the question of their secularization. Under this heading, a work of great importance is Zephyrin Engelhardt, O.F.M., *The missions and missionaries of California* (San Francisco, 4 vols., 1908–1915). A separate volume with the same title, issued at San Francisco in 1916, contains the index to volumes II-IV. While intended primarily as a history, the chief value of Father Engelhardt's work lies in the fact that it is the "great chronological source book of mission history," in which the greater portion of the writings of the friars themselves, especially those preserved in the Santa Barbara Archives, have been translated and edited. Of value for the beginnings of secularization, is *Historical memoirs of New California by Fray Francisco Palóu*, O.F.M., translated and edited by Dr. Herbert E. Bolton (Berkeley, 4 vols., 1926). For the same period, two others of Dr. Bolton's scholarly works are of primary importance, namely: *Anza's California expeditions* (Berkeley, 5 vols., 1930) ; and *Fray Juan Crespi, missionary explorer on the Pacific coast, 1769–1774* (Berkeley, 1927).

Lastly, of special value are the printed narratives of eye-witnesses who either as foreign residents or visitors recorded their impressions of California, often with greater accuracy and fairness than the native chroniclers themselves. Of these the following contemporary narratives contain materials for the study of secularization:

Beechey, Frederick W., *Narrative of a voyage to the Pacific and Beering's Strait . . . in the years 1825, 26, 27, 28* (London, 2 vols., 1831).

Dana, Richard H., *Two years before the mast* (New York, 1840).

Duflot de Mofras, Eugène, *Exploration du territoire de l'Orégon, des Californias et de la mer Vermeille exécutée pendant les années 1840, 1841 et 1842* (Paris, 2 vols., 1844).

Duhaut-Cilly, Auguste, *Voyage autour du monde, principalement a la Californie et aux Iles Sandwich, pendant les années 1826, 1827, 1828 et 1829* (Paris, 2 vols., 1834–1835).

"Duhaut-Cilly's Account of California in the years 1827–1828," translated from the French by Charles F. Carter, *California Historical Society Quarterly*, VIII (1929), 130–166; 214–250; 306–356.

Forbes, Alexander, *California: a history of Upper and Lower California from their first discovery to the present time . . .* (London, 1839; reprinted, San Francisco, 1919).

Kotzebue, Otto von, *A new voyage round the world, in the years 1823–26* (London, 2 vols., 1830).

Langsdorff, George Heinrich von, *Langsdorff's narrative of the Resanov voyage to Nueva California in 1806,* translated and edited by Thomas C. Russell (San Francisco, 1927).

La Perouse, Jean Francois Galaup de, *A voyage round the world, performed in the years 1785–88* (London, 2 vols., 1799).

Morrell, B., *A narrative of four voyages to the South Sea, North and South Pacific Ocean, 1822–31* (New York, 1832).

Robinson, Alfred, *Life in California* (New York, 1846; reprinted, San Francisco, 1925).

Simpson, Sir George, *Narrative of a journey round the world during the years 1841 and 1842* (London, 2 vols., 1847).

Vancouver, George, *A voyage of discovery to the North Pacific Ocean and round the world, 1790–1795* (London, 6 vols., 1801).

Wilkes, Charles, *Narrative of the United States exploring expedition, 1838–1842* (Philadelphia, 5 vols., 1844).

IV. GENERAL WORKS

Alamán, Lucas, *Historia de Méjico desde los primeros moviemientos que prepararon su independencia* (México, 1849–1852), 5 vols.

Arnold, Brother F. S., *The Paraguay reductions* (M.A. thesis, MS., Catholic University of America, 1916).

Bancroft, Hubert Howe, *History of California* (San Francisco, 1884–1890), 7 vols.

——, *History of Mexico* (San Francisco, 1883–1887), 6 vols.

——, *History of the North Mexican states and Texas* (San Francisco, 1884–1889), 2 vols.

——, *History of Arizona and New Mexico* (San Francisco, 1889).

——, *Chronicle of the builders of the commonwealth* (San Francisco, 1891–1892), 8 vols.

Blackmar, Frank W., *Spanish colonization in the Southwest* (Baltimore, 1890).

Bolton, Herbert E., *Texas in the middle eighteenth century: studies in Spanish colonial history and administration* (Berkeley, 1915).

——, *The Spanish borderlands; a chronicle of old Florida and the Southwest* (New Haven, 1921).

——, "Defensive Spanish expansion and the significance of the borderlands," in *The trans-Mississippi west* (Boulder, University of Colorado, 1930).

Bolton, Herbert E., and Marshall, Thomas M., *The colonization of North America, 1492–1783* (New York, 1920).

Bourne, Edward G., *Spain in America, 1450–1580*, in *The American nation: a history*, vol. III (New York, 1904).

Callcott, Wilfred H., *Church and State in Mexico, 1822–1857* (Durham, N. C., 1926).

Caughey, John W., *History of the Pacific Coast* (Los Angeles, 1933).

Chapman, Charles E., *A history of Spain* (New York, 1919).

——, *The founding of Spanish California, 1687–1783* (New York, 1916).

——, *A history of California: the Spanish period* (New York, 1921).

——, *Colonial Hispanic America: a history* (New York, 1933).

Cleland, Robert G., *A history of California: the American period* (New York, 1922).

——, *Pathfinders.* Of the series *California*, edited by John R. McCarthy (San Francisco and Chicago, 1929).

Cuevas, Mariano, S. J., *Historia de la Iglesia en México* (El Paso, Texas, 1928), 5 vols.

Denis, Alberta J., *Spanish Alta California* (New York, 1927).

Dwinelle, John W., *The colonial history of the city of San Francisco* (San Francisco, 1863).

Eldredge, Zoeth S., *The beginnings of San Francisco from the expedition of Anza, 1774, to the city charter of April 15, 1850* (San Francisco, 1912).

——, *History of California* (New York, 1915), 5 vols.

Fisher, Lillian E., *Viceregal administration in the Spanish-American colonies,* in University of California, *Publications in history,* XV (Berkeley, 1926).

Forrest, Earle R., *Missions and pueblos in the old Southwest* (Cleveland, 1929).

Gentry, Mildred D., *Expulsion of the Spaniards from Mexico, 1810–1836* (M.A. thesis, MS., University of California, 1931).

Graham, Cunningham, *A vanished arcadia* (London, 1901).

Halleck, Henry W., *Report on land titles in California* (San Francisco, 1860).

Hanley, Rev. Maurus R., O.S.B., *Relations of the Spanish government to the American Indians* (M.A. thesis, MS., Catholic University of America, 1929).

Helps, Sir Arthur, *The Spanish conquest of America and its relation to the history of slavery and to the government of colonies* (London, 1855–1861), 4 vols.

Hittell, Theodore, *History of California* (San Francisco, 1898), 4 vols.

Hunt, Rockwell D., and Sánchez, Nellie, *A short history of California* (New York, 1929).

James, H. G., and Martin, P. A., *The republics of Latin America* (New York, 1918).

Jones, William C., *Report on the subject of land titles in California* (Washington, D. C., 1850).

Kroeber, Alfred L., *Handbook of the Indians of California* (Washington, D. C., 1925).

Lopez, Pelaez, *El derecho y la Iglesia* (Madrid, 1917).

Mecham, J. Lloyd, *Church and State in Latin America: a history of politico-ecclesiastical relations* (Chapel Hill, N. C., 1934).

Merriman, Roger B., *The rise of the Spanish empire in the old world and the new* (New York, 1918–1925), 3 vols.

Moses, Bernard, *The establishment of Spanish rule in America* (New York, 1898).

——, *South America on the eve of emancipation* (New York, 1908).

——, *The Spanish dependencies in South America* (New York, 1914), 2 vols.

O'Rourke, Thomas P., *The Franciscan missions in Texas, 1690–1793,* in Catholic University of America, *Studies in American church history,* V (Washington, D. C., 1927).

Parras, Pedro J., *Gobierno de los regulares de la América* (Madrid, 1783), 2 vols.

Pastor, Ludwig von, *History of the Popes,* translated by Frederick Antrobus (St. Louis, 1898–1932), 22 vols.

Poinsett, Joel R., *Notes on Mexico, made in the autumn of 1822* (London, 1825).

Prescott, William H., *The conquest of Mexico* (New York, 1843), 3 vols.

Priestley, Herbert I., *José de Gálvez, visitor-general to New Spain, 1765–1771*, in University of California, *Publications in history*, V (Berkeley, 1916).

——, *The Mexican nation, a history* (New York, 1923).

——, *The coming of the white man, 1492–1848*, in *A history of American life*, I (New York, 1929).

Radin, Paul, *The story of the American Indian* (New York, 1927).

Ricard, Robert, *La conquête spirituelle due Mexique: essai sur l'apostolet et les méthodes missionaires des Ordres Mendiants in Nouvelle Espagne de 1523–24 à 1572* (Paris, 1933).

Richman, Irving B., *California under Spain and Mexico, 1533–1847* (Boston and New York, 1911).

Roscher, Wilhelm, *The Spanish colonial system*, translated and edited by Edward G. Bourne (New York, 1904).

Ryan, Edwin, *The Church in the South American republics* (Milwaukee, 1932).

Sanchez, Nellie (Van de Grift), *Spanish arcadia*, in the series *California*, edited by John R. McCarthy (San Francisco and Chicago, 1929).

Schmidlin, Joseph, *Catholic mission history* (Techny, Ill., 1933).

Shea, John G., *History of the Catholic missions among the Indian tribes of the United States, 1529–1854* (New York, 1855).

——, *History of the Catholic Church in the United States* (New York, 1886–1892), 4 vols.

Simpson, Lesley B., *The encomienda in New Spain, 1490–1550*, in University of California, *Publications in history*, XIX (Berkeley, 1929).

Snead-Cox, John G., *The life of Cardinal Vaughan* (St. Louis, 1910), 2 vols.

Solorzano Pereira, Joannes de, *De Indiarum jure* (Lyons, 1672), 2 vols.

Tays, George, *Revolutionary California: the political history of California during the Mexican period 1822–1846* (Ph.D. thesis, MS., University of California, 1932).

Toro, Alfonso, *La Iglesia y el Estado en México* (México, 1927).

Tuthill, Franklin, *The history of California* (San Francisco, 1866).

Wilgus, A Curtis, *A history of Hispanic America* (Washington, D. C., 1931).

V. SPECIAL WORKS

Beattie, George W., *California's unbuilt missions: Spanish plans for an inland chain* (Los Angeles, 1930).

Brackett, Frank P., *History of San José rancho* (Los Angeles, 1920).

Browne, Clyde, *Cloisters of California* (Los Angeles, 1918).

Carter, Charles F., *The missions of Nueva California* (San Francisco, 1900). *Stories of the old missions of California* (San Francisco, 1917).

Clinch, Bryan J., *California and its missions: their history to the treaty of Guadalupe Hidalgo* (San Francisco, 1904), 2 vols.

Davis, Nolan, *The old missions of California: the story of the peaceful conquest of the state* (Oakland, 1926).

Dillingham, William C., *The Franciscan missions of California* (Los Angeles, 1908).

Dillon, Rev. Noel P., *Educational efforts of the missionaries in Upper California, 1810–1836* (M.A. thesis, MS., Catholic University of America, 1925).

Elder, David P., *The old Spanish missions of California* (San Francisco, 1913).

Engelhardt, Zephyrin, O.F.M., *The Franciscans in California* (Harbor Springs, Mich., 1897).

——, *San Antonio de Padua, the mission in the Sierras* (Santa Barbara, 1929).

——, *Santa Barbara mission* (San Francisco, 1923).

——, *San Buenaventura, the mission by the sea* (Santa Barbara, 1930).

——, *Mission la Concepcion Purisima de María Santísima* (Santa Barbara, 1932).

——, *San Diego mission* (San Francisco, 1920).

——, *San Fernando Rey, the mission of the valley* (Chicago, 1927).

——, *San Francisco, or Mission Dolores* (Chicago, 1924).

——, *San Gabriel mission, and the beginnings of Los Angeles* (San Gabriel, Calif., 1927).

——, *San Juan Capistrano mission* (Los Angeles, 1922).

——, *San Luis Rey mission* (San Francisco, 1921).

——, *San Miguel Arcangel, the mission on the highway* (Santa Barbara, 1929).

——, *Mission Nuestra Señora de la Soledad* (Santa Barbara, 1929).

Field, Maria A., *Chimes of mission bells, an historical sketch of California and her missions* (San Francisco, 1914).

Fitch, Abigail H., *Junipero Serra: the man and his work* (Chicago, 1914).

Gleeson, Rev. William, *History of the Catholic Church in California* (San Francisco, 1872), 2 vols.

Goodsell, Ruth E., *California during the war of independence, 1810–1822* M.A. thesis, MS., University of California, 1927).

Hall, Trowbridge, *California trails, intimate guide to the old missions; the story of the California missions* (New York, 1920).

Hawes, Horace, *The missions in California, and the rights of the Catholic Church to the property pertaining to them* (San Francisco, 1856).

Hayes, Benjamin, *Missions of Alta California:* consisting of extracts and copies from archives—original papers—testimony of native Californians and neophytes—scraps from books, pamphlets and newspapers—also photographs, etc. Being the entire collection on the subject formed during a period of 20 years, by Hon. Benj. Hayes and by him presented to the Bancroft Library, 1873.

Hayes, John E., *The Franciscan missions of California* (Los Angeles, 1897).

Hildrup, Jesse S., *The missions of California and the old Southwest* (Chicago, 1907).

Hill, Joseph J., *The history of 'Warner's ranch and its environs* (Los Angeles, 1927).

Histoire Chrétienne de la Californie, par Madame la comtesse de . . . (Plancy, 1851).

Historia Cristiana de la California; obra traducida al español para El Domingo por el Lic. D. German Madrid y Ormaechea (México, 1864).

Holway, Mary G., *The art of the old world in New Spain, and the mission days of Alta California* (San Francisco, 1922).

Hudson, William H., *The famous missions of California* (New York, 1901).

Hughes, Elizabeth, *The California of the padres: or, footprints of ancient communism* (San Francisco, 1875).

Jackson, Helen H., *Father Junipero and the mission Indians of California* (Boston, 1902).

——, *Glimpses of California and the missions* (Boston, 1902).

James, George W., *Old missions and mission Indians of California* (Los Angeles, 1895).

——, *In and out of the old missions of California* (Boston, 1905).

——, *Picturesque Pala:* the story of the mission chapel of San Antonio de Padua, connected with Mission San Luis Rey (Pasadena, Calif., 1916).

Jones, H. Bedford, *The story of Mission San Juan Capistrano* (Santa Barbara, 1918).

Langston, Kathryn L., *The secularization of the California missions, 1813–1846* (M.A. thesis, MS., University of California, 1925).

Lowery, Woodbury, *Spanish settlements within the present limits of the United States* (New York, 1901), 2 vols.

Lummis, Charles F., *The Spanish pioneers and the California missions* (New and enl. ed., Chicago, 1929).

McIsaac, Calin H., *Santa Barbara mission* (Santa Barbara, 1926).

McRoskey, Racine, *The missions of California* (San Francisco, 1914).

Mooney, John V., *The disposition of the mission Indians after the secularization of the missions in California* (M.A. thesis, MS., Catholic University of America, 1917).

Mylar, Isaac L., *Early days at the Mission San Juan Bautista* (Watsonville, Calif., 1929).

Newcomb, Rexford, *The Franciscan mission architecture of Alta California* (New York, 1916).

——, *The old mission churches and historic houses of California* (Philadelphia, 1925).

North, Arthur W., *The mother of California;* being an historical sketch of the little-known land of Baja California, from the days of Cortés to the present time (San Francisco and New York, 1908).

O'Keefe, Rev. Joseph J., *The buildings and churches of the mission of Santa Barbara* (Santa Barbara, 1886).

Old California missions. Photographs by W. B. Tyler· (San Francisco, 1889).

O'Sullivan, Rev. St. John, *Little chapters about San Juan Capistrano* (n.p., 1912).

Powers, Laura B., *The story of the old missions of California: their establishment, progress and decay* (San Francisco, 1893).

Preta, Ludovico, O.F.M., *Storia delle missioni Francescane in California con illustrazioni* (San Francisco, 1915).

Repplier, Agnes, *Junípero Serra: pioneer colonist of California* (New York, 1933).

Saunders, Charles F., and Chase, J. Smeaton, *The California padres and their missions* (Boston, 1915).

Saunders, Charles F., and O'Sullivan, Rev. St. John, *Capistrano nights: tales of a California mission town* (New York, 1930).

Smith, Frances N., *The mission of San Antonio de Padua* (Palo Alto, Calif., 1932).

Smyth, Eugene L., *The missions of California* (Chicago, 1899).

Sugranes, Rev. Eugene, *The old San Gabriel mission* (San Gabriel, 1909).

Sullivan, Ella C., and Logie, Alfred E., *The story of the old Spanish missions of the Southwest* (Chicago, 1927).

Thomas, P. J., *Founding of the missions of California* (San Francisco, 1882).

Torchiana, H. A., *The story of Mission Santa Cruz* (New York, 1933).

Torrens y Nicolau, D. Francisco, *Bosquejo histórico del insigne Franciscano, V. P. F. Junípero Serra, fundador y apóstol de la California Septentrional* (Spain, n.p., 1913).

Truman, Benjamin C., *Missions of California* (Los Angeles, 1903).

United States and Mexican claims commission, 1869–1876, . . . Opinion del comisionado Manuel M. de Zamacona en el caso de Thadeus Amat, obispo de Monterey, y Joseph S. Alemany, arzobispo de San Francisco, contra México, no. 493 (Washington, D. C., 1875).

United States and Mexican claims commission, 1869–1876 . . . Thadeus Amat, obispo de Monterey, y Jos. S. Alemany, arzobispo de San Francisco, contra México. Reclamacion, num. 493 (México, 1876).

United States House documents, fifty-seventh Congress, no. 4442, The Pious Fund (Washington, D. C., 1902).

Vischer, Edward, *Missions of Upper California, 1872* (San Francisco, 1872).

Walsh, Marie T., *The mission of the passes, Santa Ines* (Los Angeles, 1930).

VI. PERIODICAL ARTICLES

Bolton, Herbert E., "The mission as a frontier institution in the Spanish-American colonies," *The American Historical Review,* XXIII (1917), 42–61.

——, "The epic of greater America," *The American Historical Review,* XXXVIII (1933), 448–474.

Cole, George W., "Missions and mission pictures: a contribution towards an iconography of the Franciscan missions of California," *California Library Association Publications* (Sacramento, 1910), no. 11, p. 44–66.

Doyle, John T., "History of the Pious Fund of California," *Papers of the California Historical Society,* I. (1887), 41–60.

Geary, Rev. Gerald J., "The transference of ecclesiastical jurisdiction in California, 1840–1853," *Historical Records and Studies, United States Catholic Historical Society,* XXII (1932), 101–167.

Icazbalceta, Joaquin G., "Education in the city of Mexico during the sixteenth century," translated by Rev. Walter J. O'Donnell, C.S.C., Ph.D., *Historical Records and Studies,* XX (1931), 99–158.

Loughran, Elizabeth W., "The first episcopal sees in Spanish America," *The Hispanic American Historical Review,* X (1930), 167–187.

McDonald, William E., "The Pious Fund of the Californias," *The Catholic Historical Review,* XIX (1934), 427–436.

Mecham, J. Lloyd, "The origins of the Real Patronato de Indias," *The Catholic Historical Review,* VIII (1928), 205–228.

——, "The papacy and Spanish-American independence," *The Hispanic American Historical Review,* IX (1929), 155–175.

Ogden, Adele, "Boston hide droghers along California shores," *California Historical Society Quarterly,* VIII (1929), 289–305.

Penfield, W. L., "The Pious Fund arbitration," *North American Review,* 175 (1902), 835–843.

Ramona, Sister M., "Ecclesiastical status of New Mexico, 1680–1875," *The Catholic Historical Review,* XVI (1928), 525–568.

Robertson, William S., "The policy of Spain towards its revolted colonies," *The Hispanic American Historical Review,* VI (1926), 21–46.

Ryan, Rev. Edwin, "Diocesan organization in the Spanish colonies," *The Catholic Historical Review,* II (1916), 146–156.

——, "Ecclesiastical jurisdiction in the Spanish colonies," *The Catholic Historical Review,* V (1919), 1–18.

Steck, Francis B., O.F.M., "Fray Junipero Serra and the military heads of California," *The Fortnightly Review,* XXVIII, XXIX (Dec. 15, 1921–March 1, 1922).

Walsh, Sister M. Kathleen, "The origins of ecclesiastical jurisdiction in New Spain," *Records of the American Catholic Historical Society of Philadelphia,* XLIII (1932), 101–155.

INDEX

VITA

The writer of this Dissertation was born at San Francisco, California, on December 29, 1905. He received his elementary education at St. James' Parochial School, San Francisco, and his secondary education at St. Patrick's Preparatory Seminary, Menlo Park, and at St. Joseph's College, Mountain View, California. His philosophical and theological studies were made at St. Patrick's Seminary, at the completion of which he was ordained to the priesthood on June 20, 1931. In September of that year he was sent to the Catholic University of America for a course of graduate study, where he received the degree of Master of Arts in June, 1932. During his three years of graduate work he followed courses of American Church History under Reverend Dr. Peter Guilday; Ancient History under Dr. McGuire; Medieval History under Reverend Dr. Auweiler; English Constitutional History under Dr. Purcell; and American History under Dr. Stock. As minor subjects he followed courses in Philosophy under Reverend Drs. Smith, Hart, and Sheen; and in English under Drs. Deering and Lennox.